Healing Hurt Minds

Raddery School
Fortrose
Ross-Shire
Tel. 0381 20271

Author profits from the sale of this book go to
The Peper Harow Foundation

Healing Hurt Minds
The Peper Harow Experience

Melvyn Rose

Tavistock/Routledge
London and New York

First published 1990
by Routledge
11 New Fetter Lane, London EC4P 4EE

Simultaneously published in the USA and Canada
by Routledge
a division of Routledge, Chapman and Hall, Inc.
29 West 35th Street, New York, NY 10001

British Library Cataloguing in Publication Data
Rose, Melvyn, 1935 –
Healing hurt minds: the Peper Harow experience.
1. England. Adolescents. Residential care. Adolescent psychotherapy
I. Title
362.7'32

ISBN 0–415–04943–1 (hbk)
      0–415–01796–3 (pbk)

Library of Congress Cataloging-in-Publication Data
Rose, Melvyn, 1935–
Healing hurt minds: the Peper Harow experience/Melvyn Rose.
p. cm.
Bibliography: p.
Includes index.
1. Peper Harow (Institution)   2. Child psychotherapy–Residential
treatment–Case studies.   I. Title.
RJ504.5.R67 1990
362.2'23'0835–dc20   89–10415 CIP

ISBN 0–415–04943–1 (hdk)

Contents

Contents

Foreword

The Rt. Hon. Lord Justice Elizabeth Butler-Sloss D.B.E.

In the 1950s I made several visits to Park House Approved School which then seemed to me a model of the way in which an approved school should be run. As a new patron of Peper Harow I am just beginning to appreciate the dramatic differences in, not to say gulf dividing, the present incarnation from the former life of an approved school. The existence of the therapeutic community of Peper Harow arises from the brave decision in 1970 by the managers of Park House Approved School to take the plunge and make the transformation.

Melvyn Rose was the first director of the new enterprise and in this book he reveals the stages of the transformation and sets out, in detail, the initial and continuing problems of creating a therapeutic community. As he says, it is his own idiosyncratic view of the process and he explains 'how the idea of this community came about as the result of a convergence of many different personal and social elements at a coincidental time'.

The fundamental reassessment of the objectives and the methods to achieve those objectives did not come easily or quickly and has over the years been achieved painfully by trial and error, through (as the author puts it) 'conflict and crisis'. Reading this candid and comprehensive account of the trials and tribulations, the embracing and abandoning of methods and approaches, I began to glimpse, for the first time, the mammoth task they set themselves in 1970 to turn a place, where a regime is imposed upon the inmates from outside, into a thriving community where the needs of each resident is individually considered and catered for. The emphasis is upon the communication and co-operation of the individual with the group, rather than authoritarian containment and control from above. Much more than a name had to change. The basic need was to change attitudes of both the staff and the children and the way in which this has been achieved over the subsequent years makes fascinating reading, instructive both for the expert and the layman. An example is the problem of containing the residents disturbed behaviour, while providing them with sufficient freedom to come to terms with their feelings and learn self-confidence. The author describes the effect upon the staff and upon the director himself of such problems. Formidable obstacles arose, which must at times have appeared almost insuperable. The needs of residents, staff, and director and consequently relationships, changed from time to time, as did their appreciation of each other and of themselves. Members of staff and the director have engaged in a painful learning process and in that process have fashioned the present Peper Harow.

To read the book is to be given an opportunity to see for ourselves something of the evolution in the thinking of the past 20 years over the care of emotionally disturbed children. Experiences of some children who have passed through the system have, suitably disguised, been explored.

Girls joined the community in 1980 with the consequential problems as well as advantages.

We are reminded in the preface that Harow means sanctuary. Peper Harow gives sanctuary to some of the most injured children in the country. It provides in its superb surroundings a genuine home as well as a refuge for its residents. It fills a small but essential gap in the needs of exceptionally emotionally disturbed, depressed, some of them delinquent, children for whom life has been unduly harsh, unjust, or tragic and whose right it is to have somewhere worthwhile to spend a period, with suitable treatment provided, before they reach adulthood.

The success of Peper Harow has led to the opening of Thornby Hall for younger children which has been established for about 3 years.

Melvyn Rose has now handed over to another director. Peper Harow has come to maturity. The problems have not disappeared; I suspect some of them never would and are inherent in the objectives sought to be achieved, sometimes with apparently unpromising material.

As this book records, Melvyn Rose looks back over a turbulent, exciting, sometimes depressing, but remarkably successful period of his directorship of Peper Harow. We are shown how it came to pass, warts and all. I dare not speculate what the founders of Park House, if alive, would say today. But fortunately the world has moved on and so have our perceptions of the needs of children. This book is a tribute to a vision of how in one area of need that should be achieved.

Foreword

Henry W. Maier, Professor Emeritus, University of Washington

'On Saturdays you would always find the director in the front hall, with its acres of stone flagging, with his scrubber and bucket' (p. 55). This description does not represent any preoccupation on the part of the director (and author of this book) with the cleanliness of the floors but, rather, his far-reaching commitment to the Peper Harow Community and the lives of its residents and staff. In the community, all are fully engaged in the minutiae of each other's daily life experience. In this book the manifold details of everyday group living are spotlighted. This will puzzle, engage, and hopefully instruct, the professional audience. Nevertheless the myriad of anecdotal and descriptive accounts, as well as theoretical explanations about the reader's journey through this book, however startling or enticing, are not its essence. It is the totality which is important – the internally consistent approach that shines through this story of the creation of a full communal life experience for children and adolescents.

Al Trieschman's truism: 'What is old, is new,' (Maier, 1988, p. 5) is applicable here. Readers will find vivid echoes of the teachings of earlier pioneers in the residential care and treatment fields. The author's belief in the basic goodness of people and in their development if properly nurtured is much akin to August Aichhorn's early psychoanalytic experiments (1935). However, Rose holds that unconscious forces do not have to be merely accepted benignly as in Aichhorn's days. He finds, in them, the challenge to struggle and to respond in the context of daily *interpersonal*, developmental experience. The latter is very much within the realm of contemporary knowledge and thinking where 'intra-psychic' forces are appraised within an interactional context and the emphasis is upon a developmental rather than a psychoanalytic interpretation.

In this book, readers are made privy to and become richly immersed in a communal program where human development of residents and staff alike is envisaged as a measurable ingredient in the *community's* life. Readers might then be reminded of Maxwell Jones' *The Therapeutic Community* (1953) which this book now brings fully to fruition. Community requirements that enhance individual development are always in the center. The molding of community identity is seen as essential in order that residents' and staff's actual life experience are meshed. Residential treatment becomes a true shared experience where the community is the means and context for all intervention.

Much attention is given to the symbolic meaning of physical arrangements, program structures, and interpersonal behaviors. A worker, for instance, may unobtrusively make a resident's bed; his or her purpose is neither to teach, to model, or to reinforce the utility of having a comfortable place to sleep. Instead this response is intended to deliver another important message: in our community we want you to feel physically comfortable, be welcome, and to be cared for. It is the community which has to be 'a "good enough" therapeutic community' (p. 73). This means a blending of community and individual treatment approaches by replenishing all environmental factors in each individual's life. Such content, especially the emphasis upon the symbolic meaning of all community-centered actions, represents a radical shift from contemporary steadfast concentration upon behavioral and structural variables in residential treatment efforts.

Throughout the book, readers are asked to join the youngsters' life journey rather than merely to discern these boys' and girls' complex feelings, thinking, and behaviors. Traditional psychoanalytic or current prominent behavioral/cognitive causal perspectives are shifted to a developmental situational approach. Very recent developmental psychology research is drawn upon; namely, that children at points of transition and moments of crisis require intimate personal contacts (Ainsworth, 1982). Attachment striving and struggles take priority to cognitive understanding and behavior management issues.

Particularly pioneering and noteworthy is a reliance upon playful interactions at Peper Harow as a central mode for their newcomers and other crisis-prone youngsters. Newcomers to the community are challenged to roam around, to experience the community for its people and its nurturing atmosphere. And amazingly, after months of nihilism and mere floating, they begin to enter purposefully into the community's program, including educational and therapeutic endeavors. At Peper Harow, residents first have to learn to play; then, and only then can they use play to learn. At the same time, regardless of residents' readiness to share in the daily or special community meetings, or whether in fact they see any values in contributing to the community maintenance, they must take part. The culture of the place demands unconditional acceptance and full inclusion of each resident in the community affairs.

Reflecting the tradition of Jones (1953), Bettelheim (1950; 1974), Redl (1957), and other early pioneers, staff at Peper Harow are envisaged as constitutional parts of the community. They are everpresent as both nurturing and steadfast partners; understanding and living-out such understanding in their involvement with fellow communal residents. It is not accidental that a place built upon psychoanalytical premises suggests that its staff be 'expert in broom handling' (p. 165). As with Brother Lawrence who found 'drudgery divine' while washing pots and pans, so at Peper Harow, staff variously find full engagement with a youngster while at play, in difficult joint crisis, as well as in the accomplishment of daily work tasks.

While Melvyn Rose's work at Peper Harow may help readers to re-envisage earlier pioneers' teaching; actually, a new approach is evidenced. And that is the almost everpresent reliance upon the residents' day to day life *encounters*. The central and continuous concern is the nature of each youngster's experience and its relevance to his or her eventual assimilation to the community. While the author in his accounts tends to strive for insight formation, the actual change accomplished seems to be anchored in the powerful nature of the everpresent 'joint human experience' (p. 165).

Readers are alerted to this new reliance upon the human experience within the context of each resident's life history *and* his or her immediate existential situation as he or she functions in the ongoing community group. Interestingly, the role of the peer culture, typically an enigma for any residential change efforts (Redl and Wineman, 1957; Polsky 1962), assumes frontal recognition at Peper Harow. Senior residents are the ones who are overtly the community's culture carriers. They serve much as bridgeheads for the junior residents still perplexed and adrift. Peper Harow's reliance upon such senior community members for assisting others in their development toward a well-grounded, salutary course of life may imply the need for new experimentation in long-term residential care. On the American scene, *short-term* placement and circumscribed change efforts are in the forefront.

This book is as much a biographical account of the author's professional journey over the past twenty-five years as it is an imaginary dialogue with sophisticated readers about a potent program of residential care and treatment. The meshing of an account of a person's professional career with that of his work creation is appropriate here. Peper Harow strongly represents the ideas, creative efforts, and unending commitments of its resident director, Melvyn Rose.

It is astonishing to learn again that an impactful change effort is akin to the now classical residential treatment programs of such leading greats of the field as A. S. Makarenko (1951); B. Bettelheim (1950); M. Jones (1953) and Redl (1957). Each one of them is known for his full emergence as director, as a member of the community, and the indisputable master of the program. Allegiance to the philosophy of the program and the leadership of the director are clearly instrumental to the success of the program in each case.

'What is old, is new!' In these days where token-economy, high pressure, behavioral-orientated programs, and bureaucratized level-systems hold the spotlight on the North American continent, this book's treatise may raise questions about current practices and may challenge the residential treatment fields anew. Readers may be stimulated to ask themselves to what extent must those in care acquire basic behavioral changes in order to assure a different life course.

At Peper Harow individual treatment with self-worth as its goal is anchored in the full experience of such daily human processes as eating, having fun, living as a contributor to the maintenance of the place, and continous hurdling of crises. Each person – staff, residents, and director alike – is challenged to serve as one another's keeper. In all of these endeavors, it is the attention to the minutiae of daily life which seems to make the difference.

This book presents much more than the apparent psychoanalytic approach of 'healing'. Although the terminology is essentially psychoanalytic and semantically outside of the mainstream of contemporary professional literature, *Healing Hurt Minds: The Peper Harow Experience* actually stands out for a new treatment orientation where each resident's *experience* is cast in terms of his or her immediate requirements for developmental progress within the context of the community's well-being.

Bibliography

Aichhorn, A. (1935) *Wayward Youth*, New York: Viking Press.

Ainsworth, M.D. (1982) 'Attachment: Retrospect and Prospect', in Parkes, C. M. and Stevenson-Hinde, J. *The Place of Attachment in Human Behaviour*, New York: Basic Books, Inc. (pp. 3–30).

Bettelheim, B. (1950) *Love is not Enough*, New York: Free Press.

Bettelheim, B. (1974) *A Home for the Heart*, New York: Knopf.

Jones, M. (1953) *The Therapeutic Community*, New York: Basic Books, Inc.

Maier, H. W. (1988) 'Foreword', in Small, R. W. and Alvon, F. J. *Challenging the Limits of Care*, Needham, MA.: Trieschman Center (pp. 5–8).

Makarenka, A. S. (1951) *The Road to Life*, Moscow: Progress Publishers.

Polsky, H. W. (1962) *Cottage Six*, New York: Russel Sage.

Redl, F. and Wineman, D. (1957) *The Aggressive Child*, New York: Free Press.

Preface

Before there was England, there was Peper Harow. Its name is recorded in William the Conqueror's Domesday Book, and its existence derives from the earliest pagan and Anglo-Saxon times. The second word meant a sanctuary, or a holy place, while the first was a family name indicating a relationship between the two. Whitelock (1952:23) suggests that it was reminiscent of the hereditary priest/chieftain function in old Iceland. Such places were often situated in woods, or on hill tops – something of topographic significance. In medieval times, places still retaining pagan associations in folk memory were often renamed to provide a biblical association; or churches were built over them. Peper Harow has its early medieval church, and the hill that rises behind the existing mansion has been called Mount Zion for longer than anyone can remember. There are also Iron Age burial mounds that would indicate a significant dwelling place even before the Romans came!

Men have dwelt in this setting during all the time it has taken to form an English identity. It has been central to the many levels of their experience and understanding. They hunted and fished, ploughed and prayed, and saw Peper Harow as the source of all that was most needful to their existence. In no way could this place have been inanimate. It provided all that made them and sustained them.

The youngsters who come to Peper Harow today have no sense of deep cultural roots and little sense of personal identity. For one traumatic reason or another, the ingredients of experience and upbringing that make for profound security have not been theirs. Instead, these youngsters of 13 or 14 years of age, when they arrive, are some of the most injured children in the country. They are the ones who feature in shocking press reports of child abuse, but the significance of the assaults on their essential psychic selves has often been unrecognized. Perhaps it is for this reason that the numerous, prior interventions to help them have not been successful.

However, as a result of their psychological injuries, they are profoundly damaged in the way they see other children and adults. They perceive themselves and how others respond to them unrealistically but they behave with increasing obduracy according to the way they mistakenly see and experience the world. Thus, as they grow older, the gap between their unhappy existence and the developing competence of the fortunate child increasingly widens. Disturbed youngsters' aggression, for instance, as much towards themselves as towards others is, by adolescence, too serious to be overlooked. Unless their behaviour is changed their future is dire. Yet, unless their profoundest view of themselves as terrorized, worthless beings is reversed, their behaviour cannot change and lead to enhancement, and eventually to self-fulfilment. However, they might at last find their fortune when the place they come to for sanctuary and healing happens to be inherently associated with their most needed nourishment. During their stay they will come to understand that they have a right to what Peper Harow offers. All those who lived there inherited a similar right and in that respect are their true forbears. They themselves will also become part of Peper Harow's constant history. Without having to unravel the nourishing symbol from the actuality of the place, they are offered, by both symbol and physical reality, a new understanding and a sense that hope is always justifiable.

Any human group, whether a family or a whole society, is composed of invisible but significant psychological processes. Physical forces like gravity cannot actually be seen either, though one can experience their effect. Similarly, the dynamics of human psychology have considerable impact despite being unseen and despite often being beyond the conscious experience of a particular person or group. These forces nevertheless affect the way we feel and the attitudes we develop towards ourselves and others. The baby, for example, will experience his mother's depression though neither of them may understand either the components or the way depression functions. Yet, especially because of the baby's dependence on her, the mother's psychological state will particularly affect the baby's own feelings about itself and the way in which it responds to her. This response will affect the mother in turn and their interacting relationship will also contribute to how they both function within the wider family. In turn, the relationship between mother and baby will also be affected by other members of the family. During adolescence, the psychological components of a youngster's developing personality will continue to affect the way he perceives and experiences the wider world of school and friends. But those friends and that school each affect the individual psychologically, and any group and any individual is also affected by the wider society in which they exist. Any one of these influences may have an exceptional effect on the way people come to feel about themselves and others and thus upon their fundamental sense of identity.

That Peper Harow as a place should be a significant component of the treatment process has never seemed to me to be either romantic or even particularly mysterious. While human beings are often baffled and frightened by the illogical and unintended things they do, yet the psychodynamic processes by which their feelings and behaviour are formed and function can be analysed. And through such clarification, a therapeutic recovery of the ability to live an enriching life in its myriad possibilities can be made. Yet, the processes by which that recovery occurs are difficult to describe for they include aspects that focus on the minutest experience of one unique person, and simultaneously on the inextricably complex inter-relationships between family, history, and society.

Peper Harow today has been specially established as a community that makes psychological change its main therapeutic purpose. To understand how it achieves its aim one has to be aware of all its interacting components and try continually to understand their shifting significance within the therapeutic process. In this book I have also tried to show how the idea of this community came about as the result of a convergence of many different personal and social elements at a coincidental time.

I have tried to write it in a way that illustrates not only my own experience and understanding of the Peper Harow process, but also in the way by which a resident's or a member of staff's understanding of the community begins to develop. Essentially, I see all the community's elements reflected in each definable element. Thus, psychotherapeutic insight is a major ingredient of the educational programme while, in turn, intellectual achievement can also enormously enhance the courage to grapple with one's deepest fears. These and many other ingredients, like the material environment and the closely observed human relationships, all continually affect each other. Accordingly, aspects of the book are repeated, but hopefully in a way that increasingly unfolds their manifold complexity. Examination of each new aspect inevitably brings a re-examination of those aspects already discussed. Hopefully, in the same way as it does for the members of the community themselves, this re-examination will gradually bring the reader a fuller appreciation of Peper Harow as a process that, despite its complex entanglements, can be made clear. I have included cross-references in the text to other places where the issue being examined has already been examined from a different perspective. I hope the reader finds this helpful.

There are many aspects that could be discussed. Some are omitted intentionally and some unconsciously. I regret the book's limited correlation between experience, practice, and the painstakingly achieved under-standing of major theorists, while whole books have specialized in issues such as adolescent sexuality and identity formation. Therefore, anything I am able to say of my experience of these matters is inevitably incomplete. Above all, Peper Harow's history has moved on. Perhaps that is the truest sign of Peper Harow's success – that it has a life of its own, irrespective of its progenitors or present inhabitants. Life is more fortunate or less so, at one time or another, but, as long as it continues, there is always hope of new and further growth.

And of course the book is idiosyncratic; it is my own view of Peper Harow, both of its engendering and of its development. I had hoped for room to include the direct expression of the views of staff and youngsters at different stages of the community's life, but that alone would make another book.

Above all, I have not intended to be critical, other than professionally, and certainly not hurtful in a personal way. If I appear so, I hope that the circumstantial qualification of my criticism is also noted. We are all creatures of forces beyond ourselves, so, if a particular opinion seems to judge someone else's contribution as negative, it is often the case that, irrespective of our view, or their conscious intention, they could not have been fully aware of the influences on their actions.

If this book shows how complex are the ingredients needed in the creation of a therapeutic process for profound and lasting personal change, it will have been effective. I hope though that it will be experienced as optimistic. For all our human limitations, we can still add our own labour and nurture to the human condition during our lifetime, just as our own being derives from the sum of those many unknown people who came before us.

Acknowledgements

Above all, I am grateful to the youngsters who have taught me so much over the years, and to all my colleagues. Relationships between members of staff have not always been easy because they have been subject to extraordinary stress and unusually close appraisal in the pursuance of our objective. At the same time, our work together was actually developed by our increasing understanding of ourselves and of our relationships, and lifelong friendships have arisen as a result.

I also owe a great debt to the trustees of Peper Harow for their faith in appointing me and in the kind of institution we have tried to create. In this I must particularly mention Godfrey Godfrey-Isaacs, our chairman for many years. Nor can I imagine how the project would ever have begun without Nora Murrow, our consultant psychiatrist, who had waited for the opportunity with endless patience. How I could have sustained myself without the intellectual and emotional rigour and professional concern of my personal psychoanalyst, Earl Hopper, is also beyond my imagination.

I would particularly wish to acknowledge all of my assistant directors with great affection, and without exception, for all of them have been people of outstanding quality. Indeed, every member of staff has played a vital role almost always recognized by the individual youngsters for whom they were responsible, irrespective of the immediate outcome of their relationship. I was very fortunate to share my most passionately held professional views with such a group of people.

And there are endless numbers of colleagues and friends, who have given advice and encouragement at times of need. Again, to pick a name at random is neither wise nor fair; but I would particularly mention Maurice Bridgeland for his friendship and for his initial criticism of the first draft of this book. I owe a special debt to Bill Barnes-Gutteridge, who has devoted many hours to criticizing my text. He has taught me a great deal. For similar reasons, each of my office staff deserves a very special accolade for their typing, tolerance, and tea.

I cannot let this opportunity go by without thanking my own family publicly for the many aspects of this story that they have often unintentionally shared. Whether this was through their contributions to my upbringing, or their encouragement during writing, they have all been of major significance. Undoubtedly, they paid a heavy price at Peper Harow, despite their pride at our involvement in such a commitment. If they read this book, I hope that they will feel that, despite the difficulties, they were direct contributors to something of intrinsic and lasting worth.

Finally, it must be stressed how much all of us learn from the residents themselves. It takes every member of staff some years before they come to understand the confused and frightened person hidden behind frequently appalling behaviour. That understanding makes a difference to one's ability to tolerate that behaviour when necessary. Above all, it illuminates undeniably the stark consequences of a traumatized upbringing. It is hard to learn to share the misery, the fear, and the hopeless despair of our youngsters, but we also witness their sheer courage and the miraculous changes they can make given even a modicum of personal respect. With sufficient time, it is possible to put the most shattered lives together and that is a lesson that reasserts the supremacy of hope.

In the following section there are some examples of our youngsters' backgrounds. (References are also made in the book to some thirty youngsters who were all residents of Peper Harow while I was director. I have disguised their names, and sometimes their sexes, and their background details.) They show what an enormous task lies before them when they come to Peper Harow, yet also, by implication, what a sense of privilege their eventual success inspires in those honoured by having worked with them.

A glimpse of some residents' backgrounds

Terry Herbert

Many of the ingredients that led to Terry's eventual arrival at Peper Harow were typical of an extremely stressed family likely to produce emotionally disturbed children.

Father was 21 and Mother still a teenager when they married. Both had experienced disturbed upbringings. Father had already received several custodial sentences including prison. They lived in a series of single rooms with their babies in an inner-city slum. Father was violent to Mother and the children. He lived periodically with other women and eventually the parents were divorced.

Father seriously sexually abused Terry and his brother on several occasions. Terry developed major anxieties about his own sexuality in response. These emotional problems were offered expression by the delinquent local culture and psychosomatically in terms of serious stomach ulcers in early adolescence. As some control was obtained over Terry's stealing and aggressive rages, so the ulceration became a major health problem. When it lessened, so his behaviour became uncontrollable in turn.

Terry could be charming and insightful at times, but his anger at his mother, who had done her best in the face of overwhelming odds, but who still had not been able to protect him adequately from his Father, affected his ability to benefit from affectionate relationships. At its extreme, he violently attacked those attempting to nurse him when he was ill. He found men equally threatening because his father provided not only a poor adult model but had seriously traumatized him. Terry was caught between his longing for comfort and nurture and a temptation to reject it violently.

Roddy Oliver

Roddy came from a relatively normal background though his exceptionally artistic talents showed themselves from early infancy. He was significantly ahead in all his developmental milestones and demanded continual stimulation day and night. At the same time, both parents were struggling to overcome the limitations of their own family backgrounds and undeveloped educational potential, through exceptional commitment to their careers, and through part-time education. It was their only hope of escaping from uncongenial work and home surroundings.

Father became seriously ill and the burden of raising Roddy and his sisters fell totally on Mother. Her anxiety became the family's keynote and was a major component in Roddy's early involvement with drugs. He was not helped by the self-righteous and punitive attitudes in his school, nor by his parents' sense of incomprehension and impotence to control Roddy, whom they felt to be more adult in some respects than themselves. Once he was addicted to drugs, Roddy's uncertain self-control collapsed, and with it all positive endeavours. Roddy began to steal to buy the drugs and to express his sense of worthlessness through various self-degrading activities. He had no understanding of the underlying motivations for his behaviour.

There were one or two major incidents in Roddy's childhood that could be seen with hindsight as warnings of serious problems needing to be tackled before it became too late. They were not recognized, and later recovery was seriously impeded by Roddy's difficulty in recognizing what he felt about his relationships with his parents and sisters. He was undoubtedly frightened and ashamed of such feelings. Like most very small children, he had florid fantasies about his own guilty contribution to his father's illness and about his confusion concerning the birth of his sisters. The stresses in the family, however, prevented his outgrowing them. Instead, he developed considerable fears and anxieties about the kind of person he really was and these became expressed in addiction and in the destructive, accompanying behaviour.

Johnny 'Puncher' Murray

'Puncher' came to us as a last, merciful gesture by a High Court judge who had heard of Peper Harow. The judge knew that the alternative prison sentence would probably commit him to a permanent life of violence and hatred.

When Puncher arrived he was in his late teens and in the guise of a Hell's Angel. He refused to work and was quickly rejected by his peers (Rose, 1987, 10: 156). As well as being frightening and repellent, he was also exceptionally kind – a potential noted by the judge who had received reports of Puncher's exceptional generosity to others in distress. However, he was embittered by his memories of the orphanage in which he had grown up and the appalling death of his adoptive father. The latter had been exceptionally sophisticated at helping Puncher to deal with his past, his adoption, and the exceptional problems he had in finding security in his relationships with his adoptive parents. Father's slow physical disintegration traumatized Mother too and Puncher became convinced that he was somehow responsible for the family's destruction. Yet again his response was to create situations that expressed his anger, in apparently random ways, and always ended in self-degradation or punishment. These situations were triggered by powerful and frightening fantasies about the mother his father had left behind. He was confused as to who had adopted whom and, overwhelmed by panic, Puncher could be a very dangerous proposition.

It can be seen that none of these boys was secure in his sense of being intrinsically loved and esteemed. As a consequence, they feared the implications of their angry and frightening fantasies that they felt were confirmations that they were unlovable and possibly dangerously evil. Perhaps the terrible things that happened to their families were somehow their fault. Their behaviour seemed to test the possibility of such fantasies. It was bound to become intolerable and thus would be a self-fulfilling judgement based on a complex misconception.

In a sense this kind of misconception lay at the root of all the youngsters' problems, irrespective of their experiences. Those who had been severely physically or sexually abused - a proportion that increased with the arrival of girls - were not so much damaged physically as in their essential belief that they deserved better. Their compulsive and unconsciously originating behaviour sought to test out their unconscious hypotheses, and continually brought about repetitions of the kinds of abuse they had suffered. Without resolution there seemed no way that our youngsters' own eventual children could receive an unequivocal message of esteem. Peper Harow needed to be designed so as to clarify the meaning and significance of the youngsters' behaviour and then to provide the confirmatory nurture of their essential selves. Only then might they engage with the problems of everyday life from an internal sense of secure worth.

A chronology

1850s–1920s	National development of industrial schools and reformatories for delinquent and homeless children. Many children still resident in workhouses under Poor Law legislation.
Early 1920s	Establishment of Park House School at Hayes, Middlesex and registration with The Charity Commission under voluntary management.
1933	The Children Act. Reformatories become approved schools – so does Park House School. Training rather than punishment implied as the new popular perception of need.
1951	Park House School expands in numbers and moves to Peper Harow in Surrey.
1964	Melvyn Rose appointed teacher/housemaster at Park House School.
July 1970	Melvyn Rose appointed as headmaster with remit from trustees to change the school into a therapeutic community.
1973	Peper Harow Community ceases to be an approved school under the aegis of the Children's Department of the Department of Health and Social Security. Legally it becomes a non-maintained school under the aegis of the Special Schools Division of the Department of Education and Science. It remains a charity. (See Notes, Chapter 1, 1.)
Sept 1970	First daily community meetings. New system for voluntary admission of residents.

Nov 1970   First small psychotherapy groups on twice-weekly basis.

1971   Major rearrangements of living accommodation in main house. Case conferences with local authority social workers commence.

1972   Trade training ceases to become part of programme.
Old workshops commence redevelopment as studios.
First redevelopment of front hall for Friday Night 'seminars'.
Fireplace opened up. Friday Night seminars commence.
Park House officially becomes Peper Harow Community.

1973   First development of Gold Room for community meetings.

1973–6   Redevelopment of basement completed. Temporary kitchen and dining room then becomes music room, pottery, photographic studio, group room, offices.
Redevelopment of ground floor. Gold Room, library, corridors, lounge.
Dining room and kitchen totally refurbished and redesigned for therapeutic effect.
Boys begin to qualify for entrance to higher education, etc.

1979–81   Refurbishment of conference/staff room, girls' bedrooms, bathrooms, lavatories and boys' bathrooms and lavatories.

1980   First official admission of girls.

1981   Princess Mary's Trust amalgamates with Peper Harow.

1983   Melvyn Rose leaves to create The Peper Harow Foundation.

1985   New estate at Thornby, Northamptonshire purchased. Refurbished.

1986   Thornby Hall Community opens to younger, mixed-age group.

Chapter one

Introduction

The origins of Peper Harow Therapeutic Community.
The roles of the director, trustees, and youngsters.
The history of the Trust and legislative and social change.
The inadequacy of the approved-school system in meeting the needs
of the residents.
The recognition of the need for a different atmosphere and style of
programme for treatment.

Well into middle age, I am still surprised by the influence of my early childhood on my feelings now. Unexpectedly, everyday events suddenly illuminate experiences, clarifying what I could never have understood when they first occurred. A passing comment in a conversation can trigger early memories of exclusion and worthlessness that would have 'hurt my parents more than it hurt me', had they been aware of them in my childhood. Many small children are confused by matters that are commonplace to adults. Yet, the adults' very familiarity with the world makes it almost impossible for them to see events as their children experience them. They would love to be able to guarantee their children's future, mature, and fulfilled emotional lives. Fortunately, most confusions do resolve themselves with our increasing ability to master the environment and to categorize familiar events. Some, unfortunately, remain a source of uncomfortable feelings that arouse fear and underlie later choices in ways we hardly suspect.

The artist, for instance, often has little awareness of the true source of his visual images. Why one symbol should be chosen with particular determination is often unknown. Indeed, many creative people fear that, if they understood the source of their inspiration, they would be robbed of their creativity. One could equally argue the opposite – that their work would be the richer for their insight. In my own case, the enrichment of personal psychoanalysis and the benefit of hindsight clarifies how much of my own professional commitment was determined by the unconscious but continuing anguish of my emotionally inhibited childhood. Almost

1

certainly, had my early experiences been more comfortable, my whole life would have been entirely different. Instead, those very experiences vicariously enlivened my awareness of the emotionally traumatized and socially lost youngsters who came to Peper Harow. They roused my passionate determination to fulfil a vision and create an ideal healing environment for them against any odds.

I hasten to say that as a child, no-one locked me up in cupboards, no-one sexually assaulted me, and no-one, other than a particularly sadistic headmaster, physically abused me. My parents were as loving as any and had a sense of responsibility towards their children that was greater than most. Yet, for all that, two broad factors affected me deeply and are an inseparable mixture of psychological and psychosocial issues.

My father left to fight the nightmarish Germans when I was 5 years old. That we moved from Yorkshire to London, and that my younger brother was born at approximately the same time, complicated my insecurity. Losing my father's presence became a major psychological injury, for he could have helped me cope with the stress of a new environment and with the loss of my childhood kingdom – which is every firstborn child's major crisis when he has to share mother with a new baby. Yet, it was not simply my father's absence that was injurious, but the confusion his departure caused to my newly emergent personal identity. How many generations of warriors have also made their painful farewells to firstborn children, solemnly entrusting them to, 'Look after your mother and brother for me!' A small child cannot use his sense of time to manage the pain of absence. The proud moment of their man-to-man compact quickly fades. It is actually impossible for the child to function as though he were the father. His delusory attempts to be so create an ongoing sense of confusion. To retain the paternal image within him, the child must be true to the paternal values and ideals, and to their solemn parting commitment. Yet, to try and be a replacement father and husband at the age of 5 can only produce an absurd precociousness.

In my case, I remember the archetypal women of my family huddled around the nine o'clock news and sighing like a Greek chorus as the enemy advanced across the nations, never knowing whether their absent men would stem the tide or be destroyed. We lived in fear and with the ache of absence.

This traumatic period in my childhood is one of many early experiences that have inevitably affected the way I am. It is clearer to me now how they have influenced the particular way I perceive treatment. Optimistically, such experiences indicate that both one's fortunate and one's less sanguine experiences can in the end be used to develop intuitive understanding both of others and of oneself. Engaging in the struggle to use painful experiences insightfully can shape everyone. It can develop both our ability to engage in intimate relationships and develop our sense of personal integration.

Some people, however, need very special help if they are ever to achieve this.

The children whose behaviour eventually consigns them to the Peper Harows of society have everyone's emotional dilemmas but compounded beyond measure. They have been starved emotionally, and often physically; they have been the butt of sadistic and sickening behaviour from adults. (Behind such adults' outrageous behaviour, of course, lies the terror and pain of their own unhappy childhoods.) Yet, despite the bizarre and extraordinary experiences of these youngsters, their reactions to their suffering, though extreme, are familiar to us all. The anxiety and emotional pain these children have suffered is, of course, more extreme than most people ever experience. Nevertheless, there is enough common experience of fear and insecurity to create ambivalence towards these children. On the one hand, people are shocked by what these abused children have endured; on the other, they are frightened by their own buried and confused fantasies aroused by these youngsters' experiences and behaviour.

No wonder, then, that public expressions concerning child abuse are righteous and outraged, while society responds to young people's reactions to such torment with surprising confusion. There is often little sympathy for the alienated youngsters themselves, who are often delinquent 'drop-outs' involved in the half-world of drugs – just as though these were not the same children as those who wring the flintiest of hearts when they look down from the appeal posters of the helping charities. It is the notion of innocent children attacked by alien, adult monsters that wins public sympathy. The complex reality of the disturbed family awakens personal anxiety and discomfort and is hardly welcome. The problem, lacking a more insightful societal response, can therefore only continue.

The Peper Harow Therapeutic Community opened in 1970 after a decade of social reaction to the anticlimax of the post-war years. An important part of the community's development is the story of our gradual recognition of all its members' needs, the gradual definition of those needs, and the increasingly effective development of resources that enabled them to be met. This growth, of course, proceeded in a human fashion – through conflict and crisis. Only with hindsight can it now be seen as an ongoing process. Each development tended to be initially experienced as threatening to the fragile new order.

Like everyone else caught up in the spirit of those times, we began our endeavours with a righteous sense of crusade on behalf of the youngsters. The existing establishment, from which Peper Harow sprang, was Park House Approved School. It also existed so that the youngsters could be looked after according to what were seen to be their needs. Our major difference derived from a different view as to what those needs were. However, it rapidly became apparent to us that the youngsters did not need an adolescents' paradise, however attractive a temporary retreat into such an idealized situation may have seemed. We came to see that their real need was to be part of a whole community in which adult values were often ascendant. This need may be true for every child, but it was emphasized at Peper Harow because the youngsters' disturbed behaviour became intolerable when given the free rein of blind egalitarianism. In its early days, when very few residents had developed personal behavioural controls, the demands on the adults to enforce boundaries in the face of their stubborn resistance were continuous. Irrespective of the supposedly democratic notions the staff may have arrived with, they were forced to exercise authority, from dawn till long after dusk, in order to survive, and theories about democracy and permissiveness had to be uncomfortably questioned.

It was not just the conjunction of the spirit of the times and a drive to resolve certain unconscious identity problems by its leader that created conditions in which the Peper Harow Community could germinate and take root; there was an historical context too.

As an organization it had been founded in the 1920s as a reformatory, soon to become renamed as an approved school in the 1930s. That change in itself is remarkable because it illustrates serious dissatisfaction with the way deviant children and adolescents were perceived even then. The need for youngsters to be reformed implied a value judgement about their behaviour, whereas a school approved by the Secretary of State recognizes not just that it is special but that it is a school and as such is a much more normal part of society. Unfortunately, the change that was required was not simply one of status but of attitude, and that did not take place, despite the implication of such a change of name.

The existing and unchanging attitude towards the youngsters was preserved, despite general pressure throughout the sixties against the oppressive, authoritarian approved schools. The 1969 Children and Young Persons' Act, like the 1933 Act before it, changed the name of the institutions, this time from approved schools to community homes, though the buildings and personnel remained the same. What an act of parliament cannot do is legislate to change attitudes. These, at best, paternalistic attitudes towards disturbed children – and perhaps towards disturbed and deviant people generally – are clearly visible in the Curtis Report (1946). The Report reveals the way children were looked after in the Victorian workhouses that were still in existence when it was being compiled. The Report accurately evoked an atmosphere clearly recognizable in the approved schools of the sixties. It should already have been clear that a change of name or management would change little. A different understanding was needed of how change in an individual's self-perception occurs. Only this would lead to the different organizational functioning that, in turn, would generate the hoped-for changes in the youngster.

When Peper Harow began to function as a therapeutic community in 1970, it had already been an approved school for nearly twenty years. It was called Park House School and had moved from Middlesex where it had been originally set up in the early 1920s as a denominationally Jewish approved school. In those days, the earlier wave of immigrants from continental persecution had begun to produce the recognizable consequences of the accompanying emotional as well as physical upheaval in an increased number of delinquents among its offspring. The Home Office of the time had arranged an *ad hoc* body of managers to organize a new charity, so that, like its Catholic and Protestant counterparts, the stability of religious identity could be added to its morally educational task.

By the time the move to Surrey was organized in the 1950s to meet the need for increased places in response to the general post-war surge of delinquency, there were hardly any Jewish boys in Park House School. It had earlier become interdenominational and thus provided a general community service. Its managers had always been exceptionally involved in the life of the school. For instance, extraordinary aftercare arrangements had been instituted so that leavers and their social workers, too, over whom the school had no authority at all, were actually seen by a group of managers on a regular basis after they left.

Yet, despite the managers' committed sense of responsibility, they were more aware of the well-presented and rational organization of the school than of the subculture that affected the lives of inmates more powerfully than anything else. The criteria for the success rate had been established by the Home Office as what was measurable – that the delinquents who arrived should not commit any offences within three years of leaving. On that basis, Park House had approximately a 70 per cent success rate for many years. From time to time, managers worried about the simplicity of such a measure, wherein someone who committed a trivial offence, irrespective of his background, was considered a failure and someone out of work, making appalling relationships, could be a success. They were concerned that, despite the enormous financial and programme investment in training boys for work, none remained in the job for which they had been trained for longer than a year. From time to time, rumours reached their ears of shocking bullying, for which the bullies in their turn would be beaten by the headmaster! It has to be said that, illogical though such a process may be for demonstrating the error of a bully's ways, it kept at least a superficial order. Throwing even that away without installing something more effective has often produced disaster rather than democracy.

By and large, managers were pleased at how well accepted Park House was socially. The local public school sent its sixth-form elevens over to thrash the boys at cricket and football and, at the annual sports day, even some parents came to witness their sons trundle up and down a hastily marked sports track. The managers sat in their own roped-off enclosure, of course, but they often joined in the fun by participating, perhaps in a car obstacle race with one of the boys chosen as a team-mate!

A group of younger trustees, however, were more worried by the lack of treatment for the increasing number of emotionally disturbed boys who were sent because Park House had 'psychiatric facilities'. That meant that two consultant psychiatrists visited for a few days each week and conducted individual interviews with those boys deemed to be disturbed enough by the headmaster. The two psychiatrists were of undoubted value. At the very least, the respite they provided for youngsters, persecuted by the general living situation, may have actually saved lives. Their view was that they were able to effect little real change in an atmosphere that regarded their work and those youngsters in need of treatment with contempt.

The managers became increasingly concerned that Park House should not rest on laurels whose value they themselves found questionable. They felt that Park House should become a therapeutic community, and they had in mind something like the Henderson Hospital, that Dr Maxwell Jones had set up a few years earlier. The Children's Department of the Home Office – soon to be transferred to the Department of Health and Social Security – did not want changes, as Park House was one of its star establishments. And, as the Department provided more than half of the financing, the managers were effectively controlled by central government.

The opportunity to escape from this straitjacket was provided by the 1969 Act.[1] This allowed Park House to be under the aegis of the Department of Education and Science as an independent school. This released the managers from the obligation, which they would have been under if they had opted for complete independence, to repay the capital expenditure that the government had invested since the school's inception. There were still bureaucratic difficulties to overcome as this was the only one out of 130 approved schools to choose such a course. Thus, another three or four years elapsed before this change was officially accepted. Nevertheless, as a result of this policy the incumbent headmaster successfully applied for promotion elsewhere and I was eventually appointed as his successor (see Chapter 2, pp. 23–4 for the development of Peper Harow after the 1969 Children and Young Persons' Act).

At that time, no-one was very clear about what a therapeutic community for adolescents might look like. Few managers had read Rapoport's book, *Community as Doctor* (1960). This was a serious study of the Henderson Hospital in Maxwell Jones's time and attempted to define the ingredients that made that community psychotherapeutic. However, I had worked at Park House for nearly six years, and for four and a half years of that period had been housemaster of one of the four sections into which the school had been divided. The housemaster was required to attend a monthly meeting with a regular group of three managers to discuss the individual progress of the boys of that section. There were approximately twenty-five boys to consider. Written reports were prepared quarterly, and every six months the boys actually appeared before the committee in person. The housemaster prepared a written report that detailed the issues he regarded as important. This was prepared in conjunction with the psychiatrist's report, and with those of other members of staff, such as the boy's trade-training instructor.

In some ways, taking over that house unit was comparatively easy. There was a recognition among all the housemasters – most of whom were teachers – that the boys in their care needed befriending and advising. Even the attentions of a 'Dutch uncle' are welcome in an institutionalizing environment and relationships between the housemasters and their charges, in this setting, were good. Many anxieties and much information about bullying came to light in these interviews. What was unusual in my House unit was the deliberate attempt to get the individual to perceive himself as part of a group process.

The idea behind this unusual approach was that the group's identity would be partly owned by the individual boy while, in turn, his own attitude and motivation would be considerably influenced by the whole group. If the housemaster, rather than the strongest youngster, could become accepted as the dynamic leader of that group, its orientation would actually become different from that of the existing peer group in the school. It would then be possible to think about individuals more independently than the general social context of the institution would normally allow.

Originally, that group had not been much different from the other three. The boys throughout the school stayed for about eighteen months to two years, and received promotional gradings that depended upon their behaviour and also a little on their achievements in trade-training departments and classrooms. The boys spent time in their houserooms when they were not engaged in the institutional routines of rising, washing, cleaning the House, eating breakfast, and forming the first work parade of the day. After lunch, they would parade again for classes or trade training and then shower and change for the evening meal, after which they would march off to various recreational activities, before returning to their houserooms for an hour's television before supper and bed. Weekends, too, were filled with similar activities. It was thought that, if each minute of every boy's time was filled with purposeful and supervised activity, this would somehow habituate him to functioning like that on his own when he left. Good aftercare would, of course, continually remind him to stay up to scratch.

This thinking paid no regard to the delinquent culture that enabled the boys to avoid the pain of their deprivation. Neither did it deal with the traumatic experiences of their childhood. Instead, it allowed the boys' easily roused anger to focus on any perceivably hostile force or person. Hence, school, police, and those peers in a more fortunate and successful position, could easily become their ill-considered target. The more depredatory and frightening they could make themselves, the more they would be esteemed by their underworld peers. In a private conversation with their housemaster, they might talk wanly of the loss or absence of family, or express their pain and sorrow at being unwanted, or recount some of their frightening memories of early childhood; among their peers they would brag of robberies committed, adults beaten up, girls who longed for their sexual services, and all interspersed with the argot of criminality, the reinforcing secret slang of the young lag. It was quite clear with what part of society they identified, and which activities gave them a sense of significance.

Yet, while hating to conform with the institutional system, with its sanctions of corporal punishment, and ultimately of direct transfer to Borstal without even recourse to the courts, the boys fell in with the system with remarkably little rebellion. As long as staff followed a predictable path, there were few serious riots in approved schools; rather there was an outward conformity that all those responsible for the system appreciated.

In another approved school, at which I had worked previously, a frightened elderly man used to slip twenty cigarettes at the beginning of the evening's duty to the senior boy, 'for a quiet evening'! There were 140 boys aged between 15 and 19 in that place, picked for their physical fitness, as they were intended for a career at sea. On Wednesday nights they always went to the cinema in the nearby town, marching through the winter darkness for about two miles. Within a week of arriving there, I was deputed to be in charge of this company. Under the eyes of the senior staff they 'fell-in' on parade, as fine a nautical body as could be seen. Heads up and arms swinging, they marched through the gates and into the darkness. Indeed, all went surprisingly well until the return journey. At first sight nothing seemed amiss, but about halfway back the column seemed to rise and fall some twenty feet ahead of me. Reaching the spot, I stumbled over a body. One of the boys had been kicked into unconsciousness and left bleeding and trampled. With difficulty, the column was persuaded to halt. The only response to demands for an explanation was, 'He's always fooling about, Sir!'

The anecdotes of those years now seem beyond belief, yet a similar subculture existed beneath the civilized surface of Park House. This subculture had to be overcome if any worthwhile work was to be effected.

Instead of the usual recreational activities on Friday nights, the housemasters managed their house groups for the entire evening. The book-keeping of their boys' pocket money and savings, their clothing checks, and washing routines could take nearly all of that time. However, for some months after my arrival, this was turned into a formal meeting in which I acted as chairman. Once order was regularly established, a committee was then elected and the chair passed to one of the elected boys. Various responsibilities were invented, and organized in such a way as to guard against any abuse of authority. The boys were to take major responsibility for their activities themselves. Staff worked every third weekend and permission was obtained to take large groups out on expedition training away from the humdrum routine of the institution. For a period of time, friendship was established with the warden of a dilapidated youth hostel, enabling the boys to get away for several weekends. The ostensible object was for a refurbishment project at the hostel. And indeed their trade training and their tools were put to good use, painting and plastering, and laying bricks. They had to prepare their own food, too, but joined in the folk singing that the warden organized until late on the Saturday night. What a difference the setting made. Increasingly, it became possible to discover other ways to get this group away from the others – departures straight after work on summer's evenings for rock climbing at a nearby outcrop for instance.

New boys joining found themselves taken aback by the different culture they encountered on arrival from their remand homes. The boys mixed less and less with the other house groups and developed a group morale none had previously experienced. Most remarkable was that increasingly, when their normal time for departure arrived, they each asked to stay longer!

By this time, the psychiatrist, who spent nearly half the week at the school, spent most of that time with the boys from this particular house group. Gradually, she evolved a system with the housemaster that enabled the real issues to be tackled in psychotherapy. Threatening material, normally too disruptive to deal with, was prepared for by an earlier series of interviews between the boy and the housemaster, and the psychiatric interviews were followed up in their turn with supportive ones. Gradually, as more and more boys were individually involved in this process, and as they became more senior, so a more serious group attitude to psycho-therapeutic material began to emerge.

Over a period of three years, the functioning of this house group completely changed. Though it was being emotionally sustained by undeniably charismatic leadership, much of the emotional nurture was increasingly being provided by the group itself. It had developed a sense of identity of which the boys felt a part. They enjoyed belonging to a group in which delinquent bravado played a decreasing part. Instead, they experienced a sense of comradely fun. The sustenance resulting from participation in such a group atmosphere promoted change of psychic significance. I sensed, intuitively, the timescale by which changes in the group's functioning could be made so that resistance to insight could be undermined. Gradually, insight and concern for one's individual peers became the watchwords of this previously delinquent group, and its self-sustaining power began to display itself. This, then, was a recognizable and, potentially, a definable process rather than magic.

In a sense, then, a small group of managers had some direct experience of the kind of change that could be brought about. They were involved in aspects of a therapeutic process that had not existed elsewhere in the school before. The group had become accustomed to creating a banquet in its houseroom at the end of term. The boys took over the housemaster's private kitchen in his home and the food was ferried back by car. Tablecloths and candles decorated a transformed room and all had made painstaking contributions from their niggardly pocket money to provide the ingredients. The managers, too, helped out generously, but were, indeed, rewarded by the atmosphere when, as guests, they joined these occasions at camp in the summer and at Christmas time.

My sense of a therapeutic atmosphere that could engender the courage for a boy to look at his position realistically was both confirmed and given form by several visits to George Lyward at Finchden Manor in Kent (see Chapter 3, pp. 30–1). His was the supreme example of the Pied Piper approach to such youngsters. Totally fascinating, and capable of charming a skeleton back to life, he was also an enigmatic personality. Perhaps if one had known him as a young man and in his middle years, his genius could have been more easily understood. He had bought Finchden, a small Elizabethan manor house in the Weald of Kent, in the decade before the war and it was to this quiet and beautiful building of nooks and crannies and the mystery of centuries that he returned with a handful of staff and youngsters when its military sequestration ended. What a house it was for a child! It breathed secret rooms and corridors, underground passages, and the possibility of treasure revealed at every turn. This was a therapeutic community long before the term was popular. The boys that went there nearly all originally came from privileged and talented families, but, with the years, that changed too. Giving them freedom to behave, and endless time to grow up, allowed many talents to be developed and several ex-residents have made names for themselves as artists of different kinds.

Not surprisingly, therefore, the place was full of music. The most exquisite Chopin could be heard played by an outrageous ragamuffin on a gleaming concert grand, most noticeably at dawn or midnight. Such adolescent craziness made the classics respectable, even to a pop generation. The behaviour at meal times was equally outrageous. It was not unknown for a young hulk to leave the refectory table by walking along its length among the jugs of water and place settings, and it was well-known that everyone drank out of jam jars! Beyond the oak panelling that swung aside to reveal Mr Lyward's study, all was redolent of centuries of quiet country civilization and the wildest of creatures became gentle when taking tea in the Oak Room.

Generally, the youngsters' craziest behaviour was not actually damaging, however shocking it might be to a visiting adult. Nevertheless, a new boy loaded with unhappiness and the profoundest pessimism as to his future would be convinced that Finchden could indeed be his to own in some way for ever. On arrival, he had found wild things, much like the creatures of Maurice Sendak's imagination (Sendak, 1963). Given the legitimacy of being, by Lyward's own artistry, those 'wild things' were content to be tamed in the fulness of time.

Lyward described himself as a psychologist, and no-one could have been more conscious of the nature of the inner world of the individual and of mankind. It was significant that he would invariably answer the request for his professional title in this way, and only secondarily referred to his role as a teacher, although he was in fact a quite outstandingly brilliant one. He understood a great deal about what happens to a youngster's mind under the pressures of not being acknowledged as an individual. He was the keenest of observers and was always on the *qui vive* for the opening of an opportunity for change. No knock on his door was simply accepted at face value. Any gesture or verbal slip invited the password of understanding to open the bolted door into a youngster's 'empty fortress' (Bettelheim, 1967).[2] He had infinite patience to allow the experience of a momentary shaft of light to work its magic in the gloom until the youngster became permanently open to the world, instead of defended against it. That patience required him simply to sit in an atmosphere of creativity, of intriguing fun and mystery. It was the context of Finchden that was magical. The charisma of its 'Old Magician' was an aura that actually could be analysed, and be seen as understanding and as the knowledge derived from long experience.

When it came to creating that atmosphere at Park House, I was clear in a way that I was too young to have acquired that knowledge. Two boys followed each other to Lyward's study one afternoon, both requesting a new pair of shoes. The first received a straight affirmative response, while the second was involved in an hour's diversion. He played the piano. Lyward played the piano. He took tea, chocolate biscuits, and was teased into some thoughts about the nature of his greediness and the real nourishment that he actually needed. When he finally left, it was without permission to buy more shoes. Lyward responded to the question of how he could tell how to respond to each so differently, and by such instant decision-making, with a cry of 'Forty years, my boy, forty years!' A further hour passed in which he delineated the details he knew about each boy's functioning and what he had seen in their approach. I felt slow-witted and amazed.

What was clear to me was the atmosphere, the quiet relationships between boys and staff, the context in which I might learn the patience to wait, within which everyone else would not be harmed while we all took the time to learn.

Chapter two

Setting up a new approach

The major difference between approved school's and therapeutic community's perception of causes of emotional disturbance and disturbed behaviour. The therapeutic approach regards as essential the task of making the residents' unconscious attitudes manifest. The approved school attempts to inculcate change by imposing positive social attitudes - but imposition inevitably encourages a bullying subculture.
Appointment of new director and new policy for Park House. Process of establishing the psychotherapeutic programme – resistance from government, staff, and residents.

What created the approved school's antitherapeutic style was the under-lying attitude of those responsible for the system. Any visitors who shared the staff's perspective, or who knew little about psychological develop-ment, were bound to be impressed by what they saw. They were shown houses, a full-size gymnasium and swimming pool – 'built by the boys' – they were proudly told. The place seemed orderly, as squads of youngsters marched purposefully between one place and another. There did not seem a moment in the day or night that had not been considered and catered for in what seemed a clearly managed fashion.

However, all this organized and well-burnished surface, at second glance, revealed prejudices in those responsible for the system, shared at central government level, and by those who operated it professionally. The implication was that delinquency – which meant bad behaviour, including the committing of criminal offences – arose, at its simplest, from choice. Badly brought-up children were not really trained to know the difference between right and wrong and they had become increasingly used to doing whatever they wanted. As toddlers they probably had tantrums, which they were allowed to get away with; as children they went to schools where teachers exercised less and less discipline. They lived in a society that increasingly demonstrated not hard work as a way of achieving, but

12

financial credit, and this in a work-setting dominated by the rights of the worker without regard to his responsibilities. If they were not disciplined pretty firmly and pretty soon, there would be no holding such youngsters! When they wanted something, they were simply prepared to take it. If prevented, they felt that they, not their victims, were the aggrieved party!

However, the reasons why children might become emotionally disturbed or delinquent are infinitely more complex in our society than for reasons of parental inconsistency. Nor do children exercise a wilful choice to behave badly merely for their own gratification. The parents of children who become disturbed may have been emotionally deprived in their own childhood and may themselves experience a permanent sense of being unloved. They may bear a permanent sense of resentment and envy of others. Indeed, if a parent has never been provided with secure parenting, how can he exercise an intuitive understanding of good parenting?

Carlie Crathies illustrates much of this. Margaret Crathies – her mother – was an only child. This is not in itself significant, but her daughter's development increasingly demonstrated a repetitive pattern. Margaret married early – often an indication of a wish to escape from stressful home circumstances. Carlie was born soon after the marriage, but two years later her father was killed in a car crash. When she was 4 years old, Mother married again.

Carlie's stepfather had serious emotional problems. He had a poor relationship with his own stepfather and had received some psychiatric in-patient treatment. He attacked Carlie and her mother frequently and was unable to keep a job. As a result, Carlie, her newly born stepbrother, and mother moved homes frequently. The situation worsened, with Carlie and her brother sometimes staying with their stepgrandmother and sometimes being fostered separately by the local authority. Stepfather went to prison for drug offences and Mother's mental stability began to collapse. When Carlie was eight the social worker noted 'a degree of role reversal ... Carlie had to provide Mother with a great deal of support and share the traumas of her affairs, etc.'.

As Carlie became pubescent, so a stepbrother was born. Carlie was becoming noticeably promiscuous and rebellious. On a visit, Stepfather cropped her hair when he caught her kissing a boy! Later she made allegations that Stepfather had raped her at this time. Her promiscuity, hostility, and involvement in drug abuse eventually saw her taken into care as 'beyond control'.

When Carlie's grandmother was dying she frequently confused Carlie with her own mother and with her daughter Margaret, Carlie's mother. Carlie also received numerous sexual advances from her grandfather, yet Mother kept sending Carlie to visit and comfort him. At the same time Mother implied that she, too, had been raped and that she, too, had experienced some of Carlie's problems in her early teens.

It was clear that Mother, too, found appropriate differentiation between herself and Carlie difficult. It may well be that her own rightful position as a child had also been disregarded. Lacking the secure child–mother relationship herself, she found great difficulty in offering a secure mother–child relationship to Carlie. Her attempts to explain her own position to Carlie – perhaps with consciously intended, reparative intentions – only encouraged Carlie's behaving in a similar way. Stepfather even more clearly illustrates both his own disturbed personality, and also his own undeveloped ability to be an emotionally stable and appropriately mature father.

In addition to the sheer lack of parenting ability, through lack of experience, and because of preoccupations with nagging emotional problems rather than with the children's appropriate needs, there is also an overlay of trauma. It is doubtful that Father's death, the birth of step-siblings, sexual abuse, Mother's own breakdown, the repeated separations, and so forth were ever talked through.

Carlie's anxiety outside the family in children's homes, and indeed at Peper Harow, was often expressed in ways that felt intolerable. She was exceptionally sexually provocative, engendering much abuse from the boys. She had aggressive tantrums that were actually physically dangerous and she found the pressure to face up to the suffering she had actually experienced frequently unbearable. Significantly though, all her forms of behaviour were like her parents'! It was as though Carlie was a disturbed child who modelled her functioning on that of her disturbed parents just as surely as good parents consciously encourage their children to develop according to their own good experience.

Unhappy, insecure personalities may be very ambivalent about what they provide for their own children. Ambivalence makes for insecurity in relationships and an insecure child is likely to be more demanding than normal. His anxiety and attention-seeking behaviour increasingly set the scene for conflict. As the child becomes less and less physically manageable, so others outside the family begin to find themselves confronting him. By the time adolescence is reached, much of his behaviour has breached society's boundaries, but by now he would be deemed to be legally responsible for his behaviour and therefore able to acknowledge that he should pay a price for the injuries he caused.

This assumption of sufficient emotional and intellectual maturity is unwarranted for the youngster we are concerned with, irrespective of his chronological age. The average adult may be irritated when caught committing a traffic offence. He may try to excuse himself, but is ultimately well able to accept the appropriateness of paying the fine. Not so for the delinquent. He only bows before compulsion as the cell door finally closes behind him but, fear apart, he still resents the outcome. In the approved school this uncomprehending resentment was, in turn, seen as outrageous. 'He ought to take his punishment like a man!' What was not recognized was the small child inside the adolescent that, in some way beyond expression, sensed he had been deprived of something that would have enabled him to act differently. Lacking this, it would feel unfair that he should be punished as if he had real, rather than only apparent, control over his activities. Time and again, care workers of every kind, who asked the inevitable question, 'Why did you do it?', would receive the sullen and baffled answer, 'I don't know'. The delinquent's resentment seems to assume that he is the injured person, but why this should be so lies buried years before.

It must be emphasized that the youngster does not know why he feels resentful and unwilling to accept his just deserts. He will need someone else's help if the reasons for his original attitudes are to be unearthed. Much adolescent theft is of items that are useless to the thief. Neither he nor anyone else can understand why he would want these items. Apparently he has no more discrimination than a magpie. The real problem is the youngster's irresistible compulsion to steal something – it hardly matters what. Yet, the observer can see how the roots of this compulsion lie in early childhood.

Roy could remember that he started stealing when he was a toddler. He was not aware that rooting about in his mother's purse and taking some of the coins was called theft. Nor was he aware in a conscious way his permanent state of being was called anxiety, or that the reassurance that he constantly sought could not be used by him as the comfort he needed, even if it were offered. Roy's family had always existed in multiple-stress conditions, so his anxiety was only one of the many problems that overwhelmed his mother. At times, when his mother was absent, Roy's anxiety became so unbearable that he tried to get inside her purse – as it were. His dilemma increased in complexity because he would be punished for doing this. He then stole food from the fridge. He was punished for this. Whichever way Roy's behaviour symbolically expressed his need to possess some indescribable quality such as comfort, his delinquent expression of this need resulted in denial and punishment. Perhaps, even then, his unconsciously chosen delinquent form of expression was partly motivated by some anger at his deprivation. It is not surprising that such unresolved problems from Roy's earlier life would feature still more prominently in his adolescent functioning as anger, resentment, and as a sense of great loss.

The attitude that flourished in the approved school was directed towards visible behaviour. Boys were categorized as thieves, liars, and 'weirdos'. While their behaviour often needed control, other obligations towards the youngster were often forgotten – particularly the obligation to recognize what the youngster himself could not see, and that it was therefore an essential task for the staff to help him to do so.

In the first chapter, reference was made to the daily routine at Park House that began at 6.40 a.m. Boys got dressed in one set of clothes and descended three floors to the basement, to queue at sinks for their turn to wash and shave. Those who had wet their beds disposed of their sheets in a public laundry and were made to take a shower in the centre of a huge room in the full sight of everyone else. The boys then rushed back up three floors to their bedrooms and their clothes for the day, before rushing back to the different parts of the building in order to scrub the floors or polish them – always by hand, as it was felt in some way that hard work was good for one. (That 'good' was almost always expressed as though through clenched teeth!)

There is no doubt that a group of physically fit, antisocial adolescents can be a very serious threat to anyone's wellbeing and that, if they are expected to think seriously about their lives, they will first have to hear the questions. Undoubtedly, their behaviour must be brought to a standstill so there is an essential place for discipline, yet the sooner it becomes self-discipline, the sooner will the painful, inhibited journey towards responsible adulthood be resumed.

Park House imposed discipline. But it was provocative. There was no need to get up so early. There was no need to humiliate the eneuretics. There was no need to punish anyone who talked, or to arrange for people to queue at the washbasins in order to institutionalize such an intimate activity as caring for one's body. Neither was there a need to scrub and polish the house by hand as though hoovers and electric polishers were not normal household appliances. If there was no need, then what was the purpose of this ritualistic lifestyle? I suppose it was in order to get the youngsters used to doing what they did not want to do, and used to the idea that they would be so seriously punished if they 'bucked the system' that they would eventually be forced to conform. This system bullied its weakest members into doing what its strongest required. It can be of no surprise that beneath the cleanliness was more bullying.

Generally, the staff colluded with the bullying as long as it was not too overt. Criminologists describe a hidden institutional life as a 'subculture', inevitable and arising out of the essential nature of an institution. In the case of an approved school, it was frightening and cruel and, of course, reflected the particular, psychologically disturbed fantasies of the youngsters themselves.

The weakest were its permanent scapegoats, always being set up to be humiliated. Assignations were arranged in the Boot Room. In the moments between the supervising member of staff arriving with the bulk of a group, a severe kicking could be inflicted on the terrorized youngster, who had not handed over his tobacco or his share of food at the previous meal time. Physical torture for the amusement of a dominant senior boy was a frequent though not a daily occurrence. However, at meal times newcomers were regularly deprived of their food by the voracious seniors. Most newcomers learnt to grit their teeth until, as the months passed, they arrived at the position where they could do exactly what had been done to them. The official organization, too, was partly identified with deprivation because, while the actual portions of food allowed for each growing adolescent satisfied specific dietary requirements, the boys' hunger was frequently unassuaged.

Some staff were outraged by what they knew but generally bullying was assumed to be inevitable. The youngsters often did function in a really nasty fashion and it was assumed that some of them at least were really nasty people. It was evident that, unless control were maintained, then this underworld would rule the institution in the plain light of day as well. The subculture was thus kept submerged by a gradation of punishments to provide stronger and stronger reminders that eventually the weight of society would make it an inevitable winner in a power contest.

For a few, their only refuge was in the psychiatrist's room for an hour a week. At the other end of the spectrum, another small group honed their hatred to its sharpest, balancing their sadism with masochistic triumph at the development of their inurement to more and more punishment.

However clear it may have been to an onlooker that beatings and the threat of Borstal only produced more guarded delinquent behaviour, it was extremely difficult to persuade anyone that the problems of the youngsters were simply not being addressed, or to persuade anyone that an alternative system could possibly address those issues. Obviously, if the authorities could not be sensitive to the feelings of these youngsters and thus begin to see from what roots they had developed over the years and how those boys' developing feelings had been continually made manifest by their behaviour, then they would not be able even to conceive of a system that would respond to that reality. Instead, authority could only repress, seizing the wolf of behaviour by the ears and hanging on until the inevitable day when the frustrated behaviour broke loose.

In a sense, not only did the staff collude with central government as represented by the Children's Department of the Home Office, but so did the youngsters themselves. When an organization becomes thoroughly institutionalized, then, irrespective of everyone's frustration at their inability to succeed in their task, the organization will often seem determined to resist change, even while those involved know that the necessity to change is in their best interests. Jan Foudraine (1974) describes just such an experience of how he tried to convert a long-stay ward in a mental hospital into a therapeutic one. The therapeutic ward was eventually able to allow its inmates to retrieve their sanity and wellbeing, but not without first overcoming enormous resistance by staff and patients alike. David Wills (1971) illustrated a similar process in the conversion of the Cotswold Community from its punitive approved-school roots to its therapeutic orientation.

One of the chief impediments when treating disturbed children is their own resistance to understanding their unhappiness. Indeed, this is a familiar issue for all patients and their therapists. The untrammelled behaviour of young adolescents, however, can ensure that experiments with treatment, rather than punishment, can be brought to a total standstill. When all other aspects of an institution aid and abet this resistance, the task is indeed formidable. Perhaps it is as well that none of us engaged in the Peper Harow venture knew how formidable it would be, or we might never have begun. On the other hand, our organization's other establishment, Thornby Hall, which, at the time of writing, has been open for two years, shows equal difficulties in reaching a predominantly therapeutic state of being, rather than being at the mercy of the youngsters' disturbed behaviour. A phenomenon that occurs again and again in therapeutic establishments is that everyone becomes frightened of the residents' behaviour once it has freedom to express their underlying fantasies. This occurs whether the community is one that is attempting a radical change of direction or whether it has been set up intentionally as a therapeutic community. At that point, staff wish to impose controls and rules and to expel the most recalcitrant youngsters. The staff tend to lose faith in the healing potential of a communal endeavour. They become depressed and lose faith in their own creativity. The children rapidly sense that lack of self-confidence. Their anxiety rises rapidly and their habitual expressing of this in antisocial behaviour reasserts itself. The director's main task at this stage of a community's life is to maintain the whole community's hope and to strengthen its determination not to be inhibited by its fear of behaviour.

There are usually a hoard of demands on the director at this time. He may feel under such pressure that he, too, will need regular support in order to nurture his own sense of hope. Almost always, the needs of such establishments outstrip the anticipated pace of its development and financing. Thus, its leader can see what needs to be done but his power to effect it lags behind. The conversion of Park House School to Peper Harow faced just such issues, but they were not only material; neither were they only financial, or staff, or cultural, or group-psychodynamic, or organizational issues; they were also bureaucratic issues, for the organization as a whole was not independent to make the changes consistent with its developing new activities.

Chapter one records the origins of Park House School, including the period of its first nineteen years at Peper Harow, and the time when the headmaster left to become principal of a much larger establishment for delinquents (see Chapter one, p. 6). The vacant post at Park House was then advertised in terms that indicated the managers' desire for a changed programme. It was clear that they hoped that a therapeutic process would be instituted as a predominant feature of Park House. The managers were certainly consistent in their wish to develop a therapeutic approach, though their earlier attempts to do more than establish two psychiatrists at Park House had brought continual resistance from the Home Office. At the time of my appointment, the Home Office's Children's Department was more concerned to see what choice the Park House managers would make with regards to their options of status under the new 1969 Children and Young Person's Act. That matter resolved, then central government would no longer have to bear responsibility, either financially or organizationally, for the school. The Department's view was that the sooner a new head could be appointed, the quicker the establishment would be on its way.

Those managers who had worked most closely with me when I had been a housemaster at Park House School were anxious that I should apply for the post, particularly after the first advertisement had brought an unsatisfactory response. The psychiatrist, with whom I had worked closely, also urged me most strongly to seize the opportunity to develop what we had done together still further.

Having been away at university for a year, I felt extremely jaundiced at having to return to the humdrum existence of work – and what work! In direct contrast to the heady atmosphere of university life in the sixties, the repressive atmosphere of the approved school left one with a sense of despair. The serious ill-health of the deputy head required me to replace him in an acting capacity. My own interest was in buying a property in the Lake District in order to convert it into a therapeutic community (for which I had already been offered partial funding). I judged it extremely unlikely that the kinds of change that seemed essential could be put into effect by the managers, or supported by the Children's Department. However, I eventually applied and, together with a long list of requirements should I be successful, I took my interview in turn with other candidates after a re-advertisement. The Children's Department – as required – was represented by a senior inspector. To my amazement, he agreed to all my requirements so, when offered the job, I could only accept it. I was given two months to prepare a document setting out the changes, my reasons for them, and their managerial consequences.

At that time, there were nearly eighty boys at Park House. None of them wanted to be there and all of them had arrived through the normal channels of the system. Nationally, five classifying schools, as well as one or two remand homes in cities like London, between them received most of the adjudicated delinquents and assessed their suitability for the 130 approved schools in England and Wales. These institutions then sent their reports to the schools they thought were appropriate, although this depended on how many vacancies each had.

Officially, the cost of each youngster's placement was supposed to be split equally between government and the local authority in which the youngster lived. The local authority's costs were partially met by a charge to the parents for those under 16 years old. Over the years, as costs had risen, central government's share of the costs had increased disproportionately. For instance, if the numbers of children had fallen beneath the agreed break-even figure for a school, central government would pay the difference. The number of staff required to run a particular institution hardly varied, irrespective of the numbers of children. Inevitably, then, a reduction in numbers meant an increase in costs.

One of my most important requirements agreed to at my interview was that numbers should be reduced to zero and then built up gradually.It seemed that the group of delinquents present was too set in the long-standing culture of the school to allow for much change. If the numbers were reduced below the government's 'break-even' equation to fit a different therapeutic requirement, then the government's costs would increase. The appropriate number for a therapeutic community was deemed to be fifty, implying a considerable increase in cost to central government.

At the same time, in order to maintain reasonable relationships with the staff unions, a second point, also accepted at the appointing interview, had been that staff should be offered the alternative of retraining if they wanted to stay under the new regime. After all, it was hardly their fault if the management decided that the jobs for which they had been properly appointed were to be changed. They had to be given the opportunity to adapt before any pressure was put on them to take alternative employment. It seemed unlikely that many of them could make such a transition and, despite individual discussions, none of them seemed to want to be trained for a new task.

It was clear that this proposed process would increase costs enormously for central government, so it should not have been surprising that we were turned down flat when we eventually met at the Ministry. However, on the basis that all these points had been agreed by the Children's Department's representative at the interview, I had proceeded on the naive assumption that it was only a matter of form before my document was fully accepted by the Department when we arrived at the meeting arranged at my interview.

Accordingly, I visited our most significant referring institutions and explained that we were about to receive government agreement for our policy, so would they cease to send youngsters to us until further notice. In the future, when we were open for admissions again, I would want to make my own evaluation of the conclusions they drew from their reports and I would want to interview each referred youngster with his social worker before deciding if he were suitable for admission. If the individual was suitable, then I would want him to go away and write, asking to be admitted, on the conditions discussed with him in his interview. Obviously, we explained, we would anticipate accepting youngsters whom we had actually invited for interviews. However, we were attempting to outmanoeuvre the youngsters' resistance to treatment by making the interview itself a small experience of the treatment process (see Chapter nine, pp.159–60; Chapter five, pp. 91–4). We were not interested simply in assessing whether their behaviour was tolerable or not. We were trying to engage them with the idea that treatment of their underlying problems was the purpose of their placement, and that their commitment to treatment was essential. The final heresy declared that, if the youngster said he did not want to come, we would not accept him, even if we thought he should!

At the same time I started to release youngsters as fast as possible, so that, when the chairman of managers, his colleague trustee, the consultant psychiatrist, and I went to the Department to discuss the planning document, our programme was well under way. I half expected them to be impressed with the speed with which I was addressing the task.

Instead, we were astonished at our reception. The Assistant Secretary of State in charge of the Children's Department announced that my document outlining the proposed structural changes was a nonsense. It was entirely unacceptable and we had better return to running the school as before. It was beyond comprehension why we wished it to be changed anyway. The chairman carefully explained how the managers' observations over the years had led them to this conclusion, and that now was a propitious opportunity to effect an exciting innovative treatment that would bring everybody credit. 'In any event', he pronounced, 'we have just appointed a head specifically capable of developing a therapeutic community. He was not appointed to run an approved school.'

'Well, you had better unappoint him forthwith!', came the trenchant reply. The uncomfortable senior inspector, who had agreed with the aims and changes, was then drawn into the debate and compelled to apologize for what had been a mistake in judgement on his part. He had never had the authority to make such an agreement.

Suddenly the Assistant Secretary of State started to shout. Enraged, she cried, 'Do you want me to close you down? I'll close you down this afternoon.' Everyone began trundling towards a rapid and polite termination and we trotted off down the corridors of power to the outside fresh air.

We held a rapid council of war and were all of a like mind. The chairman was our general. 'We don't, any of us, want to continue to be associated with an approved school. Let's do what we were going to do anyway. If we don't get away with it, we can all leave, but, if by some miracle we carry it off, then we will be doing the important thing, with or without permission.' Buoyed up, then, with our delinquent conspiracy, off we went to do just that.

There were many other bureaucratic clashes over the next few months, and we were warned that we would be subject to an inspection in the following year. It was clear what that meant. Some of the clashes were mysterious and some farcical.

Apparently, the local fire service regarded the building as unsafe and had been saying so for some time. They required various emergency procedures to be completed immediately or else they would invoke their power to close us. Long correspondence had passed between the fire service and the managers, who had passed them on to the Children's Department for the already agreed additional funding. Despite the increasing threat from the Fire Department, the money never arrived. As a new broom, I attempted to intervene with the Children's Department myself. However, when I spoke to a senior member of the Assistant Secretary of State's staff, I was astonished at his response. He declared his wish to be sympathetic to me, anticipating that I would nod and wink collusively with his unsavoury remarks about my managers, 'who always wanted more money from others, though they were well able to put their hands in their own pockets!'

On another occasion, a Department vehicle inspector decided the essential school vehicle should be replaced forthwith. It should no longer be used. He would make arrangements for immediate replacement funding. Unfortunately, while accepting his view, his colleagues only made enough money available for half a new vehicle. After months of wrangling, they eventually agreed that they had made a mistake.

The personal hostility of the existing staff at this time was considerable, and yet they were afraid to express it directly. My family and I lived in one of a row of staff houses and the situation was becoming more untenable for us, as the whole setting was pretty isolated, so that the hostility of neighbours was difficult to tolerate. On one occasion my 6-year-old son slipped while climbing a tree in the garden and became wedged by his knee. His cries brought his mother out to the rescue and the member of staff who lived next door. Yet, despite seeing her struggles to free the child, he turned his back and went indoors.

It became urgent that my family was moved to a detached house a few yards from the main building. In some senses this would provide less privacy, but it made a statement about our family commitment to the project. In fact, the building had been built as a sick bay and so needed some alteration in order to become a house. Its existing layout was larger than the number of square feet allowed in government manuals for the house of the headmaster of an approved school, but its conversion would cost only a fraction of the cost of building a new house. The Assistant Secretary of State would be happy to pay for a new house of the right number of square feet, but not the smaller sum for the conversion of a building that was bigger. Eventually, it was decided that the building should be converted, but that one-third of it should be turned into student accommodation, which would have been inappropriate and which would never have been used.

It felt as though my family's wellbeing was under pressure from both the hostile government department and from the staff, as a way of attacking the protagonists that they were unable to dominate personally and, at that point, I was ready to resign. Good fortune regularly came to our aid in those days and unexpectedly, the Assistant Secretary of State was suddenly replaced by a colleague from the Prison Department, who immediately came on a visit and pronounced that the head's house should be altered in whatever way he wished. His experience told him that 'you could not have a happy prison without a happy governor'!

These and many similar instances of maddening bureaucratic interventions convinced the managers that they should use the requirement of the 1969 Act for change of status, to become as independent as possible. Again, however, the Children's Department changed the policy that at one time seemed as if it would allow independence, leaving alternatives that seemed only to be, either control by a local authority, or else that we would have to find the cash to repay the Government for its capital investment over the years. Fortunately, the small print offered a third option – as a non-maintained school under the aegis of the Department of Education's Special Schools' Division (see Chapter 1, p. 6; Chapter 9, p. 166). However, no organization had been admitted under this status for many years. Would the Minister receive the appropriate recommendation from his civil servants?

The Chief Inspector was not at all enthusiastic. He knew what a school was and the whole of this set-up was too like a hippy commune for his choice. However, the Assistant Secretary of State was a very different person from his colleague at the Children's Department. (The Children's Department had itself now transferred to the Department of Health and Social Security from the Home Office.) His first visit was in the middle of the night, though he came again more normally by day. He was excited by the novelty of the situation and, despite the lack of enthusiasm from his Department, gave his total support. As a result, the Minister agreed to our changed status, though it took another two years to sort out the details.

We had anticipated that the threatened inspection by the Children's Department would be totally unsympathetic and would result in our closure. We therefore decided in advance to create a considerable support group that would cause the Department to think twice. This inspired the idea of holding our first day conference. Not only were nationally respected speakers persuaded to support us, but several hundred invitations were extended to directors of social services and education, chairmen of local authority subcommittees, professors, and professionals in many disciplines; some hundreds of whom came. At the same time, we organized a major BBC documentary about what we were doing called 'Tougher than Punishment', and several major feature articles appeared in each of the serious national daily newspapers in turn.

Our intention was to invite the personnel of the Children's Department, who, instead of arriving to see a bunch of irresponsible staff failing to manage, would be taken aback and be more guarded in their decision-making as a result of the support we would be able to gather. In the event, all this was unnecessary, as the Department agreed to our change in function, by default rather than support, but that was all we needed. A letter arrived in the spring simply saying that the agreed number for our establishment would henceforth be fifty-one – the new maximum of my submitted document. That ended the immediate arguments and enabled us to concentrate on achieving viable independence.

When we became a non-maintained school, we would be obliged to 'break even' or go into liquidation. No government department would bail us out. Meanwhile, through my policy of reducing the numbers from eighty, I had started a landslide and our numbers had in fact dropped to the lower thirties. By independence, as it were, it was essential that we should get back to break-even. Many others seem to have experienced a similar dilemma about the break-even/occupancy-level equation. There seems to be a point of balance once break-even has been reached. However, all reasonable efforts to build numbers at an even pace – as I had proposed in my original document for change – were defied by an illogical reality. Similarly, if numbers were substantially reduced for any reason it becomes extremely difficult to impose a brake. From blithely discharging youngsters as rapidly as possible, I suddenly found myself having to take anyone referred and this obviously made a significant difference to the pace of dynamic change.

While all this political manoeuvring was occurring, the actual development of the new community was also growing step by step. It was significant that even the supposed good discipline that had been the mark of Park House School had broken down. I was visited by the local police about the time I took over and they illustrated, by means of their incident map, that, whereas the nearby town was comparatively incident-free, the villages around the school were clustered with pins marking the scenes of crimes. Although it was essential to a therapeutic process for punishment to be abolished, it seemed more immediately urgent to begin by establishing control and to ensure general recognition that I, as the new person-in-charge, could effect it.

It was apparent that the night was alive with illegal excursions to steal cars, burgle houses, and so forth. I announced that anyone not in bed at the appropriate time would be punished by the usual method – corporally. It seemed that half the boys in the school were wandering around the next night and so, indeed with aching arm, all were beaten! After another night like this the numbers for punishment began to reduce. Eventually, a night arrived when no-one was found out of bed, and there was no-one to punish in the morning.

At that point, not without anxiety, I announced that there would be no more punishment. The punishment book was closed. The canes were all broken and thrown away. Henceforth, it was bravely announced that relationships would have to be different.

New staff were attracted with advertisements that clearly stated the youngsters had to come first. They were required 'to love the youngsters while not overidentifying with them'. This was a startling proposition, even for the early seventies and, although this attracted some very strange people occasionally, gradually a caring and highly educated staff began to gather together and respond to the new ideas about treatment that were being formulated.

The most major change occurred immediately after the bizarre meeting at the Children's Department, whose instructions we decided to defy. I sat down with both psychiatrists to debate what made a therapeutic community. They were both quite clear. 'A therapeutic community? We must have a community meeting.' And so, in the place of work parades, or even the more normal school assembly with which I had replaced them while only acting head, we all occupied a double circle of uncomfortable black plastic chairs that filled the dining-room. Wives of staff, occasional managers, or other visitors were all invited along and so we sat and waited for the therapy to occur.

The handful of new staff were nonplussed, but hopeful, and the majority of old timers were nonplussed and derisive. 'If I were a resident in a therapeutic community', sneered one such member of staff to a youngster suspected of arson, 'I'd burn the place down!' (see also Chapter four, p. 62 and p. 67). It seemed that time needed to be found to deal with the acting out of the staff more than that of the youngsters. So, as the end of each community meeting exploded, one member of staff was deputed to ensure the seething mass of boys and their stirred-up feelings remained in the dining-room for a further quarter of an hour and a cup of tea, while the rest of the staff were shepherded into another room for a rapid résumé of the significance of the meeting, and for a series of instructions about the methods by which to manage the expected outcome, as well as the methods by which they were not to manage them!

After that long quarter of an hour, the duty member of staff was swept aside while the tumultuous boys billowed out of the dining-room, whooping both with relief and anxiety at one and the same time.

It rapidly became obvious that the free-floating anxiety would need to be mopped up fairly quickly. We had previously thought that small therapy groups would eventually be on the agenda, but we realized that we no longer had the time to prepare and train staff to conduct them or the youngsters in their use. We would have to start at once.

The old workshops were then closed. Instead, all boys were placed in five small groups of nine or ten apiece, with the director and one of the two psychiatrists, and these were then timetabled to meet twice a week for an hour and a quarter. After a few months, it became obvious that we did not have the resources to meet twice a week and so small-group time was halved. By this time, some of the initial anxiety had reduced and staff were also beginning to find their own ways of creating positive activity with the boys, which increasingly began to look like thought-out, systematic, individual casework and so the skeleton of a therapeutic community was in place.

It was an exciting time, but certainly neither peaceful nor particularly therapeutic in any obvious way. The next two chapters describe the early development of the community identity and the large-and small-group meetings: the consequences of those developments took at least three years to reach any integrated maturity. The actual 'hands-on' experience was chaotic. The kitchen was abused to the point where it posed an obvious health risk. The furniture was rapidly reduced to matchwood. As there had never been any carpets or curtains, the crash of breaking windows and screaming tantrums echoed around the house, raising everyone's tension to fever pitch.

All old rules had been abandoned. The community had to find its own way to order and, indeed, in surprise and apprehension, the boys in community meetings rapidly reached agreements about bedtimes and meal times. But they were reached superficially, as obviously necessary organizational structures, and to defend against the overwhelming chaos. There was no consideration about the underlying dynamic significance of these daily events, so the new arrangements had little actual effect and the staff bore the brunt of the consequences. Getting everyone up in the morning for the community meeting inevitably meant a member of staff being bashed, and every bedtime required staff physically to wrestle two or three hulking youngsters upstairs to bed, from perhaps 9.30 p.m. until two o'clock in the morning.

The old staff were afraid and made plans to leave as rapidly as possible. The new staff hung on doggedly, both to principles and to their *esprit de corps*. A picture comes to mind of a particularly wild 15-year-old breaking a series of broom handles over the back of a large and urbane member of staff. 'I say, Alex', gasped our lover of literature and the high arts, 'that rather hurts you know! No, I say!', as further blows crashed down and, from gritted teeth, 'This is really a bit much, Old Boy! I will surely get a bit tetchy if you don't stop!' The more pragmatic director intervened less politely, but the bruises never shook that member of staff's caring or thoughtfulness towards the terrible Alex. Meanwhile we, the staff, had some terrific parties when not on duty!

All this time, in meeting after meeting, I was setting out to capture the boys' imagination as to what could be made of their opportunity; why they should care for each other. A picture was painted for them of themselves respected, valued, with futures they had never thought of. And, with an increasing number of creative staff, all sorts of activities were being devised that intrigued and coaxed them into a relationship with the idea of a community as something rewarding and exciting to be part of.

Amidst the destruction, a new identity was being forged, albeit not with specific clarity, but with hope and a belief that it would eventually flower.

Chapter three

A network of interrelating groups

*The development of an atmosphere that would stimulate and
highlight the community's psychodynamic life. Influential
experiences.*
*The development of the psychodynamic structure. The subgroups in
that overall structure – residents, staff, and director. Some
unconscious subgroup functioning and intergroup activity. The
eventual direction of this activity towards the therapeutic task.*

The new identity we set out to create envisaged an institution in which a
particular atmosphere would exist. Within this atmosphere a programme
would flourish that would be different from the approved school. For
example, we would emphasize art and music-making, rather than the
building trades. These different activities would indicate different values
that one might suppose were more pertinent to the boys' real needs than the
previous ones. We felt that the development of personal creativity was
more relevant to the needs of emotionally disturbed boys than vocational
training. Therefore, our programme needed to emphasize expression and
exploration, rather than finite and specific tasks that tend to support the
requirements of discipline and behaviour management.

I have already emphasized that there is undoubtedly a place for
discipline and behaviour management. There is also a place for the finite
and specific; it applies particularly in basic maths and science. These
subjects were especially difficult to establish in Peper Harow. Activity that
develops a sense of self-worth and a skill in creative expression needs to
precede the riskier task of facing up to being undeniably right or wrong.
My own views about communal values had arisen from a variety of
personal experiences.

One undoubtedly stemmed from experiences in my own boarding
house when I was at school. We had a weekly meeting on Sunday evenings,
totally managed by the boys. It was formally organized, with chairman and
secretary, and motions were put to the meeting by proposer and seconder,
which concerned, at face value, the minutiae of our school life. They were

attended by everyone, including the housemasters and frequently the headmaster, whose private quarters were situated in our house. The *raison d'être* of these regular meetings was that they were obviously educational and enabled one to practise the workings of the wider society. But, in addition to this worthy civic purpose, they also taught us a great deal about our existing personal relationships.

At one time, we boys were led by a particularly aggressive 18-year-old, who functioned at times like a caricature of a stereotypical trade union official. He had exceptional charisma, a profound sense of duty, and was hero-worshipped by all his peers. The headmaster, obviously, held him high in his affections, yet they clashed like Titans one Sunday evening. The issue seemed important to the head of house, to the extent that he was extremely rude to the headmaster, who was arguing against the proposal. The latter lost his temper and demanded an apology, which the chairman tried unsuccessfully to draw from his senior. We juniors cringed with excited and anxious glee at the gathering battle. Finally, the headmaster left the meeting angrily and it took some days before peace was restored. It was extraordinary that at that time in the early fifties such a situation could even be allowed. It was even more extraordinary that the headmaster allowed himself to be overruled by the democratic process, even though he was sure he was in the right.

On another occasion when the headmaster was addressing the sixth form about the philosophy of relationships, baffled by his idiosyncratic delivery, I sat busily playing the fool in the back row. To my astonishment, Luke suddenly roared at me to leave the room. It was vastly impressive, being so uncharacteristic. Later, when I was summoned to his study, I arrived with much anxiety. 'Please sit down', he began. 'I really must apologize for shouting at you earlier. I do hope you will forgive me. The trouble is, what I was saying seemed very important to me and I could see that I was not saying it very clearly so, as I struggled to do so, that became more important than you. I do hope you will accept that really nothing is more important to me than you and your colleagues.'

'What did he say?', demanded my eager colleagues as I left. Very subdued, I told them. 'He apologized to me!' Their waggish schoolboy's camaraderie dissolved instantly. They all recognized the essentially good man who taught us the profound lesson of the priority of personal respect in the teaching process. In his relationships with us he found the way to communicate what he tried so hard to express in intellectual and academic forms. If this need for respect is true for comparatively ordinary youngsters, how much more so is it for those who have been treated contemptuously by others and whose consequent self-respect is too low for them to conceive of themselves as worth educating?

However, while wrestling with the metamorphosis of Park House School into Peper Harow (see Chapter four, pp. 65–7 – the change of name

29

from Park House School to Peper Harow Community in 1972–3 is explained here), I was more aware of being influenced by contemporary professionals like George Lyward at Finchden Manor (see Chapter one, pp. 10–11). Unlike Lucas (1975), George Lyward never converted his antique tallboy stuffed with papers and notes into a book that would record the true value of that remarkable, educational therapeutic community. (However, a record exists in Burn, 1956.) His omission implies a great deal about the weaker aspects of his giant, but inevitably human, personality. For him, too, those for whom he cared were of essential importance. The excitement of the intellectual and academic – despite his excellence as a psychologist, a musician, a man of letters – came second.

Lyward was English to the marrow. His style was self-deprecating, never taking itself too seriously, while embracing the snobbery of amateurism that could well be afforded by an institution that reflected the confidence of the English gentry. I spent much time at Finchden during the late sixties and early seventies, gratified at being accepted into its clublike exclusiveness that is so appealing to insecure adolescents. As a consequence, I was able to disregard the serious problems that its approach posed for an organization concerned for those who were socially as well as emotionally dispossessed. Instead, my focus was on the atmosphere in which they all lived, which was more like a kind of permanent play.

From time to time, a special occasion was conjured up – a summer play, a Christmas dance – and the whole energy and attention of the community at Finchden went into converting the baronial dining room, with its two massive open fireplaces, into anything from a Chicago speakeasy to the Wealden Forest. Scenery and special lighting were created with staggering ingenuity out of nothing. Boys and staff worked all night. The 'Members of the Community', as Lyward frequently described them, very much with St. Paul in mind (Ephesians 4:25), vied to present themselves in impeccable dinner jackets, or sophisticated fancy dress. As often as not the music was supplied at professional standards from among their membership. Local girls were driven to the manor by special invitation, and were welcomed with the grace that was also part, perhaps, of the specially created fantasy. Youngsters had laboured diligently in the kitchen, to emerge with elegant collations, and the room was filled with whirling and laughing young people, themselves filled with astonishment and pleasure at the results of their work and the effervescent fun.

The deliberately shabby staff room, where unspoken rights existed over each tattered armchair, was filled with hushed conversations about the everyday activity of the community. The lowered tones almost apologized for the talking of 'shop' in the mess – as it were – yet the content revealed that the profoundest consideration was being given to the full significance of each event.

Other influences underlying my thinking about the transformation of

Park House School into such a community was Bill Curry's description of the early days of Dartington and by the writings of other founders of the progressive schools, like A. S. Neil. How accurate Curry's description was of the Dartington Moots – a kind of community meeting in which the participation of the children was of primary significance – I cannot judge. Yet, I had been left with a clear impression of the significance of their communal engagement for their individual growth. I will, of course, refer to Fred Lennhoff's significant contribution to the professional approach underlying Peper Harow (see Chapter four, pp. 53–5). Lennhoff worked with Adler before the war, and founded another remarkable school for 'exceptional children', as he called them, in Shropshire (Lennhoff, 1960).

The special events at Finchden provided exceptional opportunities for exercising the boys' creative fantasies. Yet, even their everyday experiences reflected a similar magical quality, and so encouraged the uninhibited expression of the boys' feelings. Idiosyncrasy, in an adolescent fashion, reigned supreme. It was visible in the way the boys made their living spaces into dens, whether in the stables, or in their country-house bedrooms, or in a hand-built log cabin in the grounds. And it was expressed in thunderous renditions of Tchaikovsky at midnight on the concert grand, or in brilliant jazz improvisations at breakfast. It was Finchden Manor's acknowledgement and respect of a boy's own crazy adolescent social identity that encouraged so many to take the next exploratory step on the painful journey towards understanding their past.

The first thing that had to be tackled was the totally different atmosphere of Park House from Finchden Manor. The undercurrent of bullying at Park House that was passed from generation to generation has already been described. It was endured by some boys and embraced by others, for whom it clearly expressed their fundamentally disturbed, sado-masochistic attitudes. This particular emotional atmosphere also influenced the relationships between the male staff. It showed itself, for example, in the 'macho' conversations in the staff room, in which concern and tenderness were often sneered at contemptuously. The same emotionally destructive atmosphere affected the wider organizational relationships between headmaster and managers and, indeed, between the managers and the Children's Department.

The implied requirement for the institution to satisfy certain governmental demands, which supposedly represented societal requirements, exacted a toll. The requirement to produce a brisk, containing regime in which badly behaving youngsters would be drilled into submissive and conforming workers, allowed no room for the managers to think of themselves as responsible for addressing the painful and confused internal world of each youngster in their care. Indeed, there was an expectation at Park House of a factorylike process of input, training, and discharge that, at its worst, totally inhibited the individual respect that was essential for a boy's rehabilitation.

It was increasingly clear that, if we could change Park House as we intended, we would have created an undeniable model of how to provide emotional nourishment for emotionally disturbed youngsters in the residential setting. It would illustrate the process by which a hurt individual can eventually understand why he is what he is, and how he could become what he would wish to be.

That, then, was the aim shared from the beginning by those of us principally concerned in the creation of Peper Harow in 1970. To turn that aim into reality, a special atmosphere needed to be created that would enable the pertinent, organizational, and personal questions to be recognized and explored. And, to create that atmosphere, a change in the nature of relationships between the individuals would need to occur. Such an atmosphere and such relationships are symbiotic. They feed each other, while the limitations of one also limit the other.

Trying to separate the ingredients of an atmosphere within which inter-dependent relationships will flourish quickly reveals that they are not discrete. Nor should they be because the nature of the youngsters' emotional disturbance absolutely requires a situation in which every-thing is totally integrated. Any artificially separated part, therefore, can be seen as a reflection of the overall process. Wherever one looks at Peper Harow, one sees a reinforcement of the same basic and essential concepts. These include the need to understand and the need to experience being understood; the need to be loved and to be loving; the need to forgive and to accept forgiveness; and the need to have faith in others' creative qualities and thus be able to accept others' faith in one's own creativity.

The next chapter considers the way in which an emotional commitment to these concepts was aroused among the boys. It is also important to stress how complex the manifold parts of a totally integrated therapeutic environ-ment actually are. Obviously space is limited but, if we consider the psychodynamic organizational aspects only, the complexity is immediately apparent. The unconscious processes that arise from the organizational structure can be seen to derive from three predominant entities or group-ings of individuals. They are the residents, the staff, and the director. It seems somewhat artificial to describe the director as though a single person could be a dynamic group; however, he has many roles and accord-ingly he works in many different fashions. All of these affect the different ways in which he is perceived, and in turn affect his psychodynamic significance to the other two more obvious groups of residents and staff. These two groups obviously do consist of many people yet, despite their different composition, they often relate to the director and engage with him psychically in a similar fashion to the way they themselves interrelate. They also frequently relate with each other in the same ways as they do with the director. Perhaps the director is experienced as a group because at any one time he will be reflecting so many fantasies that emanate from many individuals. Whatever the reason, it seems to be a helpful model in enabling many dynamic processes to be described.

When we move beyond the therapeutic community, engaged in its prime task of change, then the director also functions as the manager of the boundary between the internal and the external world, as the employee responsible to the trustee body for the proper functioning of the community according to its policy, and, in the eyes of wider society, as the person directly accountable for its professional activity. If we take the director as an example, the complexity of each part of the organization is underlined. For instance, the director, in his proper role, must frequently address the boundary between the internal therapeutic task and the community's overall relationship with the outside world. If he approaches trustees and the local community, for instance, while still experiencing himself as he does when he is an appropriate part of the triangular therapeutic struggle, he may create considerable problems for himself and the community.

The residents may recognize the director's external functions at one level, but their response may be dictated by the processes that arise from their therapeutic relationship. For instance, they may invest him with unrealistic status. When conducting eminent personages around the estate, I was often identified as part of the august world of the visitor. I was being used as a kind of bridge by the youngsters, whose legitimate entitlement to first-name familiarity with me enabled them to feel that some of the status of royal or ministerial visitors actually brushed off on them too. This fantasy was diametrically different from their habitual fantasy of being the least significant of creatures and, as such, could have been used therapeutically. However, the fantasies arising from the director's relationship with the outside world were not always positive. Some people felt anxious about the director's special and distanced position. The staff group, for instance, has been known to ask 'How can you invite someone of those political views here? Why weren't we given the chance to refuse to receive them? We feel we are being exhibited so that you can hob-nob with the great and the mighty.'

This, in turn, might imply that the staff group was identifying with rebellious attitudes to authority that one might have expected from the residents' group. If the staff's feeling were voiced, it might say 'Unlike you, you hypocrite, who pretends to side with the youngster, we really do, whereas you prefer to spend your time with your rich and famous companions!' Indeed, some of the residents, too, would actually feel like this, though, in such circumstances, the staff might in fact advance to them an opposite view, the very one that the director would himself express about needing the support of the visitor, or that there should be a positive response accorded to the visitor who comes as a caring friend and not as an enemy. The staff group frequently illustrated its capacity to identify

33

with contradictory attitudes: on the one hand expressing the hostility of the residents and, on the other, the mediating reasonableness of the director. This not only suggests that each group contains a spectrum of views wide enough for some of them to be contradictory, but also that each group shares a similar spectrum. The groups' common experiences enable their relationships with each other and with the third group – the director – to be worked upon positively. If one group advanced one set of attitudes, the other was likely to express the opposite. Thus both sets of feelings could be acknowledged and clarified.

Many unrealistic perceptions of daily events are likely to arise from unconscious roots that are formed from the individual's initial experiences of authority. Recognition in the here-and-now of a current, unrealistic group perception can potentially engender insight into the significance of the youngsters' (and sometimes of the staff's) earlier life experiences for them and into their consequential responses. Because the resident group's ongoing experience of reality can be juxtaposed with its frequently unrealistic perceptions, the contradiction between an appropriate response and the residents' unconsciously predetermined one can at last begin to be tackled.

The new staff at Peper Harow who began to replace the existing ones from 1970 onwards were able to recognize that much of the hostility towards them was not simply unfair: it was a re-enactment of the only way of interacting with adults that the youngsters knew. In the past, adults had usually reacted to the boys' habitually established hostility with resentful dislike, with rejection, and with the exercise of their power to punish. It was evident that a new resident might not want to behave so hatefully, but he hardly knew how to function differently, especially when the implied situational requirement was to be trusting and friendly.

If the new staff, with the aid of their intellectual understanding, and with considerable emotional support, were able to sustain themselves during the hurtful onslaught, then, above all, they could provide the youngsters with the time to discover a new 'language of relating', never before learned. The staff, too, had unresolved emotional needs. All people wanting to work in such a stressful environment have mixed motives, though this may not be clear to the new member of staff. The need to perceive oneself as a loving person may seem very important. Thus, the apparent refusal by an angry youngster to see such a staff member as anything but dangerous can be exceptionally hurtful, however clearly it can be recognized intellectually. Often this same compulsive and hurtful confrontation between individuals is expressed by their respective groups almost as though it were actually on behalf of individuals. In the same way as an individual member of staff's personal sense of secure identity is undermined by the challenge of a hostile youngster, so is the group's identity by an intergroup confrontation. However, the undermining of the group's caring and supportive self-image also amplifies the stress on each individual member of staff.

In these confrontative circumstances between the residents' and the staff's groups, the staff group soon began to find the director threatening too. He did not allow enough democracy, enough consensus, enough room for a differing view of the community, of an individual. Even the reality of his significance in a member of staff's career development, or his insistence on the need for extraordinary long hours, could be understood, but not wholeheartedly accepted. In the same way as the youngsters seemed determined to resist acknowledging the worth of their new-found relationships, so the staff, as a group, in turn reflected a similar refusal to acknowledge the worth of its relationship with the director. The staff group expressed this in socially more acceptable ways and, of course, some of its members' criticisms may also have been realistic. Eventually it became clear that much of the conflict between staff and director was an unconscious expression of what the staff group was experiencing in its relationship with the residents' group. It took a long time, however, before I, as director, was able to accept the appropriateness of this displaced stress. Indeed, I was only able to begin to do so, and then begin to understand it therapeutically and respond less defensively, when receiving personal therapeutic clarification and sustenance from outside the community.

A director who has become able to accept the projected burden of the staff's stress encourages their ability to tolerate and understand the communication that the residents' stressful behaviour is symbolizing. Not only negative feelings were transmitted and carried by one group on behalf of another. The different groups' positive identifications were often embraced too. If the staff group were less effective at one moment because of its blocked relationships with the director, the residents could often be relied upon to communicate to the recalcitrant and hostile individual among them the same message that the staff would normally make. The bullying, secretive, subcultural group of residents, described in Chapter two (see pp.16–17), always demonstrated its extraordinary power, which made it very dangerous indeed when it was functioning to defend the delinquent disorder of its members. Yet, my own experience, like many others before me, had been that the power of such a group can also be harnessed to control its delinquent members and then gently lead towards a different way of functioning (see Makarenko, 1951, that describes the supreme example of the conversion of an extremely delinquent group into a healthy and socially well-orientated alternative). Teenagers look, above all else, for the support and approval of the group of peers in which they are accepted. They will do almost anything – even the unfamiliar and uncomfortable – in order to gain that acceptance.

Unfortunately, many of our youngsters had never been able to become accepted in any group.

For such people, it is obvious that, at the simplest level, the youngster's quality of life will be improved if he can find a way to become part of his peer group and thus reduce his loneliness. But, it is also possible for the ethos of the peer group to be one in which a kind of journey back to childhood can be undertaken symbolically through the group behaviour. It will be a journey to discover not only that the past is really over, but also to find what was lost then and so learn how it can be replaced today. Indeed, I would propose that this is a normal psychosocial function of adolescent 'gangs' in helping the transition to adulthood. Such groups enable their members to commit themselves emotionally to learning through their group 'play' experience about their identity in relation to society as a whole and to other individuals. Such gangs often present themselves in fancy-dress uniform that (as well as raising adult anxiety) may also represent some dominant emotional preoccupation they wish to declare at the time.

Their behaviour denotes a 'playing through' of that emotional preoccupation and, as such, forms a psychosocial ritual normal to growing up. Nevertheless, particularly in a therapeutic community, the peer group/'gang' can also help the adolescent to recognize and clarify the difference between the real world in which the 'gang' operates and the world created by group fantasy. Such a peer group can facilitate the recognition of the parallel differences between the real world around an individual and his own internal fantasy life in which he is fundamentally trapped.

(Rose, 1983: 22; see also Chapter eight, p. 140).

This sort of group is capable of calling a difficult individual to order. In a meeting, one of the residents will intervene in another's dispute with a member of staff. Perhaps he will remind the individual of the staff member's contribution to the communal wellbeing, and will encourage the individual's recognition that his aggression is understood by others who have suffered similar experiences. The adult will feel both supported and restored in his self-image while the youngster is brought back to consider what the adult was challenging him about in the first place.

In the early days of the community, new youngsters arriving from the remand home or assessment centre attempted to put themselves at ease in their latest, anxiety-provoking situation by bidding for acceptance in the peer group. They did so in the only way they knew, by boasting of criminal escapades, of their prowess as comic-strip, macho heroes and, in so doing, they revealed their sad inadequacy all the more. When the community had begun to develop its identity, such youngsters were greeted with this kind of comment:

'You know when I came I said all the things you're saying . . . but

they weren't true.'
'Weren't true! Of course they're true! I smashed two of the Old Bill
as I came out of the back. . . .'
'Hang on! I only said that *my* stories weren't true. Actually, we don't
talk about these things here – not like that, anyway.'
'What things?'
'You were boasting about your robberies. Hang on, let me finish.
This is not a remand home. We're all here because we had a rough
time. We haven't been getting anywhere, but we're now trying to
sort things out. Tell us what your problems are.'
'I ain't got no problems. I can sort myself out.'
'Before lunch you said your dad was in prison. Don't you miss
him?'

The newcomer is then engaged in a developing discussion about the part
of him that does and the part that does not miss Dad. He is already
beginning to learn the language of the therapeutic community. The
problem was that in those early days there were few youngsters who had
any awareness so that it was only gradually that newcomers did meet a
quite unexpected culture shock. According to the records of the time,
bullying was still common a year after the venture began and the apparently
therapeutic culture of the community meeting was contradicted at night
and in other places by a delinquent subculture.

The gradual change from a regime that inevitably created bullying to
one in which the relationships were predominantly therapeutic took about
three or four years. It was not just the new boys arriving that produced new
aspirations in the community, but also new staff. These were normally
men and women who would not have dreamed of working in a penal
institution, whereas they were attracted by the challenge of being
privileged to do something really experimental and creative. Almost none
of the staff had worked in any similar setting, though some had been to
boarding school themselves and thus had first-hand experience of how
the residential situation can generate a very special atmosphere, despite
the difference in culture. The staff were largely graduate teachers, who felt
the factorylike environment of most schools limiting rather than stimulating. However, unlike the weary, cynical staff already present, they
were keen to teach by sharing their interests. It was fairly unorthodox.
Youngsters who could not add two and two found themselves sharpening
their arithmetic in day-long bridge schools! Reading Greek tragedies on
the food-bestrewn kitchen table was an unexpected way to begin to
consider the earliest relationships with parents.

Above all, staff worked round the clock! A rota had always existed. The
old staff stuck to it. The new staff stayed until the early hours. The boys
knew who really cared about them and who had their interests at heart.
Adult conversations became more sophisticated. New staff understood

that these boys could not 'pull themselves together' or 'watch it!', or even 'pull their socks up'. First they had to let down their rusted drawbridges and when they did tentatively begin to talk, at the odd times of day and night when they actually felt like doing so, they were listened to. Staff began to feel like friends.

On the other hand, the new staff had no idea how to behave like disciplinarians – like 'screws' – and undoubtedly the chaos of the transitional period was far worse than it needed to be because of their inability to say 'no' with sufficient authority and conviction. Instead, the director was ascribed the role of tyrant. He was the keeper of boundaries and was almost never disobeyed. The staff rejoiced in the tender, maternal understanding role with the boys and the conflict was largely shouldered by the relationship between the staff and the director, rather than, as in the past, when the conflict was carried by the relationship between the staff and the boys.

What a shock this was for me when I found my heroic role of slayer of the repressive dragon changed into the same dragonlike form itself! Within my own psychopathology, one could have understood why this contradiction would be so painful. The need to be valued, to be accorded recognition stemmed, on the one hand, from my deepest pathology, but, on the other, that same unresolved source produced the stubborn determination to engender a community such as Peper Harow became. I doubt such a transition would have been possible for Park House without such extraordinary drives. That desire for recognition had its own complex consequences. It was easy initially to accept the identity that the youngsters seemed to need of an exemplary cartoon of human qualities that were enormously larger than life, and therefore could be recognized even by youngsters who were exceptionally defended against relationships with adults. However, because this identity was an unrealistic depiction, its appearance could not, of course, be sustained. As the youngsters developed their own valid aspirations, such as the motivation to find their own real identity, or qualities like the courage to acknowledge their own hurt and damage, then the earlier admired heroic qualities of the tiny warrior battling with universal dragons were no longer convincing. They needed to be their own warrior. The vicarious one was no longer helpful in the same way. The director really did lose his temper at times. He really sulked when he could not get his own way. He denied psychic activity that was personally threatening - just like anyone else!

Within the community there were always people functioning at different stages of personal development. The community, therefore, no longer needed one oversimple model of behaviour, or one kind of nourishment, but a new sequence of models increasing in their realistic depiction of adulthood. For the director to be effective – just as in the same way for the atmosphere to be effective – for the individual member of staff, or for the whole group of staff to be effective – he had to find a way to meet these sometimes contradictory needs. It is not surprising that this could not always be achieved. At best it was never totally achieved, and it could never be sustained in a state of balance for long.

The director, then, was bound to be a somewhat unreal figure in terms of personal relationships. The individual member of staff was a much safer proposition in many respects. The youngster could go off for walks with him; sit down and play a game of chess over a cup of coffee. Indeed, because the member of staff knew so much about each boy, had been home with him and knew his folks, had comforted him when he was in despair, even the casual analysis of the self-destructive moves on the chessboard, for instance, could be used to illuminate the boy's general way of functioning.

Yet, if you were less in awe of the member of staff, so confrontation welling up from the injured depths of personality could also become very serious. In a sense, the sometimes outrageous behaviour of the director could be written off as unarguable. 'Well, of course, it's no use arguing with him', the youngsters might declare, 'he's totally barmy!' Yet, that phrase was like an abracadabra – a 'secret formula' devised by a boy to manage an impending outburst of his feared destructiveness. If a youngster said 'he's too barmy to argue with', he was intuitively placing the director alongside his own feared madness. The director – in the youngster's internal world – had in some way become kin. He could be experienced as the parent who could care for the mad, bad creature the youngster still believed himself to be. He could then be experienced as the positive, parental, loving and lovable, consoling and protective image that had never properly formed. By this 'magic' process, the youngster was also able to accept friendship and the director's supposed and indefinable 'understanding'. At the same time, the youngster was also able to reduce his own volcanic dangerousness by sharing its ownership. Part of my style was to play up to this and it enabled me to come to the rescue from time to time of the reasonable, caring member of staff, whose sensitive and nourishing mature adulthood was being hurtfully rejected.

One night a new member of staff was trying to shepherd everyone to bed. Trevor had spent the previous year refusing to go to bed until already tired members of staff exhausted themselves by wrestling him up the stairs and into his very bed-space. In the last month or two, he had begun to recognize the relationship between this behaviour and the way he used to get beaten by his giant and violent father. As Trev became bigger, so he had to face the uncomfortable idea that he might end up not as the poor, un-fairly treated victim, but as the aggressive bully himself. It was a daunting thought, but he also gained a lot of pleasure and excitement from the threat and hurt that he posed and a conflict remained within him as to whether he really wanted to give up this sadistic excitement, whether he would be safe if he became less aggressive to authority figures, and whether his sense of emptiness, if he gave it up, would overwhelm him.

That night, Ed, being new, was unaware of all this and found himself reduced to ineffective frustration and fear when trying to get the sadistic Trevor into his bedroom. Racing down the stairs Ed found me on duty with many other matters to resolve. He immediately started his peroration about the appalling Trev. I left him in mid-sentence and tore up the stairs to a grinning and slightly surprised Trevor. In three sentences I summarized the stark bones of his conflict about being victim, or monster, sadist or creator. How dare he renege on his hard-won insight that had cost everyone so much! How dare he bully an ingenuous new member of staff! How dare he 'demand' me to come and beat him to bed when I only wanted to care for him! 'Hang on! I didn't ask him to fetch you,' he stammered in surprise. In even greater fury, I roared, 'Did you really think I would let you throw a year's growing-up away? Do you think I care about you so little? Get to bed at once! When Ed comes round you had better save your own situation and apologize most genuinely! Good, bloody, night!' I slammed the door as hard as I could and went downstairs. Ed then returned to his task and, when it was completed, he came to my room with adulatory wonder all over his face. 'How could you transform that kid so completely?' he gasped.

What lay behind his own inexperienced question? He was satisfied with the face-saving reply that all would be possible once he had been personally accepted by Trevor in the fullness of time. In fact, Ed was anxious to be reassured about his own inadequacy; he had been frightened and needed comfort; he was intensely envious, and he was frightened of this too. Of course, it would not be that surprising if we discovered that most of us contain such irrational and unrespectable attitudes well and truly buried within us. However, in Ed's case, though he was unaware of it, he was also displacing many unresolved feelings onto me that had been stirred into life by his having been unconsciously caught up in the drama of Trevor's psychic dilemmas.

My own initial response had not been an analytic, but an intuitive one. I was furious with Ed for doing to me, when I felt overloaded, what had been done to him. After all, all he had to do was 'get a few kids to bed!' So, I chased up the stairs to 'kick' Trev in his turn but, as I did so, I recalled the progress of a year's work and gained a little insight. All that work might be for nothing, unless I could temper fury with judicious sensitivity. The half-conscious 'Watch it!' of experience, produced the exactly correct formula of observant rage appropriate for the situation. I do not use this as an example of how to deal with a challenging situation, but as an example of how all three protagonists brought their own unconscious dilemmas into the play. Unconsciously, these began to be projected from one to the other and back again. Intimate familiarity with the other Trevor in other circumstances intervened, and the straightforward, habitual, behavioural re-enactment of the past was interrupted. An alternative and reparative process was instead set in train.

This reflects the overall process of a therapeutic community when it is working well. Similar processes between individuals occurred daily, but these processes also functioned in group forms. As classic Greek chorus and antichorus symbolically represent the contradictory arguments and conflicting emotions that individuals enact on the stage of shared daily life, so in the same way the residents, staff, and director interact with one another. Catharsis occurs as the result of the clarification of these unconscious issues whether in the therapeutic community or the small city state. It is a very old, sociopsychological human process.

Whenever unconscious group interactions were made plain in the community, as the pain in classic tragedy is eased by catharsis, so a similarly relieving, healing, changing, and growthful process occurred. The community meeting, for instance, also formed a live and compelling rite into which its participants were absorbed by their group response. The girls and boys at Peper Harow were recently shown a film of those early days. Despite the intervening fifteen years, what struck them all was the similarity of the process. They shrieked with laughter at the long-haired director, at the totally outmoded teenage 'uniform' of the time, but they remarked thoughtfully about the similarity of the process.

The same antisocial behaviour occurs in the community today, as the result of the same forces on similarly damaged youngsters. The community gathers together its individuals, its groups, and its population as a whole, re-enforcing its psychic and social strength at each integrating level. It thus absorbs the impact of the behaviour, eventually gets in touch with the feelings underlying the immediate reactions, and takes another step forward on the unending journey of human experience in gathering insight.

Of course, the process is not often straightforwardly optimistic. In the same way as it was impossible for the director to sustain in reality the variety of conflicting and not clearly understood roles, so does the whole process frequently only totter hopefully towards its goal. Nor are the problems that arise because the process is in some senses so uncertain merely insignificant. At times it feels as though the community were functioning to reinforce antitherapeutic processes!

Almost none of the youngsters coming to Peper Harow has an intact family. Whatever the reasons for their having disintegrated, the consequences have been very injurious. The shock of losing a totally trusted parent in childhood can raise permanent doubts about the trustworthiness of human relationships and thus impede an adolescent's ability to manage intimacy. Many of our youngsters have been paralysed with horror while watching parents fighting. Not only have the blood and the symbolic wounds caused by words been terrifying and incomprehensible, but the impotence of the child's ability to halt those occurrences leaves him again deeply uncertain of his ability to control or to manage relationships at all. Time and again, a youngster's unconscious compulsion is to re-enact these often repressed, traumatic experiences through his behaviour. In addition, his emotional incompetence to manage age-appropriate needs, because he has failed to grow emotionally beyond these early traumas, in itself ruins his life increasingly.

It is obvious that the tantrumming two-year-old, in the shape of an hysterically screaming young woman, or one in the shape of a berserk six-feet-tall young man, needs containment. Yet, the pain of the underlying anxiety also needs endless reassurance and, above all, the environment in which this occurs needs to be consistently integrating of their fragmenting personalities. Yet, there is no way to ensure such reassuring nurture, except through the consistently positive functioning of the community itself. However, when the group itself is at its most anxious, it no longer tends to contain and reassure, but to express its anxiety through various group psychic mechanisms. Like an individual's disturbed behaviour, the unconscious purpose of these mechanisms may be as a defence against anxiety. Realistically, they usually make the situation worse.

If the staff group and director appear to be embattled, for instance, the residents' group may forget the containing, reassuring, and integrating way in which the community often functions. Overwhelmed with its anxiety, the residents' group may instead try to split the two adult groups who, in the residents' fantasy, are now being experienced as parental figures. Yet, they desperately need to retain the symbolic and united parental model of these two adult groups if they are to grow the needed psychic resources for future relationships. Other unhealthy consequences may also occur. For instance, developing, unconscious and omnipotent fantasies that they might actually be powerful enough to separate their warring parents never was a realistic way of defending themselves against their suffering in the face of quarrelling parents. On the other hand, that fantasy may be exciting and so tends to generate an increasingly absorbing obsession with it. The strengthening of this kind of defensive fantasizing is inhibiting of emotional maturation. Whether the initial unconscious objective of the compulsion to split the 'parent' symbols was to save each of them from the feared consequences of their conflict – they might kill each other – or whether it was to save the 'child' himself from such fearful consequences, the end result leaves a seriously emotionally impoverished personality, preoccupied with the need to defend through controlling others rather than through engaging in creativity. His inevitable and regular failure to achieve the control he obsessively seeks is bound to result in his developing the kind of personality of someone who can never achieve what he most wants.

Such entangled psychic dilemmas are what become enacted again and again in times of stress. Actually, the stress often recurs as a result of the

actual functioning of the adults in the community. Their personal interactions, as in any group in an intense situation, may create problems that
may not even be capable of being verbalized by either adults or youngsters. If the resolution of such problems is bound to take some time, then
the youngster's habitual pathological functioning is likely to be triggered
in response to the rising but inexplicable anxiety in the community.

Someone then lights a fire. The uncertainty as to who is the culprit, and
the fear of death by asphyxiation, or from burning, causes more and more
wild behaviour. It creates the desire to punish extremely, or to run away.
Scapegoating and absconding, petty theft, and physical attacks abound.
People seek sexual gratification, but at a level of emotional functioning
that is infantile rather than that required for interpersonal, adult and
adolescent relationships.

The basic anxiety each resident carries within him is triggered by the
normal process that exists within any normal group. People leave, people
arrive, and all groups throw up human problems from time to time.
However, our residents have not developed the repertoire of psychic
response that normal life experiences require. For them, new residents'
arrivals are experienced as though they were actually displacing new
siblings, and familiar residents and staff leaving cast them into their past
traumas of loss. Consequently, their reactions to these processes are
unbelievably extreme. Yet, we have to remember that the community is
designed to allow this to occur. A regressed infantile group that will not
clean the house, that will not produce meals on time, and will not get on
with its studies is regarded as normal in the therapeutic community.
Coping with this abnormal 'normality' is the bread and butter of the
therapeutic task. Nevertheless, when even by those standards life is being
intolerably difficult, the necessary solution will develop as the unexpressed relationships between the adults become clarified and begin to
resolve.

In fact, there should be a permanent dialogue between the staff and the
director about the centrality of his role. If the director is too overtly
significant in every situation, then the staff will tend to feel that they are
less mature than they felt before coming to the community, or that
they are being treated as though they were, themselves, disturbed 'kids'.
The director may perceive his role too managerially. This may be argued
as his attempt to enhance the significance of the staff. However, if he denies
the dynamic significance of his role in the overall community, then the
youngsters will cease to be held to the therapeutic task.

If communication between the adults about these issues ceases, then
individual members of staff begin to act out feelings in ways that seem to
be imitative of the youngsters'; a member of staff loses his keys or another
comes to work late, while another threatens to strike a youngster. More
secretive and delinquent behaviour occurs. In the early seventies, young-

43

sters visiting a member of staff's house discovered the remains of cannabis smoking in his grate. The youngsters were furious. Yet the reasons for their anger were often very difficult to unravel. In that instance the residents' reaction complicated the community issue about the adults acting out unresolved conflict between themselves. In those early days, drug-taking was a major threat. Other communities had been closed as a result. Involvement in drugs for excitement or to pacify anxiety was also in total contradiction to the therapeutic process. However, it was also seen as culturally trendy, particularly if adults took a stand against it. Any actual adult ambivalence needed clarifying and countering if the youngsters were to feel safe. If the adults, instead of supporting the staff's public stance towards drug taking, smoked 'dope' themselves, then the youngsters' ability to behave in a way that enabled them to stay in the community was undermined. Perhaps more serious was the conflict that this produced between staff and the director, because this fuelled the unresolved anxiety within the youngsters, which stemmed from their early experience of warring parents.

One member of staff had falsified his application form and had succeeded in misleading his appointments panel. Despite an impressive beginning, his behaviour gave increasing cause for concern. Eventually, he was suspended, in order to give time for the most appropriate resolution to be reached. During this period he was required not to communicate with the two boys for whom he had special responsibility. However, he insisted on inviting them to his house. This provoked anger in all his colleagues and he was given a written warning. His escalating response was to arrive in the main building as though on duty. He was formally dismissed. Although the two boys concerned remained for nearly two years after he left, they were never able to make an attachment to anyone else, and their commitment to the community, and therefore to interacting with it as they needed, never fully occurred. Both eventually left to a feckless future instead. In their case, their impregnable resistance was aroused by a quarrel not between staff and director, but between their member of staff, whose behaviour none of his colleagues agreed with, though several were very sympathetic to him personally, and the director and staff combined.

In a recent staff group, the members were discussing the director's absence with some trepidation. The youngsters' behaviour had indicated their anxiety at not having a clear central figure who could control their behaviour. There had been several examples of sexual activity between individual youngsters that were felt to be beyond what was acceptable in the community. After a responsible community meeting, in which the youngsters had been exceptionally open about their feelings, the staff in their own meeting felt somewhat daunted. Nevertheless, they jauntily reassured themselves that they could cope. But then they began to express their anxiety that, if they managed the community too well in the director's absence, he would not be needed any more! Would they have caused his disappearance? Anxiety was then expressed as to whether he would actually return. If he did, would he punish them out of jealousy or in revenge for their own competitive feelings?

This staff meeting illustrated two frequent modes of group functioning. As the staff began to recognize them, so their understanding of what the youngsters were feeling about the director's absence became far more accessible. The initial staff group response of simply feeling inadequate – perhaps as the youngsters had felt – masked the group's depression aroused by the director's absence. But then they began to express their competitive fantasies. These eventually provoked the staff into thinking about the extent to which they really did possess such feelings. Finally, they were then able to evaluate the extent those feelings were also being expressed on behalf of the youngsters, who had found it even more difficult to verbalize their anxiety at the director's absence. The youngsters had only been able to be 'good' and responsible in their meeting. This had followed their initially depressed reaction to the director's absence, followed by delinquent behaviour. Now the community could be properly managed because the staff, recognizing what they had been unconsciously asked to carry, now found themselves able to encourage some further expression by the insecure children themselves of their more covert anxieties.

In Peper Harow's early days it was undoubtedly necessary for the director to function with forthright authority in addition to his personal charismatic style. The endeavour was under attack from all quarters. Its controlling governmental department was completely hostile, as was a proportion of the managers. Most of the staff – several of whom, significantly enough, were stealing the school's property – thousands of pounds' worth were never recovered – were frequently deliberately undermining. The boys themselves who had been sent to an approved school could only respond to the anxiety aroused by the total change of their familiar, institutional environment in their habitual, delinquent fashion. Nor were those who were potentially responsive to psychotherapy able to resist a delinquent response to the general anxious chaos, because no alternative culture had yet been established to help them. Thus, the odds in the battle for a therapeutic victory were almost overwhelmingly negative. In such a situation, a single-minded charismatic leader was essential. However, once the antagonistic element had been reduced to the appropriate therapeutic battle against the boys' propensity to neurotic and delinquent sickness, then such a centrally authoritative role was no longer consistently essential (see Chapter ten, pp.196–200). We were neither skilled enough nor experienced enough to recognize that there is actually a subtle difference between charismatic leadership and autocracy. Lacking this recognition, the two adult 'groups' increasingly fought between themselves. The director felt betrayed by those he had appointed as allies, and his ability to trust the staff and to encourage their development decreased. Meanwhile, the staff undervalued the director and complained about being exploited. One of them put it, 'I always feel somehow diminished in your presence.'

Often this battle took place in the community meeting, where staff, attempting to silence the director or compete with him, often dominated the meeting – in the way that they said that he did. This battle allowed the residents little opportunity to speak and, if they did, the staff addressed them in hectoring, punitive tones – again illustrating how the staff perceived the director. The therapeutic development of the community slowed down, as the boys became depressed by the inevitability of their past experience being repeated between those they had tried to love. Occasionally, the boys would produce some delinquent behaviour, and the staff and the director would then unite!

We were, however, gradually able to use an exceptionally good consultancy service that eventually enabled us to gain sufficient insight and understanding to overcome the impasse. Not only did the mutual problems of the adult groups then become acceptable, but ways were found in which the staff could make a considerable contribution to the development, both of the treatment programme and to its underlying policy. The decision to admit girls arose very largely out of the staff working as a team on the issue for nearly two years prior to that decision.

Perhaps, more important, as a result of the unlocking of this clash between groups, was the recognition, not just of the personal and organizational elements that had created that clash, but the recognition of the intrinsic dynamic representation by this triangular group constellation of the archetypal, familial scenarios.

Thereafter, when staff meetings began to feel uncomfortable once again, the first step its members took was to examine the contents of the morning's community meeting. Almost always, they found themselves repeating some of the youngsters' behaviour in a more overtly respectable fashion. The staff group was thus beginning to perceive its function as a psychotherapeutic tool that looked to its own activity for at least part of the explanation of the group issues in the larger community.

The staff for some time had a good working notion of transference between the individual and the therapist (see Chapter 9, pp. 161–2). As a consequence, individual members of staff had been able to withstand enormous amounts of aggression from the individual youngsters for whom they were responsible. Their tolerant ability to enable the expression of unreasoning hatred, that also frightened and baffled the youngster himself, allowed that youngster's innate aggression to be examined safely. In addition, the staff coped with the youngster's idealizing, or even the idolization of, his beloved adult, too, by recognizing it also as a compulsive but necessary expression of the youngster's internal and chaotic feelings, and not a demand on their reality relationship. As supervision of the staff's casework developed, so were they increasingly able to recognize the part played in the relationship by their own unconscious, emotional investments in the relationships. But what was new was the concept that the subgroups within the overall community also unconsciously transfer their pre-occupations from one group to another. The continuing existence of this unconscious process is usually a sign of the psychic maturity of the community, which enables the process to become another mode of effective therapeutic functioning.

The whole process, we have to remember – from the *de facto* revolutionary coup under a charismatic leader to the sophistication of a series of psychotherapeutically interrelating groups – was not a smooth process. We learned as we proceeded and as a result of pain and conflict, self-doubt, and fear. Neither the difficulties nor the growth proceeded at a constant pace. A well-known phenomenon of therapeutic communities is their propensity to oscillate (Savalle and Wagenborg, 1980: 137–47; see also Chapter ten, pp. 195–6) between poor and successful functioning. A live community is never static.

Communities can petrify. However, the oscillating periods of high and low functioning gradually became institutionalized and I suggest that one reason for this relates to the context within which the interpersonal and intergroup dynamics occur. Concepts like transference and counter-transference, splitting, projections, scapegoating, and all the other concepts that seek to describe complex unconscious processes are only helpful within a certain context. This is a context where the atmosphere of the community is exciting, full of symbolic representations of what is happening to its members, and where the atmosphere is designed to match the cultural life of its age group. Once a community becomes institutionalized, then the once-helpful technical concepts themselves add to the institutionalized way of functioning.

One of the problems of some hospital settings is that they are not exciting, but depressed; they are starved of good furnishings and cultural activity. And they are not exciting to work in, because they are part of a bureaucracy in which idealism is grossly undervalued in comparison to what can be proved as cost-effective in the crudest of terms. In this kind of atmosphere, what mends a broken leg most efficiently is much easier to understand than why it costs so much to mend a broken heart.

The possibility of psychotherapy becoming an accepted and appreciated notion at Peper Harow arose out of the changed relationships between the individual adults and young people; and it arose equally out of the fun these new relationships generated. Like Finchden Manor, Peper Harow developed its galaxy of feasts and special occasions, each demanding an amazed response from the youngsters at what they had created. Their creation was shared with staff who, unlike their predecessors, believed in the youngsters'

47

human potential. So, the staff joined in the youngsters' activities. They had fun together. In the silence round a smoking campfire by a river, or as the last candle was lit in a transformed dining room as the doors swung open to admit the revellers, the youngsters felt understood. This feeling was a small step towards feeling lovable and towards being loving. It also aroused their recognition that others would 'make it' and so encouraged their belief that they themselves could 'make it' too. Nurture the context and the possibility of psychotherapeutic change exists. Let it wither and the most sophisticated vehicle for therapy will tend towards aridity.

Chapter four

The development of community identity

The residents lack the psychological development essential for the formation of an age-appropriate sense of self. If they can use a communal identity transitionally, then anxiety can be reduced, behaviour controlled, and compulsive resistance to emotional nurture overcome.

Managing the development and application of an effective community identity is a major organizational task. Consequent problems for staff and their families arise from their own unconscious functioning and the boundaries of appropriate involvement.

Further history of Peper Harow's struggle to establish a therapeutic organization illustrates the impetus needed to overcome different kinds of social resistance and indicates a series of events that would integrate the individual's identification with the community, e.g. the community meeting, Friday Night seminars, the Christmas Feast, Dragon Night, change of name, etc. These are enriching but also symbolize growth and achievement in the individual and the total community. So they further define the community identity and illustrate its atmosphere.

It would be misleading to describe the creation and development of the environment as if it were a stage production. Simply to think of the 'atmosphere' as though it were theatrical 'business' is to trivialize its potential. Many people recognize the dramatic effect that can arise from an emotionally stimulating setting, but, unless this potential can be integrated into that of the specifically therapeutic task, its impact, like any single factor, will not remain effective.

An appropriate atmosphere will stimulate self-awareness in the individual and in the whole group. Such an atmosphere makes the style of living, become effective because it is exciting. Caught up in it, youngsters and staff begin to identify with that lifestyle. When remarks are made such as 'Well, that's the way we do this here!' a community identity has been formed. 'Here' has become a particular and special place. 'We' relates the members to it. For this identity to be therapeutic, it will need to reflect an age-appropriate, socially acceptable image while simultaneously meeting unconscious needs. Those whose psychological development is at best fragile can nevertheless recognize the combination of factors in the community's identity that they intuitively know they need. Lacking their own internal resources, it is essential that the community's clear sense of identity can be shared. From this will derive the sense of security that will calm their anxiety and control their behaviour. Eventually, when they have developed their own internal resources, they will be able to manage stress independently.

Before I worked at Park House I took a group of extremely delinquent boys from an approved school on a climbing and canoeing expedition to Scotland. One object was to take a couple of days to canoe the length of Loch Lomond and, in addition, to climb some of the surrounding peaks on either side. We took considerable time before we set out, practising our canoeing as a group in the local harbour. However, we had not thought of working on the nature of the relationships between the individuals. Though the itinerary had been planned to produce novel and exciting experiences, I had not thought out what specific significance those experiences would have held for each individual.

The approved school had been visited by the Duke of Edinburgh in person, and it was enthusiastically committed to a variety of activities connected with his scheme.[1] Not surprisingly, in that approved school setting, the scheme's notions of creativity and of public and personal service were less developed than its notions about what supposedly encouraged manhood. Tough expeditions to the hills or toiling at the oar of a whaler in the face of a squally winter's sea spray – these were the business of real men. So this Scottish expedition, in the eyes of the institution, was valued as an enhancement of this male image and the fact that it took place beyond the institution's gates also enhanced its status in the imagination of those left behind. Youngsters would swear to anything in order to escape the boredom and the grind of institutional life, and for the attention that their tall tales would attract on their return.

I, too, was keen to escape the grind and depression of the bullying approved school but I also envisaged the fantasized adventure with excitement and with, who knows, how many romanticized fantasies of myself as a hero leader. One result of this particular trip was that I began to grasp what potential for insight and change was engendered by the atmosphere that such activities can stimulate.

The weather was golden in Scotland that September. The sunlight burnished the wavelets on the lochans, revealing basking brown trout. Stags at the end of summer's feeding rose almost good-naturedly from the tussocky heather as we approached and we camped at last on a northerly islet in the courtyard of a ruined castle. The boys splashed about in the icy loch waters and charged for warmth to a huge fire built on the sandy beach. We baked potatoes and told stories until supper time. It seemed to have been an idyllic week until we discovered a singular absence of food the night before we were due to return, because one of the party had stolen it.

The culture of the institution tore among us as suddenly as a wolf from the surrounding wood. Under its baleful threat, kit bags were emptied and inspected until the disciplinary search revealed the stolen supper. Suddenly, we were conscious of our imminent return to the institution the next day, as the incident soured our comradeship. By morning, one of the boys had disappeared. His canoe was found drifting towards the road shore by an anxious fisherman. Reaching the nearest road, I prayed he had run off and not drowned and, a mile later, at the nearest telephone box, had my entreaty answered, for the telephone had been torn out recently!

I breathed murder and threat, as much for my personal anxiety as for his welfare. I was anxious that I would be jeered at by my colleagues for my lack of disciplinary control. Yet, at the same time, I was baffled and hurt by the boy's response to such a marvellous trip. I had thought we were closer together – a band of brothers in adversity. My blind enthusiasm had been partially undermined earlier in the week when, nearly at the summit of a particularly tough climb, it turned out that another boy had deliberately smashed his shin against a rock until the skin split along its length. He had to be carried several miles to the nearest doctor. I was completely baffled by his betrayal, too, and I completely failed to see that our being prevented from reaching our goal and our inability to enjoy an unmarred experience was symptomatic of a serious personality problem in the group's identity.

Part of the problem could be defined as denial of reality. In actuality, the boys were not manly heroes ranging the land for the grail of adventure, but were seriously disturbed and delinquent adolescents on a journey only to Borstal and prison. Yet, despite that, I feel sure that those boys will always remember the mysterious castle ruin, the bonfire on the beach, and the mountain-top views across the Trossachs. Such memories may be astounding theatrical experiences, but they had merely occupied the youngsters' attention briefly; in no way had they affected their inner lives. Nothing of the programme would rub off simply by contact. Each individual would have to become a functioning part of the group. The staff would need to enable the experiences arising from such an expedition to become significant and effective for each boy. This therapeutic consequence would not occur by chance nor would it come simply as the result of the intuition – however inspired – of an enthusiastic member of staff.

The primary experience of residential treatment should be within an environment designed to contribute to and stimulate psychic change. However, to ensure this psychic change, an awareness both of the task and of the purpose of the environment needs to be constantly made plain by staff. Yet, ideally, this has to be communicated in a way that is apparently spontaneous – one that arises from the natural responses to the lifestyle of the community. This lifestyle, embodied by its many activities, thus becomes meaningful to each youngster and so produces a sense of self-worth that the individual could not generate personally, for he is empty. He has no internal sense of riches that would make for self-respect. Therefore, he must begin by being able to experience and value the riches that surround him and to identify with those riches' contextual life until he can eventually internalize them and be free to regenerate them from his own resources.

The self-worth and the emotional strength that is necessary to cope, other than defensively, with the daily issues of a stressful living environment are poorly developed in the community's youngsters. Therefore they begin their journey with no familiarity with the kind of psychological functioning that would regenerate their emotional being. Yet, if these youngsters could belong to a group that does experience a sense of its intrinsic worth, and a sense of its ability to cope with great difficulties, then each of them could generate the hope that in time they, too, will find their personal way to enrichment.

The entire life of the community thus needs to symbolize and express its therapeutic intention through each of its aspects. The experience an individual might receive from his small group of self-worth and self-confidence can also be re-experienced by him through his participation in all aspects of the shared daily life. Meal times and bedtimes too can be specifically designed to promote and reinforce the positive feelings hitherto discovered in some other kind of community experience (see virtually all of Chapter 6). Such positive feelings will also become material for consideration within the small-group context, where the group will seek to ensure that the individual will not compulsively resist these positive feelings. Aspects of the community's identity will thus become part of the individual's identity too. He will share the community's preoccupations and concerns as well as his own. However, through his participation in the group process that contains and manages the community's concerns, so he, too, will simultaneously learn that an individual's problems actually can be managed also. The youngster will learn that he need no longer be enslaved by them. He will eventually discover and be convinced of his own intrinsic worth.

Of course, a community of human beings only rarely, and then only momentarily, achieves perfection. A community, too, is subject to the rivalries that split families. The very survival of a community also depends on how it manages itself in the wider societal context; how it copes with departures, separations, failures, betrayals, human inadequacy. All these experiences exist both within family groups and within each individual. If the emotionally dispossessed are to regain their individual ability to be fully human, they must come to experience their environment as an emotionally dynamic one, and then be able to cope with it just as more fortunate people function within their families.

Perhaps the first task on this therapeutic journey within a therapeutic community is to address the reality of pain and inadequacy, because to do so is to unlock the door to personal freedom and joy eventually. This is true for adult or youngster, and whether the journey is taking place in an individual context, or in a bedroom, a meeting, or during a meal. Confronting pain and inadequacy is hardly a desirable activity and it usually meets with intense resistance. However, in the same way that words expressed in poetic images create a shaft of indefinable insight, so can charismatic persuasion convince the dubious of the verity and worth of the struggle. It is the charismatic conviction that momentarily bridges the gap between belief and doubt. Yet, something of it – its passion perhaps – can arise from everyday experiences as much as from an obviously outstanding event.

The experiences that fire a defeated adolescent's imagination do not have to be exceptional. A sense of contact and relationship can be generated by even trivial experiences. 'They don't know the kids!' declared a domestic cleaner with decades of experience in residential settings, 'Leastways, not the way you do when you are standing next to them doing the washing up!' She was talking dismissively of exceptionally qualified senior staff. Both her knowledge and their knowledge are, of course, important. Yet, unless they are equally acknowledged and supported, then the community will lose some of its dynamic vitality and its ability to work change, for it will not be totally therapeutically orientated.

Such change-making, therefore, is not the magic that the outsider so often wonderingly perceives, but results from the enlivening of each life experience, as consistently as possible, and as ingeniously as can be devised, within an integrated totality of experiences. It is difficult to describe such an amalgam, or the process behind its creation, without sounding pretentious. However, enlivening a community's self-awareness so that everyday experiences can be recognized as being therapeutically significant arises from the way intellectual understanding of psychic need can be expressed in physical and material terms, as well as in verbal ones. Thus the staff obviously need to be intelligent and well-educated in order to embrace new and complex ideas. Yet, without being able to handle a broom with equal skill, they may never become the most useful therapeutic member of staff! Sweeping and simplistic this may be, but I came to see the truth in it a long time ago, and my experience was occasionally reinforced by staff who were not able to engage with physical and material experiences in a way that could embody their care and insight.

'How you like our PE?', Fred Lennhoff demanded of me at Shotton Hall School one day. He spoke in a gutteral German accent that in no way disguised his origins in prewar Berlin. When he pretended not to understand, or when he pretended to be able to express himself only in very limited English, you knew he was then disguising some arcane objective that would eventually surprise you! Not yet having learnt this lesson, I replied that I thought it very institutional.

'All this standing in lines. "Astride together! Astride, together!" at 7 o'clock in the morning, was', I thought, 'a little outdated!'
'Oh, you think so? How very interesting. Sadly, we all get out of date so quickly. Well, we will have to see what a modern teacher can do. You be here tomorrow morning in time and you can take the class!'
'Hang on', I exclaimed in alarm. 'I teach English, History. I have never been trained in PE!'
'Well, tomorrow you start!', he roared. And so I did.

On another occasion Lennhoff engaged me in a long conversation about the Royal Canadian Mounted Police, who had demonstrated at the County Show the day before.

'And they had, how do you say it – Ach! mein English. These idols, from the Indians. What you call them?'
'Totem poles.'
'Ach! Ja! Totem poles. What you know about these?'
'Well... Freud wrote a book called *Totem and Taboo*.'
Lennhoff leapt to his interrogative task. What had Freud said; what did he mean; what was the significance, the psychological value of totems in primitive cultures? How could they generate psychic health?
'It would be wonderful if we had some of these here', he said smiling. 'They would be fun, but they would also stimulate questions and thoughts. Well', he said, as though suddenly stumbling on an idea, 'You will make some.'
'What? Make a totem pole? I'm no good with my hands. They take years of skill .'
'Find a way', he bellowed. 'Make with your hands. Otherwise all you do is just talk.' And he strode off contemptuously.
'No', he snarled the next day, he would not provide money for tools. I had a week to complete the task.

To my utter amazement, I gathered one or two youngsters and together we made three totem poles in a week! They stood only 5 or 6 feet high but, painted and carved as best we could, there was no doubt as to what they were and they lasted for years. The lesson he taught me has lasted a long, professional time. At the time I would rather have murdered him than make totem poles, or devised physical exercise that was good fun, yet, within my affronted exasperation, I knew that he was right and that values that ascribed all skill in therapeutic work simply to knowledge and sympathy was, on its own, pretentious. So, for years at Peper Harow, when it came to Saturday morning cleaning, you would always find the director in the front hall, with its acres of stone flagging, with his scrubber and bucket.

On the one hand, the staff should sympathize deeply with the adolescents, should care enough to have endless patience to stay up all night with the boy or girl who needs containment, and they should be glad to play games with them. On the other hand, while the staff should want to do all these things, they must still be able to retain professional objectivity and an adult identity, rather than identify with the disturbed youngster. Perhaps the same disturbed adolescent that fires such commitment still lurks within the member of staff, too, – certainly, the community's group dynamics tend to make the adults a little regressed. Yet, although the adult should be prepared to return over his completed journey to adulthood, back to where the adolescent stands paralysed, the adult should only do so in order to take that adolescent by the hand and lead him towards adulthood. He should not return simply to rejoin the youngster (see Chapter 5, pp.54–5). The adult, too, must continue to grow; he also has personal responsibilities for forming relationships, perhaps for nurturing his own family, for example.

Consequently, issues about personal and functional commitment, such as whether members of staff should live on or off the estate, in or out of the main house, are difficult to balance. It is understandable that those who design new residential facilities, who remember appallingly depersonalizing total institutions, tend to ensure that all staff live in the wider community and not in the institution. Although it seems clear that no single factor such as this makes for institutional health or sickness, living away from the institution often speeds a recovery of reality for the member of staff. It makes a distance of perspective more easily achieved.

On the other hand, living within the community boundaries, with one's family, also contributes enormously to the youngsters' acceptance of the staff's commitment. Above all, it creates an atmosphere that counters the youngster's tendency to feel that he is part of an outcast group. He can appropriately instead see himself as a member of a kind of normal community, and this adds enormously to the residents' sense of self-regard and security. If the families are relating well, then such a community setting can often be an ideal circumstance for sharing the upbringing of one's children with other people who have similar views and similar insights. There is no doubt how powerfully this can add to the cohesiveness of the whole atmosphere with mutual benefit to residents and families.

Establishing the boundaries between when families' involvement was wanted and when it was not was one of those painful experiences that contributed to the development of the community's identity. In the early days, wives of new staff, often similarly professionally qualified, very much wished to participate. They always took full part in their husband's interview procedure. Their importance was undeniable, for staff would often need their spouse's support to an extraordinary degree. They came to community meetings; at times of crisis they added to the comforting resources, and they helped to prepare for open days, while staff wrestled with the recalcitrant youngsters' lack of motivation.

Yet, it was often difficult for parents to know where their own children stood in all this. Were they not entitled to the same resources as the community's disturbed children received? Yet, there were occasions when the picture of mothers cuddling their babies and encouraging their toddlers were almost a torment to the deprived residents in the community. In some circumstances, the residents' fantasies – stimulated by their juxtaposition with normal families with prior claims on their personal member of staff – were so disturbing that their sense of security and their confidence in their ability to manage their own impulses were seriously reduced rather than increased.

Each member of staff was responsible for a small caseload of two or three individual youngsters. These knew the member of staff's family well. They often went to his home for special birthday meals, or a special meal before a holiday, so that a family coming into the main house for the opening night of the annual exhibition, for example, or perhaps a wife coming to join her husband at the Christmas feast, were always welcomed with familiarity. There were about fifty youngsters in the community and thirty-five staff (if one included the support teams of clerical and maintenance staff). It was sometimes a little overwhelming when, perhaps, a further twenty adults joined in such community activities. Yet, the sense of everyone being part of a unified enterprise that arose from this coming together seemed crucial to the community's early success. After the feast, staff and their spouses changed their party clothes and got stuck into the mountain of washing up. This often lasted until three in the morning and, despite the accompanying case of wine, it required a real commitment, which the youngsters recognized. It certainly meant a great deal to them.

In those early days, we also met on a fortnightly basis for study seminars. The object was to try to consider our work from a more objective perspective. Each member of staff prepared and led these seminars in turn and, of course, their partners came when they were able, and that added immeasurably to the serious way in which all the adults in the community related to the task.

Other communities and, indeed, Peper Harow in recent years, have taken a view that such commitment denies what the family needs for itself alone, denies the professionalism of the task, and thus is a denial of reality. 'Work is work', they would say. One should not raise confusing and artificial expectations of entitlement in the youngster. One is more able to give to them when one is more refreshed. There was always a tension between taking a view that being at Peper Harow was a vocational commitment or that it was a job – a highly professional job perhaps, but with proper boundaries between work and home. I have no doubt that the adults' commitment made a great deal of difference to the youngsters' belief that the staff were truly sharing something of essential worth with them. It was also much harder to indulge in a fantasized relationship that one owned the member of staff if the experience of that member of staff's family was an undeniable reality.

That the member of staff had to be shared with his or her own family was, undoubtedly, a painful problem for disturbed children. On the other hand, it was also more difficult for anger and frustration to turn into real violence against the person who was going to be one's host at supper time in his own home. Nevertheless, a cautionary story of John Gittens – late principal of Aycliffe School:

A member of staff took a delinquent boy into his home almost as though he were adopting him. Before they left for a holiday, when the boy was to be left at the school, the boy stole his child's money box. The member of staff remonstrated about his betrayal, lack of gratitude.... That night the boy broke in and stabbed the child in her sleep!

It was essential that the staff came to recognize the significance of the youngsters' behaviour so that they could interact with residents in a way that reinforced the communal message. Like Finchden Manor, Peper Harow, too, had its overgrown, tantrumming children, whose early ability to evaluate situations had never been developed. These youngsters would misinterpret everything, it seemed. One approached them on eggshells and, sensing this, they would roar away at the implied message that one was scared of them when they felt themselves to be the only ones entitled to be scared. It is small comfort when nursing a bleeding nose delivered from a 14-stone young bull to be told that he is more frightened of your friendly smile!

A staff-room discussion at Finchden Manor one evening between two experienced members of staff about a new colleague illustrated both the necessity of confronting such youngsters with reality and the necessity of developing a strategy for achieving it. The new member of staff at Finchden had become quite angry about the blackmailing, physical threat that one bullying youngster constantly posed. After a series of such events the member of staff responded to the final one – a flicked bread pellet – by grabbing half a pound of butter and hurling it accurately at the offender's chest. This was an unusual, spontaneous response and caught the youngster totally by surprise. In terms of his development, its timing was accurate too. It was the first time that the youngster was able to see and accept a confrontation about his behaviour, and thus begin to consider what was underlying it. It was an absurd thing to do and both the youngster and the young member of staff, after their mutual gasp of astonishment, burst into laughter that was followed by a serious discussion.

This kind of 'conversation' was common at Finchden, and was exemplified by many legends of Lyward himself. His staff understood this message to the point where they could eventually repeat it in their own human idiosyncratic way rather than as a stilted caricature. It is a form of play psychotherapy and it enables behaviour, and what underlies the behaviour, to be tackled in a way that is perhaps more real than words alone could manage.

Fed up with the insensitivity of a particular visiting student, Lyward suggested it was time he departed. After a few days the suggestion was repeated, but the student was still there when Lyward made one of his lunch-time forays into the dining room, with a much-used copy of Milton in his hands. The older boys gathered round, ready to learn, and the younger ones to be included in the 'gang', but also out of a new curiosity. *Paradise Lost* and the regaining of sight are live issues for such audiences. Lyward often taught by a Socratic method of question and answer, which eventually became a symposium. It was interrupted by the student on the edge of the crowd. 'Mr Lyward, Mr Lyward', he called, with no sensitivity to what Lyward was creating, or why. Mr Lyward, then in his seventies, rose to his feet, grabbed the water jug, and emptied its contents over the student's head and thus returned to Paradise Regained!

Such drama could be said to be still more unfair when, in later years, I shouted at the butcher's delivery boy in one of Peper Harow's early community meetings. We were struggling to create an atmosphere, which, day after day was being wrecked by one delinquent jack-in-the-box or another. However, the point that I was insisting on making, and that I insisted would eventually be accepted, was that nothing would be allowed to interfere with the community meeting. Like it or not, there we would all be for an hour every morning, for the opportunity, at least, to deal with what arose between us. One morning the butcher's delivery boy barged in and tried to shuffle around the double row of chairs in the direction of the kitchen. 'Please go back and go around the outside', he was told. But, he was not a butcher's boy for nothing and he began to argue – no doubt to hide his embarrassment – that he always went this way.

'Out!' I roared leaping to my feet. 'Out, at once!' in tones that brooked absolutely no denial.
He fled and half the staff were appalled.
'How could you set such an appalling example?' said one. 'You made me feel ashamed of you. If this is a therapeutic community, I'm not sure I want to be here. I'm really surprised at you.'
'Not at all', said another. 'I'm not remotely surprised. The moment the guy came in I knew he would get something like that. No, I'm

not appalled either. It was hard luck on the kid, but he ought to know better than to think he can stomp through someone else's house, and the lesson was pretty important for our kids.'

'What lesson? Such appalling manners and unkindness.'

'Not at all. The lesson that "No means No". We all need them to be absolutely sure about that.'(See Chapter eight, p.141–2.)

It was difficult to establish a communal sense that we were really entitled to live as a therapeutic community at Peper Harow. The boys had little sense of being entitled to anything. At one level of functioning, that was why they stole so much. That they had rights seemed hardly credible and many of them, as well as some staff, would have been prepared to capitulate to outsiders' expectations.

Opposite the mansion, though no longer part of the park, was a local cricket ground. It attracted snobbery, as well as interest in the game itself, for this club had been associated with the aristocracy who had once owned it. The same grandiose associations applied to the parish church, that was geographically very much part of the estate. The drive divided the cricket ground from our elegant front lawn with its specimen cedar trees and well-kept flower beds. A good view could be obtained of the match, which was perhaps part of the reason why visitors, without a moment's thought, parked their cars on our lawn. We, in turn, received complaints, with some cause, that our radios were too noisy, even from 200 yards' distance. However, the tone of the complaints often implied an underlying assumption that our obviously bad youngsters certainly had no entitlement to prior consideration. That they lived in our noble mansion was viewed with a mixture of envy and contempt and that attitude above all was intolerable to accept for boys who already viewed themselves contemptuously.

Seeing cars on our carefully mowed front lawn one sunny summer's afternoon, I remonstrated with the member of staff on duty, 'Why haven't you turfed them off?' I demanded. His look implied that it did not matter and that to get so worked up was an indication of unbalance, at least. It would also be very embarrassing for him to tell those people to leave. Far better to pretend not to see them, or that it did not matter if they took for granted property that was owned by those who cared for such riff-raff.

'Get rid of them', I demanded.

'Right now?' he questioned.

'Immediately!'

He strolled to the near edge of the lawn and in stentorian, American tones he bawled,

'Da Boss says, git off da lawn!'

At which point he turned away, prepared to leave the issue. Furious, I came out of the front door to do the job myself. He then began

trotting ahead, anxiously calling as he went and gesticulating as
though Nemesis were following.
'Dere yer go. Whadidda tell yer? Here come da Boss! Here come da
Boss!'

While the community had rights, it also had obligations. Out of the
chaos of the early days it was quickly accepted that, whereas empty rules
were no longer appropriate, when the community actually came to an
agreement – such as the one that you did not leave the premises without the
agreement of a member of staff – then in the community meeting you
would certainly be called upon to explain yourself if you had breached such
an agreement. The disciplinary function of the community meeting will be
discussed later, though one needs constantly to remember that the meeting
served a variety of purposes, at one and the same time (see Chapter eight,
pp. 141–52).

Yet, all the different functions that the community meeting fulfilled
together formed a very powerful focus for the new identity that was to be
established. Above all, the community meeting was a situation in which
everyone was called upon to exercise responsibility for their own and each
other's behaviour. This was a totally different way of perceiving authority.
Hitherto, authority had been punitive and was of the sort that instructed
youngsters how to behave. But when they misbehaved, instead of this
being understood, they were abused. Simplistic attempts were made to
deter the repetition of bad behaviour by beating such disturbed youngsters
with a stick. Occasionally, youngsters even had to be held spreadeagled
over a table by several adult males in order to be so assaulted. This
discipline was all unidirectional. Only the hatred passed back up the
hierarchy in a reverse direction.

To get such a community to accept the ownership of its behaviour, and
to get it to cease to punish that behaviour, was difficult enough. And the
community meeting, and, to a lesser extent, the small therapy groups,
played an essential role in bringing this about. The change in the functioning
of the staff meeting above all else allowed the community meeting to
function. That change took some time to occur because several of the old
staff were busy sabotaging the endeavour before they finally departed.
This change of attitude of the staff towards the youngsters was bound to
take a long time, and so the community could only gradually come to
function in a therapeutic way. Once it had done so, the community could
then be described as a system of interrelating parts. Much of its functioning
was unconscious and difficult to identify in a specific way. Nevertheless,
what could be defined – the small groups, the attitude of staff to residents,
the specially designed physical surroundings, for instance – could be seen
as mutually reinforcing. Because this was frequently an unconscious
process, setting out to change the way the group was functioning, or
avoiding being caught up in its mutually reinforcing processes, was

equally difficult. Additionally, there are other reasons why a disturbed group of youngsters prefers life in a system that works according to rigid, judgemental values about behaviour and that also inevitably punishes breaches of its synthetic code! The underlying sense of being worthless and unwanted; the terrifying sense of chaos and disintegration; these feelings create a desperate but confused desire for order, for a simple way of achieving a 'good' self-image, and thus of entitlement to a place in the hierarchy. At least the old approved school attempted to provide that structure; undoubtedly, some youngsters did gain a relief from it. Yet, the most disturbed children were only partially restrained by its structure because it did not address the underlying reasons for their compulsive, destructive urges. The most benign and creative atmosphere will not be adequate either unless something in that atmosphere can address within it the underlying reasons for such attitudes and behaviour.

It takes a long time to establish a staff attitude that is predominantly therapeutic. The staff need to view the youngsters' behaviour in terms of what it reveals about therapeutic need. At one time a youngster might need control. At another it would be important to understand that even bizarre behaviour is only an unconscious attempt to manifest internal confusion or fear. Thus, behaviour provides an opportunity for the member of staff to help relieve anxiety, or to help the youngster clarify what he is actually feeling. Concerned objectivity is always difficult to achieve. Staff need to become aware of their own feelings and prejudices in order to step aside from their influence and stay in touch with the therapeutic task.

It can be argued that all staff, whether they choose to work in a therapeutic community, or in a repressive regime, have many unconscious motivations in addition to their objective intentions. The supposed activity of addressing the youngsters' problems and underlying attitudes can also become vicarious ways of supposed self-examination. The member of staff may never have fully resolved issues of authority and of discipline. He may also have other unresolved dilemmas from his own childhood or adolescence. Unconsciously, at least, identification with the rebellious or the abused child and the opportunity to pay exceptional attention to a child's unconscious processes offer staff respectable ways of addressing their own problems. Like any child, adults are also resistant to addressing painful and frightening psychic dilemmas directly. Yet, having to deal with such problems daily inevitably stirs up their own inner world. The member of staff may not be aware of any unconscious tendency to approach his own problems through the youngsters. Yet, with proper supervision, the member of staff can increasingly recognize the differences between the child's problem and his own. The gradual and ongoing clarification of his unconscious motivations is also of great maturational significance for the member of staff personally. As it occurs, so his objective attention to the youngster will be enhanced. Their separate but mutual journey can then become of mutual value. The member of staff will be in closer touch with his own most vulnerable feelings – such as inadequacy or helplessness – as well as with those of the youngsters.

For those staff who have been working in a system in which everything reinforces a defensive way of functioning, it is unrealistic to expect them to make such a diametric, professional change. The more such a staff member's emotional stance is challenged, the more he is likely to respond with an increased level of delinquent functioning. For new staff, however, at Peper Harow in the early days, their passionate and ideological - but also unconsciously motivated – desire to introduce the therapeutic mode of functioning, was bound to be inhibited by the increasing conflict between them and the original staff. Neither was this simply a debate in the staff room. It was enacted throughout the communal life and predominantly by the youngsters. It was as though the youngsters' increased delinquent behaviour 'spoke' on behalf of the threatened old staff group.

There were several fire-raisers among the youngsters, only one or two of whom could be identified. During one period of about three months, some thirty fires were lit, of varying seriousness. In fact, it was actually reported that one member of staff had addressed one of the recorded arsonists as follows: 'I can quite understand how disturbing all this therapeutic stuff must be to you. If I were in your position, I would feel like lighting fires all the time. I wouldn't blame you at all.' (See Chapter two, p. 25; also this chapter, p. 67.)

Another member of staff became so anxious at her teenage daughter's interest in one of the residents that she took the boy's file home one evening to reveal details of his disturbed sexual activities in order to put the daughter off. This youngster found himself jeered at a week later in the street, when visiting the local town, by the daughter's school friends.

Some of the youngsters eventually began to verbalize this conflict. I remember one member of staff being bitterly castigated in a small group, for his 'two-facedness'. Angrily, one of the boys complained that the idea that such a group should be described as a place where one's most sensitive feelings could be revealed was the grossest hypocrisy. 'You don't seem to have any idea what it feels like when you make jokes outside the group about something I have said.' The member of staff was frightened and embarrassed at this public revelation about his apparent misdemeanour. He was also sorry for his consciously unintended hurt. He was simultaneously baffled and confused as to how he found himself in this situation, for he saw himself as a kind, caring person. Then he became angry and defensive. In different company he would have begun to remonstrate, 'How dare you talk to me like that!'

Years later that same boy took me to task. He had left prematurely, he said, because he felt the contradiction between public statement and private functioning was driving him crazy. He listed some examples and found it nigh impossible to accept that they were all news to me. 'But surely you knew everything that went on!' he declared.

I am still sorry for my ignorance at that time. I, like most people in the community then, tended to see the issue as a battle between the repressive 'baddies' and the heroic rescuing 'goodies'. The more difficult the behaviour became, the more narrow became one's focus on the issue of managing it. Hindsight reveals that painful and frightening necessity only slowly clarified one's understanding of the ongoing experience. It is clear that, at the time, my sense of the nature of the boys' functioning and my acute appreciation of the quality of experience that would respond to their need was intuitive. Thus, my determination to create an environment that would embody that manifold experience was envisaged in artistic terms. I did not understand the nature of the underlying reasons for the contradictory systems of the community's psychodynamic functioning. I, too, was caught up in the judgemental fight. I was aware that the consequences for the youngsters of these symbolically warring parental groups was, indeed, antitherapeutic, but my answer to this was that I should win the battle as soon as possible, so that the good alternative could then begin to flourish.

Looking back, it seemed that this victory occurred one evening when a special meeting was called between the staff and the managers. The meeting was called to consider the future careers of some of the older staff who, anxious for their position, were enthusiastically declaring their total commitment to the new regime, despite the fact that everybody knew that they were busily undermining it. One member of staff, who was making this declaration most fervently, called upon a new member of staff to verify the sincerity of his commitment, reminding him of their conversation in the pub a few days earlier. However, the new member of staff denied that this had been the case and, indeed, went ahead to quote the various things that had been said, which implied the complete opposite of the present public statement. There were some further difficulties as these members of staff sought trade union support for their position. But, from this moment on, their opposition became decreasingly effective and the balance began to swing in a therapeutic direction.

The therapeutic community movement as a whole was, in those early seventies, still imbued with a messianic spirit. But, even if I had been objective enough to have recognized that the dynamic interplay between the community's subgroups was a process by which psychic growth could actually occur, I doubt if it would have changed my view of the kind of management of that process that was needed at that time. The director's task, as well as enabling the subgroups' interplay, is also to seize the appropriate moments for change – particularly when new ground has to be broken. Thus the director's management style was bound to be experienced as arbitrary and perhaps despotic. There was so much change required in that situation. Each aspect of change had been debated endlessly but, because there were so many antitherapeutic convictions among managers, staff, and boys, few of whom had any awareness of the motivations underlying their views, the impetus for change would have been drained away if we had waited for consensus. I read Terence Morris's *Pentonville* at that time, and accepted that it was a grim warning (Morris and Morris, 1963 – nothing presents more clearly in this book than the way a megalithic institution can blanket all possibility of change). My priority was to keep up the pace of change and allow nothing to hinder it before the opportunity slipped away. Nevertheless, it is often very difficult to acknowledge both the extent to which real change so often depends upon an individual's personal determination and energy, and the extent to which we envy that individual's charisma and thus feel compelled to denigrate it.

The consequences of this partially blind cavalry charge were in some way hurtful for everyone associated with the community. I was aware of this at the time, but hoped that the price would be felt to have been worth the paying by all of us, when our land of promise was eventually reached. Some managers must have thought I was intolerably autocratic; others recognized that I had a vision and felt they should support it unquestioningly. Those managers who could not do so resigned, raising the general anxiety still more. Some managers remained and so did their uncertainty about the validity of this process.

In a sense, the biggest change was as much in terms of our external image as our internal one. I insisted that my title was that of director – not headmaster. Indeed, the title 'managers' seemed to me inappropriate. It was a professional and full-time occupation to manage the task and the resources to support it. The term was also redolent of the whole approved-school system. We needed to be recognized as a charity rather than a penal institution. Those legally responsible for the affairs of a charity are called trustees, but it took three years before the managers could accept a change of their own title. It is a small example of the way institutions resist change. Meanwhile, without consultation, I had brass and marble memorial plaques in the front hall, erected to the memory of dead chairmen, removed and stored. The silver sporting cups were put away and, above all, the relationships with the youngsters began to change.

Most of the trustees had, as managers, been members of progress committees. There were four of these, corresponding with the school's division into houses. The managers arrived monthly in the evening and sat with the head or deputy, the matron or assistant matron, and the respective housemaster to review the progress of a quarter of the boys in each house group. Sometimes the boys got a 'wigging' for their lack of effort or praise for their excellent behaviour. The managers felt that they were in close touch with events, though the subcultural activity rarely showed itself to them. Some committees were arranged magisterially behind a vast desk.

The boy sat on an upright chair before them; his housemaster, like a solicitor, to one side.

I decided that this system, which my own group of trustees had modified significantly when I had been the housemaster, was totally inappropriate. The kind of reports submitted should indicate not behaviour *per se* but its implications for the individual's psychological condition and development. If we were to have any awareness of the family's significance, the boy's social worker should be present. Indeed, we felt, there should be a regular review of each resident's development, but it should be a professional case conference, rather than a night of judgment before the board.

It was, perhaps, unfortunate that no alternative structural opportunity to enable the trustees to relate regularly with the youngsters was devised, yet I still cannot think of a situation that could specifically inform trustees of the psychic issues except through the mediation of the director and staff. It confuses the nature of psychotherapeutic authority if the trustees require a manifest engagement with the residents on a personal basis. The presenting social and behavioural issues of the youngsters tend to inveigle and fascinate any visitor. Unlike the staff, the trustees do not constantly have to reflect on their own unconscious responses, either as individuals or as members of a subgroup, in a shifting kaleidoscope of relationships. The staff, on the other hand, must be in touch both with the youngsters' and their own psychic functioning, both in individual and group terms. It is a central professional task.

There are other ways in which trustees can engage personally with the whole community, some of which occured after the progress committees had been terminated. One trustee came and taught regularly; another even came and worked as a member of staff for a few months; certain other trustees participated in camp, but several of them still felt they had been deprived of contact with 'their' children. The conflicts over ownership were kept alive, despite harmonious appearances.

A still greater challenge – especially for those trustees whose families had been associated with Park House School for years - was my insistence on a change of name. With my vision of Finchden Manor much in mind, I wanted to sell the estate and move elsewhere. This, I was persuaded, was financially impossible – we would have to do the best possible with what existed. The question above all was how to get the local neighbourhood, the professional world, as well as our own organization, to see the institution afresh. Without this change of perception, no material or organizational change would have any effect. The rest of the approved-school system merely changed the titles of its institutions to community homes, but had not changed their individual identities, and so it was not surprising that little else changed either.

The search for a unique and apposite identity was rewarded by one unusually fortunate circumstance. The house we lived in and its lands were called by a name that was older than memory. By owning the estate, we automatically owned the name just as much as our predecessors had done throughout the centuries. Therefore, through our similar relationship to our home and our land, we could relate ourselves as a community to all who had been there before us. The present house was two hundred years old, yet it was only the latest embodiment of Peper Harow, which every house on that site had been called since before it was recorded in the Domesday Book. The very earth was Peper Harow. Those people who had lived there, like the hills and the woods and the river, were one part of that Peper Harow. They had entwined their individual and group identity with it, whether they had lived in a wooden Saxon long house or in a Palladian mansion. Those timeless roots were now available to be owned by those who lived there today.

Yet, several arguments were advanced as to why a change of name was not possible. For instance, the occupier of the home farm had appropriated the name to his farm house. I did not feel that avoiding trouble with a neighbour was worth the sacrifice of what made Peper Harow itself unique and was thus of priceless symbolic value to those with no sense of identity. At first the heading on the official paper was agreed as Park House, Peper Harow, but the next batch of paper simply bore its proper name. This became amended in the trust deed much later, and it was as Peper Harow that the infant community began to approach the outside world.

The outside world did not know how to respond to this change. Our neighbour eventually acquiesced in allowing the name on the notice board of the gate to be changed. The vicar was less happy when compulsory churchgoing was abolished. It was difficult for him to accept that no boys would want to go to church voluntarily. Perhaps the atheistic staff were dissuading them, at the very least! If so, it was certainly not conscious, though memory of the time when the boys were herded in the half dozen pews at the back of the church to allow a suitable gap between them and the respectable local population was very recent. Those boys who had to borrow a penny for the collection, having been found wanting at the prechurch inspection, were caned for their omission afterwards. It was not a memory to be cherished. At Rogation-tide the normal church congregation was swelled by hundreds of others, who came with the Salvation Army band and many coaches for a tour of the estate. At several ritual points the procession halted, sprinkling symbolic water and blessing upon the trees, the lawns, the river, and the still overgrown kitchen garden. That this immemorial invasion should be stopped, too, as though those who lived at Peper Harow were entitled to the privacy of a real home, came as a great shock.

Other local people were equally appalled when the local hunt was ordered not to trespass on our land. Though the hunt's members met on the edge of the estate, they really were experienced by the community as the outside enemy. On one occasion a fox was reputedly brought in a sack and released among the assembled pack. There is no doubt that, however it arrived, it was actually torn to pieces in the sight and sound of the community. We were all shocked by this! It certainly raised many questions about the generally judged identity of our own residents in comparison with the respectable company at our gate.

There is nothing like an outside enemy to unite the group within (see Chapter nine, pp. 166–7). There is nothing like a convenient scapegoat to enable all of one's anxiety, guilt, frustration, and fears of inadequacy and failure to be carried away. Nevertheless, encouraging such processes for temporary gain is like a compact with the devil – expensive later. No doubt the boys were aware of these battles, ostensibly on their behalf, and no doubt they were gleeful at the activities of their champion who could so discomfort those whom they saw as so far above them. To some extent these affairs were unifying, with a conscious objective, passionately declared over and over again. The intention was to defend the youngsters' right to have a community that was theirs; to feel that they were worthy to have a stake in an estate that was older than memory; to share roots as deep and as secure as that. If their source of greatest authority – the director himself – was insistent that that was their entitlement, their rebirth-right ... then perhaps they, themselves, should begin to review their self-valuation.

This ringing declaration and the nature of their relationship with the community was pronounced every Friday night. The Friday night session was the major charismatic activity for about ten years (see Chapter five, p. 77). This activity commenced at the time when we were having an increasing number of fires (see Chapter two, p. 25; also this chapter, p. 62). There were nearly thirty in a period of three months and each fire was guaranteed to raise the community's anxiety. Several people were involved, but not all of the arsonists were known. It occurred at a period of maximal chaos during the transition from repression to therapy. So many feelings were being expressed in delinquent behaviour, as no more appropriate form of expressing them had yet been achieved. How much of the fire lighting was a direct response to frightening situations in the community, and how much of it was the habitual response to any anxiety, was not known. However, it seemed to me that the expression of this anxiety needed to be given a legitimate form as well as requiring control. Simply uttering imprecations against unknown people in a situation one had to acknowledge was difficult for them would merely demonstrate one's impotence.

It occurred to me that, if we had a legitimate fire in the house, it would lessen the hysteria about fire in general and would reassure the unknown perpetrators that their compulsions could be managed. With much difficulty the fireplace in the front hall was unblocked and, for the first time in many years, flames danced in the grate. It provided an opportunity for gathering in a different way from the community meeting. We eventually made some communal and upholstered benches for the boys to sit on and each week we met and ate cream cakes, and settled down for a story. Sometimes I read a book that had allegorical overtones of our life together and at other times I would make up stories on the spot. I used to have great difficulties every Friday thinking of what I might say, bearing in mind that the sequential weekend might be affected by it. Sometimes I would arrive without a thought in my head, but when the time came I could always get going.

Never could one have asked for a better audience. It didn't really matter what I said: 'You always end up singing the same song', they said time and again. I agreed. Often my story was long-winded and boring, but my audience was patient. It was clear to me that the exercise itself had deep meaning for these emotionally starved youngsters. The regularity of it, at the end of the working week, produced reassurance. No decoration had occurred in the house for years and it had certainly taken a battering in the previous year. We eventually sorted out the recalcitrant chimmney, decorated the room – the first to be redecorated in the house, obtained a grant for curtains that hung the full 20 feet from the ceiling, and installed a system of lighting that increased the comfort and highlighted the dramatic relationships of the meeting. The group around the fire was contrasted with the dark room by a dimmed floodlight. The fireplace and director were spotlit. A dramatic setting had been created and the participants joined together in the weekly ritual of story within it:

> On the hill behind you, out there in the rain and the darkness, still stand three cairns. Under those mounds lie three chiefs who each lived here, with all their people, before we came. While we have been gathering here tonight, have they also stepped silently down the hill? Are their spirits out there beyond the curtains and the locked front door, standing incomprehending in the darkness and the rain? Could they, invisible, be watching us by the fire that they once used to know? Do they remember how in their time long ago, their gratitude stretched towards the warming flames and the glowing embers that cooked the deer they caught in their sun-bright mornings? They are our brothers and our sisters from an older time and I will tell you a story about them.

Then would follow some tale that spoke of persecution and suffering, of the tribes coming together for the gift of understanding and protection, of achievements and adventures, of journeys across the seas and mountains, of magic and metamorphosis. And then the spell ended. We all trooped upstairs to bed. Going from room to room the same comments were made, 'You always tell the same story.' 'Yeah. Last week it was about the

Japanese Samurai Brothers. It is always the same. Yeah, really it's us, isn't it?' (Rose, 1988: 14–15).

What was occurring on these Friday nights was predominantly an understanding response to behaviour at an intuitive level, that contributed significantly to an atmosphere that was designed to engage at a preconscious level. This engagement recognized unconscious need and responded in a way that had psychic meaning. In other words, the symbolism of the interaction was alive to the youngsters, because it illuminated both their chronic need and, at the same time, the possibility of its being fulfilled, at last.

A community calendar of such regular events was gradually developed. The next major occasion was the Christmas Feast.

One Christmas we chose as the motif for our feast decorations 'The Cave of Ice', and the idea was that, despite the chilly surroundings, we could, together, generate immense warmth. The tables were covered with fresh linen and then loaded with an amazing array of cutlery and glittering glass for each place setting. Enormous, colourful decorations and bowls of fruit filled all the rest of the candlelit space. The whole vast area itself had an internal shell built of chicken wire, covered with silver foil and, at one end, down a cataract of foil, constructed in place of the removed twelve foot high window, ran a stream of water which passed through the centre of the room to turn a ten foot high water wheel, as though part of a mill, before going out of the opposite window!

Many of the boys were involved in this crazy inspiration. The atmosphere during construction was often hysterical with the same quality of excitement that the boys had previously experienced perhaps when taking away and driving stolen cars. At one point the whole wire structure emitted blue flames as it was electrified by one megalomanic adolescent. But in the end, the whole Community gathered in the 'cave' together, utterly amazed at what they had done and aware that the intensely enjoyable memory of this occasion would last forever.

This was the menu: Ogen Melon with Parma Ham, followed by Velouté d'Asperge, made with asparagus from our gardens. The Fish Course was Smoked Salmon and was separated from the Roast Duck and Orange Sauce with Chestnut Barquettes and Potatoes by a Champagne Sorbet. In turn, the Entrée was followed by Christmas Pudding, brought in decorated with holly and flaming in brandy of course, together with real Rum Butter and accompanied by Mince Pies and Cream. A Cheese Board was brought round after that, while Coffee and Cream were served. There were beautiful receptacles on the tables which had been specially made to go among the sculptural, thematic decorations and candles, and these contained frosted black grapes and home-made sweets, and chocolates. The correct cutlery and glassware were laid appropriate to such a banquet. The crockery had been brought out of store – a different design from that of everyday use. Two kinds of wine were served. Although, of course, every attempt was made to buy these costly ingredients as cheaply as possible, quality was not sacrificed to cost, nor to inferior cooking or presentation, the standards of which would have done credit to a very sophisticated restaurant. It can be seen that this is another example of the kind of fantasy we create but, for it to be truly meaningful, there is no pretence – a banquet is a banquet indeed! And nobody there could imagine that it was called one thing but that they were being foisted off with the second best. It's usually very difficult for the new boys to accept such an occasion {see Chapter five, p.75}. Not having become so identified with the Group, they cannot throw themselves into the craziness of the occasion in the same way as those who have experienced it before. As far as they are concerned, they are being offered something which is far beyond what they deserve. So, usually, they refuse most of the food which is on the table and spend the whole three-hour meal pecking at the sweets and smoking surreptitiously. When they have learned to enjoy themselves with unfettered enthusiasm, they may remember the agonizing quality of a Community Meeting, but they also have the enriching memories of this apparently purely material extravaganza which, of course, is one of the many examples of how fantasy can be created and used. The Feast is an extravagant gesture, yet engaged in by boys whose movement is more usually constrained than comfortable and free. For all the familiar hysterical and perhaps delinquent excitements involved, these have been harnessed and re-directed towards a recognition and involvement of the creative individual and the communal talents. Perhaps the implication behind such an occasion is to suggest that, as part of this Group, each boy would, in the end, be able to find a way to turn his own inner resources into something creative.

> (Rose, 1987: 38–9 – originally written for Lectures at the
> Universities of Liverpool and Newcastle-upon-Tyne)

Another feast was organized each summer to end that term when, because of its greater open-air opportunities, there was room for all the families to join in. They all arrived in November, too, when Guy Fawkes Night eventually found itself being called the 'Dragon Night', as it became an occasion special in its own way to Peper Harow. The 'Dragon' arose from a Friday night story as a creature of wonder and mystery. It was unclear if it were good or bad, strong or gentle, a friend or foe. It would require care and respect and might share a treasure that was also undefined.

> Our Bonfire Night consisted of a torchlight procession from the House to a point overlooking the River. The torches were hurled flaming into the immense edifice and, as it reared sixty feet into the air, the barbecue began to provide under the nearby Cedar Tree. As this supply waned, so everyone wandered back to a further feed of toffee apples, home-made fudge, and so forth, in the fire-warmed entrance hall. Then, on the Terrace before the open door, traditional games of apple-bobbing, pillow fighting on a greasy pole, and slapstick-humoured obstacle races took place.
>
> (Rose, 1982: 83)

At Easter one of the assistant directors, with folklore aspirations, reinvented the northern cult of 'Pace-egging', especially for Peper Harow. Everyone in the community had to be provided with their own painted egg. Armed with sticks, every member of the community was lined along the south lawn terrace and, at the signal, whipped and prodded their eggs down the hill towards the river. A ceremonial presentation of the first to arrive was made at the special tea that took place afterwards. This was felt in recent years to have lacked the vitality that would have spontaneously arisen from this activity had its symbolism related directly to the experience of the individual members of the community.

What it did contribute, however, was to a series of occasions that marked the year's passing. Youngsters began to recognize that they had 'been here before'. For some who had more homes than their actual number of years, this was an astounding realization. Every autumn there was a major creative art exhibition, to which members of the public were invited. The object was to involve as many participants as possible. Many of the newcomers were not prepared to join in, especially as the standards of so many of their peers were extraordinarily high, and thus somewhat daunting. What the participants could see in this exhibition was the enormous development that they had made in the previous year. Their work, almost always, symbolized their personal, psychological growth.

In the very early days the whole community was set by its ears when we agreed to make a fictional film adapted from one of Rosemary Sutcliffe's stories. Two years later a major documentary was made by the BBC. These were notable and exceptional occasions, like the annual day conferences that occurred over a five-year period. On each of these occasions several hundred visitors attended. But although these presented the community and its activities to the outside world, in a form of which its members could be proud, perhaps it was the regular celebrations of the passing year that gave a sense of stability and established a framework for the youngsters to use as a measuring stick of their many differently developing personal skills and abilities.

They represent, between them and the many other special occasions in the community, the two sides of community identity that say so much about the individual's emerging sense of self. On the one hand, they indicate something to the outside world. They make and test a statement about what the community sees itself doing, why, and how. On the other hand, it also illustrates to the youngsters their own gradual, internal integration. They have the increasing evidence of their worth in their changing ability to cope with stress. As newcomers, for instance, they were almost always overwhelmed by the Christmas Feast, but they eventually came to regard it as one of the experiences that belonged to them personally. The stress of being offered such riches is enormous for those so certain of their worthlessness. To respond as though entitled represents a diametric change in self-perception and a significant therapeutic victory over their compulsive resistance to change.

Nor are the members of the community really deceived by these crazy events, whose very craziness excuses the individual from his usual resistant stance. The often spectacular presentation practises the youngsters' rusty ability to wonder, but, at the same time, the residents are aware that the events also symbolize the passing struggle, the tears, the despair, the anger, the shameful and sadistic ill-treatment of others. These occasions embody a totally serious message about the therapeutic environment. Such activities help the overall programme to generate an atmosphere within which people and their worth can be experienced afresh, thus freeing the despairing adolescent from his past enslaved identity.

Chapter five

The development of individual identity

Treatment requires specially adapted psychoanalytic, nurturing, and social ingredients.
Resistance; culture-shock; the community as container; the significance of community identity for the individual.
Erikson's concept of developmental stages of growth enables clarification of individual's therapeutic needs.
Individual casework with staff limited by insufficient psychotherapeutic skills. Staff's limitations compensated by community context. Relationships between individual casework and residents' experiences within group and general environment.
Director's input – the initial interview.

In coining the phrase 'a good enough mother', Donald Winnicott reassured us that one did not have to be perfect to rear a child successfully. Since then parents have tended to become more relaxed about the imprecise process of child rearing. Winnicott reminded us that, in fact, ordinary, non-expert people always have managed the process of child-rearing without needing to understand how complex the growth of a child actually is. If they provide a tolerable environment, things will eventually work out well. Since Winnicott began writing, it has also become more widely recognized that the mother's and the baby's relationship is also part of a significant family system that adds another dimension to the complexity of how growth actually occurs (Winnicott, 1964). The benign and relaxed spontaneity of the 'good enough mother' arises as much from the family's psychosocial system as from Mother's personal emotional stability.

A 'good enough' therapeutic community partly fulfils its healing, nurturing, and educative task in a similar way to the healthy family. It is essential to remember that individual rehabilitation and growth takes place in the psychodynamic context of the whole group (see Preface, p. 10). Such a therapeutic community can provide the spontaneous, restorative qualities of healthy family life, because it is consciously structured to incorporate a complex, psychodynamic process.

We always need to remember that the youngsters who come to such places are not developing normally like their more fortunate, normal peers. They misunderstand their surroundings and the people they encounter. They often experience frightening symptoms of their disturbance, like acute anxiety, sleeplessness, and sudden unexpected and alarming outbursts of rage. It is obviously important to understand what is specifically happening within each individual, as well as within the nurturing and containing overall environment. These two requirements require the therapeutic community to be significantly different from the spontaneously good enough family.

Most of the essential ingredients of the good enough family have been missing from the lives of our youngsters. A community that has obviously warm, caring, and very personal relationships, and that operates socially and emotionally as a total group, will, as a result of the group strengths, have an extra healing potential that is rarely required in an ordinary family. That potential must be much more consciously exploited if the combined individual and group process is to be harnessed most effectively.

This healing function by the nourishing, everyday, communal life experience is neither easy to operate nor easy to understand. In an ordinary family a hungry or exhausted toddler may be difficult to get to feed or to sleep. The child's frustration or anxiety will have temporarily changed its normally relaxed relationship to life around it. The child will need much containing reassurance from its parents.

Our youngsters, on the other hand, have often been in care for years. As a result, non-institutionalizing surroundings and relationships pose a threat, both to their passive acceptance of isolation and to their sense of worthlessness. The simple implication that normal relationships are actually available for them, too, demands in turn that they respond normally, but they are out of practice. Previous hopes, even for a successful foster placement, for instance, have crashed again and again. Hope extinguished leads to the pain of despair, especially if it was hope of the essentials of emotional life, and especially if the trauma of deprivation and of loss of those essentials has been repeated each time hope has been reawakened.

Thus, the good food of such a community tends to become wasted; the warming fire allowed to die in the grate; the soft furnishings dirtied and torn. Preserving the inherent nourishment of these things, in the same way that staff have to preserve their tenderest caring despite endless hostile rejection, requires very carefully managed boundaries. For our youngsters, that management is as essential a part of the psychotherapeutic task as the gentle encouragement to discover buried feelings and put them to the work of reassessing one's self. Overcoming resistance to becoming hopeful takes a long time. Very skilful and continuously reassuring coaxing is essential. The youngster is, at the same time, almost by osmosis, absorbing the good experience of the community's life and so becoming stronger. He has increasing emotional energy to engage in the risk of experiencing the available relationships. He is increasingly strengthened internally, and so can increasingly respond to compensatory ingredients for growth that potentially arise from those relationships.

It can be seen that the youngster needs to be recognized in two guises all the time. In one of them, he is always a part of the total community – a varyingly effective social person; in the other guise, the youngster is an individual with his own needs. The 'social' person will increasingly give to others and to the environment, and equally receive from it. The individual, however, will need to lay the 'ghosts' of his own past in order to understand why his perception has been distorted, in what way his ability to understand is injured, and how these half-sensed 'ghosts' lie behind so much of his actual behaviour. After that the youngster will be able to search for his own identity. To be sustained in the pursuit of this task, the youngster must continue to be provided with the emotional resources that will specifically nurture this process.

Thus, treatment is both sociopsychological and psychoanalytic - and all within the same communal life experience. The youngsters need to be actively engaged in the everyday life of the community. They also need to be receptive to it. Their resistance to nourishment and to change needs to be circumvented so that they can take in those elements of their new experience that will help them to grow. Many – perhaps most – of the definable ingredients have a dual function. Their significance to the youngster varies according to his readiness at any particular time to function in one way or another.

Newcomers to the Christmas Feast rarely can tuck in (see Chapter four, p.70). They tend to be slightly stunned by the occasion. Sometimes they spend more time running to the lavatory than sitting in the dining room. They pick at the fruit or sweets on the table and refuse the actual courses. They become subdued and may feel like small children among the conversation of their older peers and the adults. All this is part of the culture shock they experience when they are new to the community. The culture shock can be used to great advantage in the residential context. Many view the culture shock of residential placement as another of the several, inevitably negative features of the residential experience. Yet, culture shock is not necessarily damaging. It depends on whether the sudden stress of the unfamiliar directs the young person towards something therapeutically intended and whether he is emotionally supported at the same time.

In the old approved school a newcomer very quickly felt at home, despite his distance from dilapidated urban estates. The delinquent culture may not have been very comfortable, but it was certainly familiar. So, the newcomer felt at home despite the distance from town and despite the institutional size of buildings that so exercised the anti-residential advocates. The youngster would consciously look for the head of the pecking order.

'System-wise' from years of care, he would establish himself in his niche with delinquent boasting that confirmed his habitual values to be the same as his peers. He could settle down rapidly into the stereotyped responses to institutionalized living and advance patiently up its hierarchy (see Chapter two, pp. 16–17).

But this was a warehousing experience. Change, however, requires new ways of thinking and feeling, and a new 'language' of understanding and response. Yet, people with serious emotional problems are compulsively resistant to change. In a new situation they will always try to re-establish a familiar, habitualized way of responding. The culture shock of a therapeutic community robs the newcomer of this defence. His anxiety to be accepted puts great pressure on his learning the community's new 'language' – whatever its particular culture actually is – as soon as possible. The habits of a lifetime, particularly those he created to defend himself against the pain of what he was really experiencing, cannot be easily changed. Once the shock is over for a newcomer, the old habits begin to re-establish themselves, unless the difference in culture has been sufficiently established to allow the community's new mode of functioning to become sufficiently accepted.

To the newcomer each new experience seems crazily unfamiliar at first. If the whole structure of the community is to confront the newcomer's negative response in ways that he can tolerate, and if the community can then hold his hand and lead him towards a new way of functioning, the youngster will gradually learn the language that will guide him through his therapeutic journey.

A recently arrived young thief broke into a neighbour's kitchen and stole her handbag from the baby's pram while her back was turned. George, one of the senior boys, knew who had done this and brought great pressure in the community meeting for Bertie to confess. The culprit, finding no collusive colleagues, felt obliged to do so. Thereupon, even more astonishment awaited him, because the community responded with total delight to Bertie's utterly unaccustomed honesty. Praises were heaped upon him and the community offered various suggestions as to how the crime could be put right. This was another story indeed! For Bertie had expected not a pressure to own up but rather that other delinquent liars would protect him from any chance of discovery.

Several things were happening here. First, the newcomer was constrained by boundaries he would not have been able to maintain himself. The community's role as a container requires it to cater for the needs of each new boy or girl. A community that cannot sufficiently contain the behaviour of its residents may have to close down altogether. The community's need for behavioural containment is an essential need of the very new boy or girl. Second, in this situation the young thief was also experiencing that admitting his mistakes did not bring about rejection and, more surprisingly, he found that it did not bring about a familiar sense of worthlessness or shame, or dependent vulnerability. Indeed, in the incident above, Bertie's peers were most concerned to discover elements of worth in him that could only have been discovered as a result of his unacceptable behaviour! Third, discussion of this incident in the community meeting allowed others to see themselves through someone else's dilemma. Fourth, still more senior boys could by now understand what would make Bertie defensive and understand why he had to be completely open, and so they were able to deal with him in a way that would enable him to respond appropriately.

The gathering in the front hall around the fire is another illustration of the multiplicity of meaning that one event has and is an example of its potential for feeding different individuals' needs at one and the same time. The description in Chapter 4 is of early days at Peper Harow. A community identity – the most important part of a system within which individual change is possible – was still in the process of being built. The director, in his Friday night session, was deliberately fostering the environmental atmosphere that would help to engender a positive community identity. The youngsters were unarguably together because the seating had been designed to ensure that they were in physical contact with each other as they sat shoulder to shoulder. They had just shared something unusual to eat – shop-bought cream cakes – which in itself suggested that this was a special occasion. The predominant feeling when everyone sat down was of having been sensitized to something special. As well as being aware of their physical oneness, the youngsters all shared the same physical perception of warmth, the crackle of logs, the scent of pine resin, and the drama that the object of their mutual attention – the director – was about to relate.

If the imagination of a unified audience was caught, so also was the imagination of each of its members when the Anglo-Saxon saga of Beowulf was related to their group experience. How much more significantly could they relate to its personal message as they became caught up in the story and as they identified with its protagonists! This story could have been equally familiar to the early settlers of Peper Harow, whose place and name we had inherited. It was easy to imagine those former warriors gathering around their fire to listen to this very same story. It did not require such a vast leap of imagination to see their shadowy ghosts in the dark beyond the fire, beyond the curtains on the walls. They, like our youngsters, would have had their personal experiences of loss to grieve over. Although the boys' experiences were different in detail from those of the warriors, they were not different in essence. The lament of King Hrothgar for Aeschere, his counsellor and friend, could touch the heart of anyone who knew loss and grief today, as it had done for those who sat in that same place a thousand and more years ago.

The universal questions that keep such literature alive are valid for all who hear them. They address our essential nature. Do we fear a monstrous

Grendel within ourselves, or do we aspire to the heroism of Beowulf? Do we acknowledge in ourselves any element of Unferth the Envious, or do we strive desperately for the idealized generosity of King Hrothgar?

Perhaps adolescents will respond especially to stories of simple heroes, for they seem to be so certain of themselves. They make unequivocal judgements – as the naive adolescent often does. Beowulf, however, introduces more sophisticated questions about family obligations and loyalty – both reasons for his journey to Heorot – as well as his desire for adventure and the fame that would follow his success, both of which ideas would also appeal to adolescents. He expected to defeat the monster! He had optimistic youth and strength on his side. Though the seeds of Beowulf's engendering were far removed from our own rootless youngsters' beginnings, because both belonged to the same physical place, the youngsters could allow the deep associations of that place to become in some way theirs too. Here, then, was a magic transformation – created by an unfamiliar and therefore irresistible situation and culture – that allowed the group to perceive itself in a new way. Once more the therapeutically convened group created the folkwise possibility of transforming ugly duckling into swan.

And the transformation did not only affect and enhance the group; it was significant for each individual's nurture too. Something of the enriching experience of the small child being read to was also present in this generally accepting and identificatory experience. The strength of the group, when it is functioning at its best, seems to provide the most nurturing of cocoons but the greatest question, perhaps, is whether any permanent personal transformation will be recognizable when the cocoon is no longer present. Redl and Wineman (1951) describe the process of such change in Pioneer House. Here we read of the manifold shifts and twists that the youngster's personified delinquent ego gets up to in order to avoid change. Finally, the 'delinquent ego' gives up the struggle and conforms. A dramatic change in behaviour occurs, but this phase, warn the authors, is the stage to be most wary of, for it is likely to be only an 'apparent change', although it can easily fool the adult onlooker who will see exactly what he had been wanting to see since the impossible child arrived. Now butter would not melt in the youngster's mouth. Yet, out of sight of the nurturing community and its available identity, the old panic anxiety in response to stress is likely to re-emerge. This reappearance also associates with past stress and triggers the old response. Permanent change must stem from a changed internal way of experiencing one's life and one's self.

Thus, each resident must also be considered from his individual perspective. It seems self-evident that a one-to-one relationship is as important as the peer-group relationship. The member of staff, however, almost certainly loses sight of the trees because of his close proximity to the wood. He may be responsible for the individual's wellbeing, but he also has to remember his own part in the total process (see Chapter four, p. 55). Nevertheless, if the member of staff's special relationship requires that he identifies the youngster's needs more specifically than his colleagues, and if the staff member is to make a useful, personal contribution, then an understanding of the theory about psychological development and functioning would be of great help. The appropriate application of that knowledge requires that the staff member has ongoing supervision. We all need others to help us recognize our own unconscious interactions.

As it happened, my own insight and knowledge were minimal when Peper Harow was formed so that ignorance limited my ability to identify with any particular school of thought.[1] Magpie-like, I built the community 'nest' with whatever idea seemed to fit the immediate pressing need. As a consequence, I was often surprised at the categorizing comments of quite different visitors. 'I see you are very Rogerian', they would say, or, 'psychoanalytic', or, 'heavily Freudian', or, 'Jungian, Adlerian, or anthropological' and later, when the new kitchens were completed, many Kleinian insights were attributed to us. My surprise lessened when it became apparent that, in a sense, at any one time all of these theoreticians' approaches and models had validity in this context.

Before they came to Peper Harow, few staff had been in contact with any concepts about unconscious processes, either within themselves or as motivaters of group activity. At their interviews they were assessed as people whose sound common sense would recognize the irrelevance, within our setting, of judgemental responses to behaviour. Moreover, they would quickly come to understand that behaviour had much to tell us about the nature of unconscious feelings. In time, theories about the existence of systems of unconscious relationships between groups also proved to be essential equipment for staff when trying to retain their balance in the face of much stress. As we developed our recognition of the community as a complex system, so could we begin to understand how the group's behaviour mirrored the unexpressed feelings of its individual members. So also we came to understand that the inexpressible fury a youngster felt towards his parents might be more safely expressed towards an individual member of staff who could help the youngster consider the source of that anger. Thus, the group of youngsters, made particularly anxious by some unacknowledged event in the community, for instance, would express their group anxiety towards the staff group. This, too, would be an unconscious way of drawing the staff group's attention to the unspoken anxiety the youngsters needed to acknowledge. The staff's recognition of this mirroring process enabled them to be closer in touch with the youngsters' specific need and so help them to become clearer about it.

Obviously, having a wide knowledge of the many relevant theories would speed understanding and enhance or release both the group and the individual. Theoretical knowledge might even be essential to enable one to reflect more objectively about one's work. Practice could be said to be the application of others' thinking to the specifically rehabilitative and growthful task. If the youngster is to become emancipated from slavery to the past, and if he is to come to see how his present feelings and behaviour arise from his past, and if the youngster is also to discover his potential, then the member of staff certainly needs an understanding of the normal process of psychological development against which the carefully observed resident's development can be compared.

For me, E.H. Erikson's (1959) concept of phaseological development was particularly helpful. Although theories of psychological development have tended to focus on pre-adolescent and adolescent functioning, most people would at least agree that one's adulthood is considerably predetermined by what has occurred before. Erikson perceives such pre-determination as arising from sequential psychological conditions, or states of being, that are normally attained during each of a series of developmental phases. These psychological states may be positive or negative, but, in either case, they affect sequential developmental phases, until a particular kind of adolescent personality is created and thereafter, a particular kind of adult.

Erikson identifies these pre-adolescent developmental phases as: I Infancy, II Early Childhood, III Play Age, and IV School Age (see Figure 5.1). The positive, sequential, psychological achievements that are generated by these phases are, in turn, trust, autonomy, initiative, and then industry. The ability to be independently initiating, acquired in successful childhood, encourages the child in his growthfully experimental play fantasies. Erikson shows how the child's positive curiosity arises from a well-rooted sense of trust and of personal autonomy. Successful play, in turn, develops into successful, goal-orientated work. This industriousness also derives from the original self-confidence that created the child's initiatory activity. At each stage of the continuum from play to industriousness, the individual is rewarded with great pleasure at each new discovery. In adolescence we thus have a youngster who anticipates achievement, is able to explore his current and future roles creatively, and is gradually able to develop an increasingly clear and integrated sense of identity with regard to sexuality, authority, and social ideology.

Alternatively, if no trust develops in infancy, then there can be no sense of autonomy to underpin play and work activity. Instead, a sequential train of mistrust, self-doubt and shame, guilt, and a sense of inferiority are set in train. In that case, we eventually find an adolescent with a diffuse rather than an integrating sense of identity, who is confused with regard to sexuality, creativity, and ideology and who tends towards work paralysis, and to a negative sense of self, and so on.

Of course, polarizing the alternatives as starkly as Erikson does

Figure 5.1 Erikson's epigenetic chart of developmental phases

	I INFANCY	II EARLY CHILDHOOD	III PLAY AGE	IV SCHOOL AGE	V ADOLESCENCE	VI YOUNG ADULT	VII ADULTHOOD	VIII MATURE AGE
I INFANCY	Trust v. Mistrust				Time perspective v. Time diffusion			
II EARLY CHILDHOOD		Autonomy v. Doubt, Shame			Self-certainty v. Identity consciousness			
III PLAY AGE			Initiative v. Guilt		Role experimentation v. Negative identity			
IV SCHOOL AGE				Industry v. Inferiority	Anticipation of achievement v. Work paralysis			
V ADOLESCENCE					Unipolarity v. Premature Self-differentiation; Bipolarity v. Autism; Play Identification v. (Oedipal) Fantasy Identities; Work identification v. Identity Foreclosure; Identity v. Identity Diffusion; Solidarity v. Social isolation			
VI YOUNG ADULT					Sexual identity v. Bisexual diffusion	Intimacy v. Isolation		
VII ADULTHOOD					Leader polarization v. Authority diffusion		Generativity v. Self-absorption	
VIII MATURE AGE					Ideological polarization v. Diffusion of ideals			Integrity v. Disgust-Despair

clarifies psychological issues, but they may suggest an oversimple picture. Despite the seriously inhibiting factors in our youngsters' backgrounds, there are also nourishing ingredients. Some of our youngsters do partly achieve the qualities relevant to Erikson's phaseological development while, at the same time, they are certainly seriously frustrated and limited by the negative polarities he describes.

In the circumstances of a therapeutic community it is surprising how many children who have been consistently deprived of secure, trustworthy relationships nevertheless are able to display real elements of trust towards their individual members of staff. Their personality surprisingly seems to have developed some of the positive conditions to which Erikson refers rather than the negative ones alone. However, the more complete development of these positive states of being seems to be impeded by the damaged youngsters' ambivalence and confusion in addition to their absence of trust, or initiative, or autonomy that may have arisen from early deprivatory life experiences.

A new girl was given a watch as a Christmas present by her member of staff. Within hours she had smashed it! The relationship that the gift symbolized was too threatening to her sense of embattled isolation. Tilly was then overwhelmed with rage, arising both from her anguish at what she had done and from her sense of persecution by the member of staff who had put her in such a dilemma. Nevertheless, the fragmentary tendency towards trust that her rage attempted to resist was also the foundation for its rehabilitation after the fullness of much time.

A boy was overwhelmed by shame whenever his perverse sexual behaviour re-emerged. Yet equally, Shaun was also able to experience himself autonomously on occasions and to remember the deliberate and positive choice he had made by coming to Peper Harow. Others, supposedly defeated by guilt, could nevertheless take significant initiatives in their creative and academic work.

Many youngsters clung tenaciously to a particular memory of one good fostering experience, or one caring member of staff in a foster home, and that minimal, nourishing experience remained the source of a total shift from Erikson's negative chain of development to its optimistic counterpart.

It is often this contradictory mixture of psychological development and inhibition that creates the youngster who apparently does well in the therapeutic environment, but who does not internalize the strengths necessary for the transition to independent adulthood on leaving. Several of our youngsters in the past achieved significant success – especially when one considers their beginnings – yet, that success still has not yet enabled them to achieve the creative adulthood that one might have expected.

Despite arriving at Peper Harow as seriously educationally retarded, many developed their embryonic sense of self-worth and of an entitlement to success. They achieved examination successes in two or three years that their normal peers managed in seven. So, like them, they have gone on to university and even gained good honours degrees. Yet, in the end, some of them have been unable to allow this success to affect other areas of personality. Their adult psychosocial functioning, in Erikson's terms, would seem pathological.

It is equally important to remember that many of our youngsters have continued to grow successfully after their departure. Yet, the negative experience warns us not to be too easily misled by the development of visible, healthy functioning within the community. The truly successful youngsters are good reason for hope that change is possible for such damaged young people, many of whom suffered exceptionally badly in early infancy. Part of the treatment problem is simply the limited time available. To imagine that a youngster, who has had a consistently disturbed life history, until he arrives at Peper Harow at the age of 14, can rework all the growth of infancy, childhood, and early adolescence in four or five years, after having experienced all the regression needed, is, indeed, optimistic!

Nevertheless, for such optimism to be warranted at all, great attention has to be given to the psychotherapeutic task for the individual. It is already accepted that, both for resistance to be overcome and for trust to be established in the individual staff and youngster relationship, it will have to be well rooted within parallel, mutually supporting, group relationships, and all this within the nourishing and containing, overall community.

The accompanying adaptation of Erikson's epigenetic chart of developmental phaseology (see Figure 5.1) simply organizes categories of complex psychosociological states of being. If we imagine what questions would have to be addressed in order to assess the extent by which the individual's ability to function age-appropriately has been inhibited or enhanced, we can see a daunting task ahead. For a start, it is difficult to describe emotionally nourishing ingredients so that they can be formulated in a quantifiably useful fashion. In any event, ensuring the youngster's prior motivation and receptiveness requires exceptional patience and skill, as well as much time. And, irrespective of the youngster's tendency to resist the painful insights of pyschotherapy, adolescents are inevitably moody and inconstant. Although the staff themselves gain psychotherapeutic skills and insights surprisingly quickly, their average stay of four to six years limits what they can achieve psychotherapeutically. In the therapeutically designed residential context, their vigour and enthusiasm are of exceptional value, but their lack of psychotherapeutic experience and timing is significant. In the face of these limited treatment resources, the possibility of the youngsters reversing their deepest psychological attitudes towards themselves and their environment seems doubtful.

Yet, though it may be difficult to convince the reader otherwise, having witnessed major change despite these limitations, one is compelled to recognize the exceptional effectiveness of the interacting network of group experiences within the context of an integrated total community. The inspiration, nourishment, continued growth, resourcing, and management of that network are yet other problems, but the power of those integrated group experiences for real change is truly amazing. The integrated total community provides the opportunity for behavioural regression; it provides the analysis of the meaning of that behaviour, and it provides the reassurance that such behaviour can be contained. The properly functioning community ensures that those and all other experiences are made significant for the youngster, and it gradually enables him to internalize that recognition, understanding, and strength.

One of the inhibiting factors of a member of staff's contribution to that network arises from the likelihood that only the newest member of staff will have time to take on a new resident. And, if one takes into consideration that the different identificatory gender needs of girls and boys have also to be matched with available staff, then the priority of other treatment requirements, like the emotional fit between the member of staff and the youngster, are likely to be further reduced. Obviously, these requirements are further indications both of the need for a large staff of exceptional people and of the high costs that must therefore be incurred. A major advantage does derive from new members of staff having to take on the casework of a new resident. They at least are unlikely to begin the relationship with superficial 'interpretations' about his behaviour. Such a commentary is very likely to feel persecutory. It is difficult to imagine how frightening premature revelations might feel to the youngster. Yet, our highly educated staff had often been brought up to expect that 'to know is to understand'. New members of staff often desperately grasped for some specific knowledge that would resolve the insecurity they themselves experience through their lack of understanding or of knowing what to do for the best.

The newly arrived resident does not need cognitive understanding; he needs people who can play with him and communicate intuitively through such 'play'. 'Play' may consist of a recreational activity like rock climbing. The new resident may find himself terrified on a rock ledge with apparently only a member of staff and the rope between him and horror. Yet, if the eye-to-eye contact, the tone of the voice, and the enabling, secure tension on the rope say the right things, then the experience may achieve the therapeutic development of months. It has the potential to say 'I know you are scared. I know you have been as scared as this or worse in other circumstances. We are in this together. We will play our respective parts. You'll succeed'. The hand-clasp at the top of the climb seals the achievement. The hearty replay around the camp fire at night reinforces the relationship with an adult. The symbolic significance of the eye-talk; the symbolic demonstration that mastering fear is possible are in turn further psychotherapeutic opportunities that arise from this kind of 'play'. The 'gang' too can be similarly effective sociotherapeutically, because of the familiar cultural comfort its way of functioning can bring to the adolescent. The brave laughter and raillery that a group of youngsters may generate can be very similar to the bravado of the individual youngster boasting of his criminality in order to find a place in his expected group culture (see Chapter three, pp. 35–7). Often this group excitement is only generated to fill the youngsters' sense of emptiness and isolation. The community 'gang's' excitement can be harnessed by the staff, who can not only provide individual role models, but also a significant relationship with an adult group. This is a truly therapeutic alternative to the artificial but defensive device of self-generated group excitement.

Everyday life provides many opportunities for important communication between the individual member of staff and the youngster for whom he has special responsibility. For instance, the squeezed shoulder at bedtime can be very reassuring for the sexually abused youngster. Nevertheless, because the everyday transactions between a resident and his 'guru' are of such importance they will not be used by the youngster only as a form of nourishment. The youngster's disturbed personality may compulsively attempt to control adults by many manipulative devices. Sometimes the actual form of manipulation may also illustrate an area of the youngster's unresolved anxiety. For instance, the youngster apparently decides not to get up one morning when his member of staff is on duty. This develops into a confrontation. The member of staff, with determined humour and perhaps a touch of exasperation, tips the youngster out of bed, or pulls the covers off him. In an instant the youngster may re-experience this as a sexual assault and as though it were the same as actual childhood experience.

The accusation will not feel very comfortable for the member of staff. However, the member of staff and the youngster are not left alone with this experience. The community meeting will enable it to be examined in the light of reality and may even begin the enquiry into how and why the whole sequence occurred.

When the member of staff later on thinks carefully and honestly about his intervention, he might indeed recognize some personal excitement arising from the exchange. And that may increase his personal anxiety. Such anxiety is likely to reinforce the youngster's fear rather than resolve it. In fact, the member of staff's anxiety may not be fully justified. Many feelings are generated by the therapeutic relationship. They may not originate from the member of staff. Whatever may have passed between them, if the member of staff is able to locate its actual source, with the help of his supervisor, or of the staff group, then such knowledge will shed light both on his unconscious processes and motivations and on those of the youngster. If a five-year training experience in the management of these unconscious interactive processes is obviously impossible between appointment and picking up the post, it can be recognized that staff at least gain experience at the rate of 8 hours a day. That is probably four times as much time as the usual training for psychotherapy. However, the incident of tipping the youngster out of bed underlines the kind of reflecting, encouraging, supervisory, and teaching support that is necessary to enable the member of staff to make constructive use of his ongoing experience. A great deal of this supervision can be structured among groups of colleagues so, although the resource requirements are indeed considerable, the organizational compromises need not be totally inadequate either.

To the extent that individual counselling or psychotherapy can be described as a journey in which a member of staff accompanies the youngster and shares the youngster's burden and the memory of his intended direction, then to that extent is his four or five years' shared journeying of enormous worth. He and his pilgrim begin together, both uncertain. They may both leave together, but their mutual accomplishments on the journey will also enrich both of them individually far beyond expectations.

The description of the Friday meeting in the front hall is an example of the way in which the individual gets drawn into into an identification with the group (see Chapter four, pp. 67–9 and this chapter, p. 77). The main purpose of the meeting was to enable the sense of identity that arises from the group to be regularly experienced in a particular way. Such an occasion fires the imagination in a way that would not be possible in the one-to-one relationship alone. But whether the groups are informal like the Friday night meeting, or whether they are formal groups like the community meeting, or the regular, small, psychotherapy groups, they can all serve a very special psychotherapeutic function. The technical psychotherapeutic word for the interaction between the individual and therapist is called transference. Its positive management requires considerable skills that the individual member of staff may not possess; nor may the youngster be sufficiently secure to engage in such a relationship.

In the normal one-to-one psychotherapeutic setting, as the therapeutic bond changes, so the immature aspects of an individual's personality become increasingly obvious to the individual as well as to the therapist. Often, in this therapeutic context, the individual actually experiences the therapist as one of his parents. What the individual reveals is not his current adult self so much as the undeveloped child self of long ago. Thus, he reveals how he actually experienced his parent at that distant time. His sense of inadequacy, of helplessness, of incompetence to function in an age-appropriate way arouses a variety of consequential responses. His envy may focus on the therapist; he may wrestle with a sense of utter inferiority, or contemptuous, compensatory omnipotence. This state may alternate with an idealizing of the therapist as beyond fault. The therapist may become the adored star in the patient's limited constellation. Yet, all these moods, as they become fully experienced, function as a process that can be seen as a kind of Eriksonian 'play', and rehabilitate the natural positive process of growth from trust to identity integration. The therapist can help the 'play' onwards but as often as not he himself is the object that is being 'played with'. He functions like that part of the individual's self that actually seeks change and insight. An identification with the therapist followed by a complete rejection of his views is thus part of the alternating 'game' through which the individual eventually establishes his sense of self.

It can be seen how skilled the proper management of this game called transference must be. It is somewhat unrealistic for the inexperienced member of staff to engage deliberately in a process he has not experienced as a major part of his own professional training. In that training, he would not only discover what it is like to be a vulnerable 'patient' but he would also discover that the feelings and the interactions of his relationship with his therapist uncannily reflect feelings and responses whose origins were in his real family. An equally essential awareness that could be developed by proper training would be the ability to recognize and evaluate his own 'counter-transference'. This term sums up the feelings aroused in the therapist. Some of these feelings may exist in the therapist's unconscious being. Others arise directly from the psychodynamic relationship with the patient. Evaluating the differences enables the therapist to bring his objective judgement to the psychotherapeutic setting. Yet, the member of staff in a therapeutic community for adolescents will also be 'played with' in this fashion, irrespective of his lack of knowledge or his ability to manage the play. He will need great faith in his personal stability and worth.Fortunately, the group setting, and the community as a whole, can also provide this play relationship in large measure. The resolution of a youngster's helplessness and inadequacy does not have to occur in the one-to-one relationship alone. For instance, time and again you hear youngsters cursing the community in disparaging terms. 'This place' is then taking on a load of feelings that is far in excess of what could be ascribed simply to a geographical location. On the other hand, called to explain their reason for hope to a visitor whom they are showing around, their identification with 'This place' can alternate eulogistically! So, the identificatory hat can be hung on any peg – the place, the director, a senior youngster who 'did my interview', and of course, his personal member of staff. Obviously, skilled staff actively promote their therapeutic role, but all aspects of the community can fulfil a similar role in the overall psychotherapeutic process. In some way the part of the youngster that is being 'played with' comes to understand that and comes to be able to co-operate. When a senior resident is asked to help with music practice or homework, he will probably be aware that in some way the request is a vehicle for the kind of play that is explorative of identity and is a major part of the ongoing psychotherapeutic process. Similarly, the therapy group, at first angry at its disruption by one of its members, may eventually conclude that the disruption is another form of identity play. Of course, the content of the interaction, if properly analysed, will also reveal a great deal about what has confused the individual in the here and now.

Thus, the community, the member of staff, and the small group can each be used as a 'play object'. There are manifold experiences on summer camp, on adventurous expeditions, in the various creative art studios, as part of an instrumental music band – which also allow the individual to play with various roles and personalities. Over a period of time an observer could see an individual's play identification develop into work identification. Adults, too, may also continue to use play to resolve some psychic dilemmas, but they also have the ability to 'work things out', indicating that their psychic competence and resources have been developed age-appropriately (see Chapter 7, pp. 117–24 – which discusses some of the underlying personal experiences that prevent development of age-appropriate psychological conditions and limit psychic resources).

We can also see how different aspects of the residential experience specifically address the other phaseological needs, so clearly identified by Erikson. To start with, the very initial interview sets out to establish trust as the basis of the autonomy that will allow the sequential, internal psychic states of being to be built up. The relationship with the member of staff, the small therapy group, the community meeting are as much opportunities for the development of trust as they are occasions for play activity (see Chapter eight, pp. 148–9, for further discussion of the experiences that need clarifying through these several kinds of therapeutic play – as it were – for secure identity to be formed). In the next chapter specific reference is made to the physical and material significance of the building and grounds.

Because many of the first relationships of our lives are conducted in physical and material language rather than in an intellectually verbal language, it is obvious that the physical feel of the environment has to be designed to reflect the trust that would normally be established in infancy through predominantly physical experiences. How can the lavatories and bathrooms be designed to encourage a youngster's sense of his individuality and worth? Each new experience can be perceived as stimulating the development of one or another psychological capacity. Lying on a thick carpet by a real fire encourages the day-dreaming aspects of fantasy. The 'mother' kitchen reassures because the fundamentally mistrusting youngster needs unlimited reassurance that there will be enough food. The kitchen's very food-providing existence also underlines the issues of dependence and differentiation between mother and baby and arouses some of the unresolved feelings relating to these, which can often be seen in the youngster's behaviour in the kitchen (see Chapter 6).

The adolescents at Peper Harow do the cooking – there are no special kitchen staff – and so themselves become identified with the providing mother. They are also being the fed child on the days when it is not their turn to cook. Whether this scenario encourages the first steps towards autonomy, normally taken in infancy, or whether this process reinforces the faltering child, whose traumatization at a later stage of childhood caused him to regress towards an earlier dependency, varies from individual to individual. The situation potentially helps a youngster towards the clarification of his own deprivation, while at the same time it may be offering experiences that will strengthen another boy or girl who may often be overwhelmed with their sense of inadequacy.

What is critical, however, is that each youngster is made sensitive to whichever message is most apposite at that moment. It hardly needs repeating that the way this interpretation is made is critical, whether it is conveyed by a member of staff or the small group, or by an *ad hoc* group of youngsters who may be gathered around an individual perhaps refusing to cook or refusing to come into a meal. Most of the time the way to make a youngster aware of his experience and of its significance for him individually, and also for him as part of the group, is not through intellectual explanations.

We used to insist that the public parts of the House had to be kept impeccably (see Chapter six, p. 111). They belonged to everyone. One's right to individual expression existed in one's bed-space. If one chose, this could be the biggest pigsty in the world. The variations between one bed-space and another were enormous and often reflected an individual's development. The evidence was demonstrated by the artefacts, from teddy bears to volumes of Homer, or superb ceramics achieved after years of developing the skill. The bedrooms also offered powerful clues about the general state of the optimism, or despair, anger, or sense of growth in the community generally. The member of staff and often senior residents in a room would have half an eye on their junior neighbour. His bed was allowed to stay unmade for days if they knew that it was part of the youngster's expressing the depression that he had defended himself from hitherto. Irrespective of their own experience, staff and other residents would have acquired real knowledge about the youngster's family background and specific information perhaps from his group meetings about his current state of mind. On the other hand, the unmade bed might express a sense of infantile helplessness that required psychotherapeutic intervention, where the member of staff made the youngster's bed, for a while, or helped the youngster to make his own bed. This physical activity communicated to the youngster something clarifying about the source and resolution of his distress. For instance, a member of staff might go to the youngster's bedroom during breakfast time and make his bed.

'Who made my bed?'
'Your member of staff', another bedroom colleague might reply.
'Why did you make my bed?' the puzzled youngster might enquire.
'Sometimes it gets very hard to get on with the everyday chores
when you are feeling awful. I thought I could make life a bit easier
for you by doing you a favour.'

Later, the youngster might wreck his bed once more, to see if the
member of staff would feel repulsed and hurt, or to see if the member of
staff would really make the bed again. The destruction could also be saying
countless things about the youngster's confused relationship with his
mother. A member of staff at bedtime might say:

'I'm sorry you spoilt your bed. I thought you would enjoy getting
into a clean, comfortable bed.'
The youngster might reply with a curse, 'You stay away from my
bed!'
But after the lights had gone out the others would remonstrate:
'Why were you so rude? The guy was doing you a favour.'
'My mother always used to buy me off like that. She'd pretend she
really cared about me by looking after my clothes and things, when
really she just wanted to keep me quiet while she got on with her
new boyfriend.'
The other youngsters might ask a lot more about this. Some would
offer their own similar experience and show that they both
understood and shared the feeling. However:
'Old so-and-so isn't your Mum though. He's really like a good
mum and he obviously cares about you a lot. Maybe you could talk
about this in tomorrow's group. I'll help you say it if you like.'
The newcomer had been able both to clarify the meaning of his own
behaviour and to receive some appropriate 'medicine' that would
allow the development of trusting relationships despite feelings he
had retained from the past. Yet, if several weeks later the same
behaviour was being enacted, the other boys in his bedroom might
respond more angrily.
'It mucks the whole room up! We're trying to look after our living
area and you wreck it. We're entitled to some consideration too.'
Once the youngster's unconscious use of the experience had been
clarified, he would be expected to function in a more socially
appropriate fashion. Self-indulgence was certainly not appreciated.

Of course, as in the best of families, experience is not always consistent.
Indeed, in a community where all the residents are needing to express the
endless hurt done to them, and where confusions entangle their inner lives,
there are bound to be many occasions when the way in which their
disturbance is expressed will be at the expense of others. The new resident,

full of admiration for the way another youngster intervened in his initial interview, is stunned to see the same youngster some time later storming off, breaking windows as he goes. What trust can be engendered here? Staff often angrily castigate the youngsters for their lack of care of the cultural environment. The staff's defence of the fragile environment may be motivated by many things. For instance, the staff may be experiencing what the youngster's own group is feeling. That feeling may be that the staff are not contributing. What underlies this is probably complex and should not be accepted simply at face value. What the staff must reinforce is the recognition that the community's value system needs to be experienced as fundamentally secure, or the individual will collapse before its betrayal of his trust.

The appalling behaviour that may invade the community in its ongoing struggle with the self-destructive resident is often shocking. It would be reasonable for the insecure resident to lose his tenuous sense of trust. Yet, though the community's process is fallible, like all life, in time it does become apparent to the resident that, on balance, the community is trustworthy. When the resident is able to trust the community in a mature way that will help him towards adult relationships, he will not be seeking those relationships out of desperation or panic, but having recognized the need to share responsibility in a relationship and having also developed an ability to be dependent. Reaching that mature perspective takes the full length of time the resident lives in the community. His trust only becomes sure after enough time has encompassed enough of his vacillation for him to know that this is all part of a predominantly worthwhile life.

Nevertheless, this mature ability to use trust appropriately is at least suggested in the youngster's very first experience of the community – his initial interview. Many attempts are made before this meeting to establish whether the youngster has sufficient motivation to use the opportunity. In a sense, the preparation for the experience is as important as anything that takes place later. Referring agents, however, are often overwhelmed by their immediate tasks and have neither the time nor other resources to do a good job. It is very evident when a social worker has actually taken appropriate care to prepare the youngster for the issues that will be raised in the interview.

Though it was enormously time-consuming, as director I conducted almost every initial interview personally (see Chapter two, pp. 20–1 and Chapter nine, pp. 159–60). I read almost every referral document and conducted most negotiations. For me this established the youngsters as the community's priority however important other issues were. I needed to know as much as possible about the youngster before he came. I wanted to understand what had made him the way he was – and indeed, the way he actually was! It was with that understanding that I would best be able to respond to the scared youngster in a way that was felt to be understanding, and in a way that might strike a light of hope in him and kindle his interest in what he might involve himself. Obtaining such information was not very easy. There were rarely psychosocial reports that related the social aspects of a child's life to his psychological condition. If a psychiatrist's report was obtained, it usually said no more than that the youngster was not suffering from any formal illness. If one obtained psychological reports, they often suggested that test results may be inaccurate. Occasionally, a psychologist would reveal a hunch and such reports usually turned out to be the most helpful.

In the early days, when referrals usually arrived after a period of assessment in a special centre, there were lengthy additional reports about the youngster's behaviour in that institution. On the basis of the assessment centre staff's past experiences, their note added that they felt this was 'Your kind of kid'.

We used to send the youngsters a prospectus with coloured photographs of the community and a description that tried to answer the questions they might ask. It was surprising how carefully many youngsters read the prospectus and how frequently they asked questions arising from it. We tried to get the referring agency to get someone to visit and discuss whether the youngster's needs matched with what we were trying to offer. In phone calls and letters we tried to describe the interview procedure and why other youngsters were involved; and the basis on which parents should or should not be invited to participate. We tried to get the referring agency's representative to understand that the object of the interview was to see if we could get the youngster to understand the nature and purpose of his proposed relationship with the community and the essentiality of his own commitment. We were often surprised at the difficulty a local authority might experience in understanding why we should take such trouble to engage the youngster in a treatment relationship. They often seemed to think treatment was something you somehow imposed upon a youngster!

If the parents came, they and usually the referring social worker were met by the member of staff who would look after the youngster if he eventually were to come, and they were also met by two residents, one of whom would be fairly senior. The visitors were divided into three groups and taken on a tour of the whole estate. The visitors all then had lunch with the community and about an hour later began an hour's interview.

Usually the youngster had decided by this time that he was going to come – few chose not to. Whatever the decision, it was difficult to get the youngsters to restrain their anxiety and to think about what coming to Peper Harow would entail. We would not have been offering an interview unless we had already thought they needed treatment such as we could offer. The issue for us was whether they could ever be brought to an acknowledgement of how they were and of what they needed. The discussion focused on just these issues, with the residents chipping in to help the frightened and the tongue-tied. At the end of the hour the visitors retreated to tea in the dining room while the interviewing panel made a decision and then told the candidate. If we were offering a place, we would await the youngster's letter confirming his wish to come, and conclude thereafter the final financial and contractual arrangements with whoever was sponsoring the placement.

Initial interviews were frequently moving. The participating residents in particular took personal risks often beyond their contribution in their therapy groups. They struggled hard to put the newcomer at ease. Often the contrast between their culture and the newcomer's was so great that the newcomer felt himself to be in a world far too inferior ever to allow him to be worthy of being on the same planet as his interviewing peers! He was pressed quite hard to verbalize his problems. Sometimes, when he was overwhelmed by shame, it was made clear that in time he would have to deal with such problems or there would be no point in his coming.

If the interview could not be brought to a successful conclusion, the participant residents became very depressed. They became desperate to admit someone, recognizing as never before the mess the interviewee's life was in and the likelihood of this being not resolved outside Peper Harow. If the interview were successful, that was sometimes harder. Now the residents would feel bound not to let the newcomer down. They were envious of the good treatment that they had fed him with, yet hardly ever did they spoil the opportunity for new understanding being offered to the interviewee.

The huge mansion seemed daunting as the newcomer drove up the long driveway. It was far more imposing than the picture. Inside, the non-institutional furnishings, the first name relationships with the staff, and the youngsters' apparently unsupervised freedom often astounded them. All visitors were astonished at the way lunch was apparently prepared and cooked, served, eaten, and cleared up by those whose turn it was, with no-one having to encourage them to do it. They were most astounded by the sophistication of the residents who showed them around. Their peers had never before asked them about their feelings or revealed the personal aspects of their own life, not in compensatory, boasting fantasies, but in the stark insecurity and inadequacy that was the miserable truth.

Never had the visiting youngster had such an experience. The place; the way it functioned; the way the staff approached you; the way the residents felt they owned a real stake in the community; the way the visitor had been made to look at issues he had never thought of before; all these experiences amounted to a real shock, and finally the youngster was being told to go away and think carefully before writing to say if he wanted to accept the offer. He would still be able to withdraw after a term. He would want to leave many times after that if he had decided to stay, but every pressure would then be brought to bear to keep him to the task. The community's offer was unconditional, but he had the choice. Occasionally this would all be lightened with a joke – for instance, to a youngster with overdeveloped intellectual defences and rather puritanical inclinations towards pleasing parents perhaps, 'But in your case there is one condition. You will not be allowed to do any school work for ages!'

I did everything in my power to charm such youngsters personally. These were youngsters who were almost more afraid of being offered anything of worth than of a life of misery. The latter they could endure, or they could end it; the former required trust, attachment, and commitment and the youngsters had little sense that they could respond appropriately. We knew this, of course, but were teaching a lesson from the start. Our lesson was that no-one could change anyone else. You cannot really impose teaching on people or heal them, or do anything to them, but you can stay at their side until they themselves are ready to take up the struggle on their own behalf. You can remain at their side when they fall in despair, and you can remind such young people of their forgotten aspirations when they become overwhelmed and confused. That is the professional specialism such youngsters need. Almost all of them responded thoughtfully in their painfully written letters. A few turned the offer down – they did not come. Those who did were already intrigued by the possibilities they perceived but rarely understood. What they had seen were groups of youngsters with real authority. What they had felt was intense personal attention and all of it was in an environment that was full of wonder.

Chapter six

A therapeutic house

*Those making residential referrals need to understand the
ingredients necessary for psychological change. The residential
setting can potentially provide these therapeutic qualities because of
its size, difference from normal life experience, and distance from
the family setting.*
*Youngsters resist psychotherapeutic examination of the past.
Managing behaviour and circumventing resistance is too complex
for staff without support systems.*
*The whole atmosphere and physical design of the environment need
to symbolize the psychotherapeutic relationship.*
*The development at Peper Harow of these principles in the design
and use of kitchen and dining room, lavatories, bedrooms, and
bathrooms, and other public areas of the house.*

Many false assumptions frequently underlie the decision to place someone
away from home. If a youngster's behaviour is difficult enough to be
described as 'behaviourally disturbed', then he is often felt to need
'specialist provision', which is often a euphemism for 'residential provision'. Yet, the last few years have witnessed many social workers
adapting slogans such as 'residential placements don't work' and that they
'do more harm than good'. Social workers who feel like this must be
uneasy when recommending a youngster's residential placement.

Undoubtedly, there are great difficulties in designing residential
programmes that exercise proper control and yet do not depersonalize the
residents. Yet, residential facilities are worth the expense and effort of
coping with the design and ongoing management of programmes,
provided these are capable of addressing the real psychological needs
of the residents. Unfortunately, those responsible for such major decisions as placements often have little understanding of what makes a
child or young person behave as they do. It is, therefore, almost
impossible for them to conceptualize the kind of treatment programme
that would address those needs. The predominant pressure on the social

worker too often is that 'so-and-so' is intolerable where they are. The issue then becomes one of finding 'a good place'! They are concerned as to whether they will be left trying to find somewhere for the youngster during holidays or, even worse, whether that place will throw the youngster out if his behaviour becomes as intolerable there as anywhere else.

The thinking underlying what makes a good place often seems confused. One hears that, if someone has to be removed from home, then their placement should be somewhere as much like their home environment as possible - and preferably in the same neighbourhood. It will rarely have been recognized that, for change to occur, the springs of the youngster's being will have had to have changed. But, for that to have been possible, all aspects of the residential experience – including the physical environment – will have required very careful construction if they are to achieve such profound change. So, if children are not removed from home as a punishment, but rather because there is something they need that cannot be met in their own home, the social worker should only look for an institution that is actually designed to provide for just that need. The location may, indeed, be important, perhaps if maintaining very frequent contact with family is the top priority in that individual youngster's case, but not in order to pretend, somehow, that a major event has not really occurred.

The social worker's first visit to Peper Harow often causes shock. It is difficult to grasp exactly what creates the general atmosphere – what stems from the obviously sophisticated staff, and the relationships, and the activities and what stems from the physical and material design. It is often very difficult to see how the usually inarticulate youngster whom the social worker may be trying to place could match up with the lively young people who show him around. It is even more difficult to understand exactly how this atmosphere could permanently reorientate the way the youngster thinks and feels and behaves. If the unexpected culture shocks the worker, how much more will it dumbfound the youngster? Yet, the culture shock is potentially one of the community's most important therapeutic assets.

However unhappy the problem adolescent is, he is nevertheless highly resistant to acknowledging the sources of his unhappiness. Treatment in the 'day setting' is often completely ineffective for those who defend themselves against insight. Such young people compulsively seek someone or something to collude with them against their treatment setting. In the day setting, surrounded by their familiar environment, little of their functioning is challenged except by adults whom they perceive as hostile. The streetwise, often drugwise, and delinquent culture of their environment is at the door. A stressful day with antagonized and, perhaps, overwhelmed staff can precipitate even worse relationships at home in the evening. Less obviously, the contrasts between a therapeutic group and a group of the youngster's neighbourhood cronies may well feed an unhealthy way of functioning, enabling the youngster to split experiences into polarized extremes, thus frustrating any real therapeutic effect. The 'good' behaviour stays in the day treatment unit, the 'bad' at home. The youngster's 'good' people, as they are unconsciously characterized, seem to be in one place, and the 'bad' seem to be in the other. The children of warring parents often try to clarify their own confusion, in fantasy at least, by characterizing one parent as the 'good' and the other as the 'bad'. Indeed, this polarization reflects what the embattled parents may themselves feel about each other. Yet, if a child is compelled to take sides, he may then be left with a significant problem of guilt. Even worse, he may be forced to deny his need of the discarded parent's qualities. He would then tend to grow up as half a person with real difficulties about integrating aspects of both parents into his own personality. For boys and girls, both masculine and feminine personality qualities are necessary in order to promote the important role-experimenting activities of adolescence. A young person who does respond to parental conflict by trying to discard the 'bad' parent needs therapeutic distance to be able to focus on this problem. The real distance of the residential setting may be able to provide this more easily than a treatment setting close to home.

Many youngsters who have never experienced a secure, loving family become extremely uncomfortable in a surrogate one. The warmth of an intimate foster family situation recreates the pain of their own contrasting family experience, counterbalancing the foster home's qualities and good intentions. Their hurtful responses and their resistance to the foster family's therapeutic qualities too often become uncontainable and another broken placement ensues. Such children actually need the less personal containment that a large group can offer. They need greater emotional room – as it were – and they need to act out feelings that cannot be expressed in coherent language. Such acting out is likely to be intolerable in any ordinary family (see Chapter seven, p. 120).

The choice of treatment setting should be assessed individually. The setting should depend on the way by which personality integration can be best effected for each particular youngster. For those who are too disturbed to acknowledge their needs fully, living in a therapeutic community is perhaps the only realistic approach. The integrating function of a therapeutic community will be further examined later. Nevertheless, therapeutic integration can only take place if the whole process of the residential community is consistent in all its approaches to the youngster, so that he experiences something of the good fortune of the child with parents whose relationships are generally harmonious. The residential community by virtue of its greater totality has the potential to provide such consistency and on a scale that is perhaps necessarily larger than normal life.

There will, of course, be constant attacks on this consistency. Delinquent behaviour may break out when the community is supposed to be peacefully asleep. The lavatory that has been designed to feel secure and a pleasurable place to be in may be attacked with pent-up anxiety, represented by smeared faeces. Youngsters will attempt to disrupt their therapy group, or break their special member of staff's birthday present.

Yet, whichever way they will 'despitefully use' those who love them, this behaviour is an unconsciously disguised response – yet a legitimate expression within the therapeutic community – to the acute anxiety and confusion within the youngster. He will need to be reassured that he cannot ultimately destroy the community. (These youngsters often suspect that somehow they have been responsible for the death or departure of a member of their family and that as a consequence they are deservedly likely to be destroyed in turn. Certainly their guilt is aroused when, instead, they are offered the very things they long for most.) They will need to discover for themselves that explanations do exist that will clarify the reasons underlying their bizarre behaviour and that, incidentally, also frightens and shames them as much as it frightens those on the receiving end.

The biggest question for staff is how to communicate such an 'explanation'. How can understanding be achieved for the youngster that will lead to insight? Insight and self-awareness enable self-management of the feelings that have writhed within for years. They also establish the conditions that make new experiences acceptable, and for the feelings that the new experiences promote to become well-rooted within them. With increasing insight, the balance starts to shift towards growth, creativity, and achievement.

What occurs among so many youngsters' often crazy behaviour and its consequent staff reactions is often so confusing that staff struggling to keep their own balance tend to 'interpret' events as though from the depths of oracular wisdom. Such staff may indeed have grasped the essence of a situation but, while attempting to maintain their clarificatory perception and the personal relief that arises from it, they should be careful not to 'kill' it with their omnipotent pronouncements. Such pronouncements are frequently more intended to reinforce themselves rather than to provide relieving insight for the youngster. Far better to crack a joke, or tell a story, or play some kind of game. Greek mythology or biblical parables inherently demonstrate the greater effectiveness of their symbolic message. Unlike confrontative commandments, they outmanoeuvre resistance and denial.

The therapeutic community, therefore, also needs to be experienced symbolically. The community should function allegorically like a story that coincidentally – as it were – reveals much about the nature of its characters and their activities. All groups influence each of their members very profoundly. This is true whether the groups were specifically created for that purpose, or whether they arose in some natural social setting. The intrinsic potential of any group makes it possible to highlight and clarify the way a person relates to others. The way a group encourages this is as much through its mood – through unspoken communication – as through spoken language. The story of the community's life – as illustrated by its activities and by the hard-won social values it demonstrates – are all symbolic statements about its complex psychological needs and functioning. In Peper Harow, we deliberately set out to design the physical environment to represent a similar function also. It was to express, through its own symbolic language, the same message that could be expressed, verbally or nonverbally, in individual or in group relationships. It, too, was to offer symbolic experiences that communicated more than words alone could do. It was to convey another part of the consistent message that all aspects of the community were to convey: that the individual can be made safe enough to risk experiencing the psychic activity that lay behind the relationships and the daily events. He could do this by engaging fully with the physical aspects of the community. And this could be done, whether privately in the bathroom, or as a member of the group cooking the meals, or as a member of the group cleaning the house that day.

When I used to take youngsters out for the day from the first school in which I taught, my remit was 'to do adventurous things with them'. That was adolescent language for the word 'play'. How transformed were these lower-streamed adolescents once we gathered around a fire to roast potatoes after a game of hide-and-seek in the surrounding woods. They talked as no-one ever heard them talk in school. Indeed, they came to life in the way my encouraging headmaster had anticipated. Similarly, I noticed when taking expeditions from various approved schools that the quality of discussion away from the actual establishment was completely different. The slightly insolent air born of anxiety and resentment gave way to a more normal interchange. Yet, the biggest difference occurred around campfires or by rivers as the evening gradually shifted into silence and darkness. Inevitably, youngsters seemed able to respond to the atmosphere and talk relaxedly, almost as in psychotherapy. Nor was my discovery remotely new. I had simply made contact with an experience so familiar to humankind that we tend to forget its immense potential. In the most distant time our ancestors' experience of the atmosphere of forest glade or awesome mountain found its expression in a pantheon of deified beings. Through them some symbolized sense could be made of human impulses and fantasies. Thus, the myths that embodied this process enabled the societal group or the individual to make sense of their inner worlds through their symbolic dialogue with the natural world. Years of expedition work with youngsters and my experience of Finchden Manor guaranteed that I would not overlook the significance of atmosphere in the design of a residential setting.

When I was originally interviewed for my first appointment at Peper

Harow I set out to find it the evening before, in order to make absolutely sure I would arrive on time. If I had approached on foot rather than by car, my pace up the long drive would certainly have slowed to a halt as I came to the final corner, for indeed beyond it was an awesome sight. Across a vast, open space of several hundred yards of lawn stood the dominating Palladian grandeur of William Chambers' great house. His original design had been more restrained – smaller, more elegant, fitting neatly into the surrounding landscape. Since the eighteenth century, the owning aristocratic potentates had grown still greater, so the house had grown in size to match them. I knew nothing of eighteenth-century architecture at that time and was less aware of the building's beauty; only of its lofty authority. I carefully and quietly reversed my car. Could this really be the approved school at which I was trying to get a job? I half expected some stentorian voice to boom its authoritative demand for an explanation of my presence. When I reached the main road I breathed freely again.

When eventually I became responsible for the estate I wondered how it could possibly be changed. How could it be more welcoming, friendly, engender an atmosphere like Lyward's Finchden Manor for instance? It soon became clear that to sell the estate in exchange for another was impossible for many reasons. We would have to make the best of it. In those early 1970s it looked as though there was not going to be much left for anything to be made of it. As indicated earlier, control of the boys' behaviour had begun to deteriorate some time before the transition to a therapeutic regime was set in train. Once this change occurred, they really set about wrecking the place with a will! A visiting speaker spoke ironically of therapeutic communities 'as places notable for the permanent sound of tinkling glass at the end of long drives' (Millham, 1973). It was hard work keeping up with the broken windows, with no money with which to replace the broken chairs. We rescued some dozen institutional armchairs and locked them into what later became the library, and struggled amid the echoing and cavernous reception rooms to see what could be done. It was not immediately apparent how to develop a more congenial atmosphere and how to conceptualize the therapeutic use of the building.

The front office was turned into the first staff room. However, it then changed its function several times more before eventually becoming the front office once again. A basement storeroom became in turn a therapy-group room, a coffee bar, a music room, and eventually a photographic darkroom. And so we struggled to adapt this crumbling pile into a therapeutic environment that would foster a sense of the kind of home that our youngsters had never experienced, but in a form with which they could relate.

Despite its national architectural importance, Peper Harow had not been looked after in a professionally responsible way for many years. Within a month or two of my appointment in 1970, we discovered one whole wall, from sub-basement, basement, first, second, third, and fourth floors to the attic roof a hundred feet above, to be riddled with dry rot. One of the joists, the girth of an oak tree, and intended to support a corner of the building, had rotted right through! Clearly the building was going to occupy a great deal of our attention simply to work out how we might use it for our daily programme of living and how to get it into decent order. The acres of bare boards were devoid of carpets, while the 20-feet-high windows were like gaping holes. In such a cheerless place, that created so much anxiety and so little comfort, it was not surprising that the house itself invited so much aggressive behaviour.

We responded by lighting the first legitimate fire in the front hall. Thereafter it was a permanent feature. Then we began to tackle the problem of bringing the dispersed living quarters together. During the approved-school era the boys' washing facilities had been in the basement and their bedrooms three floors above. Immediately below their bedrooms almost the entire floor had been occupied by the headmaster. At first it was occupied by a member of staff but, as soon as he could be moved, these best rooms were converted to boys' bedrooms, and the top floor and the basement were closed! The boys now lived in the middle three floors, while I as director moved to another converted building about ten yards from the house.

These changes began to integrate the physical living space. At the same time, the closely-knit gathering on Friday nights and the verbal statements in community meetings deliberately emphasized that the solidarity of the group was essential to its members' future lives. Thus, the physical development of the house, and the verbal content of the formal and less-formal group therapeutic activities, were more co-ordinated and so became mutually enhancing.

The practice of beginning each day with a regular community meeting emphasized the message about the community's changing identity. More will be said later about the meeting's manifold significance within the community (see Chapter eight, pp.141–52). As the community meeting became dynamically alive, so important clues as to the next integrative steps that needed to be taken arose from its transactions. What these steps should be was directed by specific issues arising from the need to manage behaviour that, in turn, was expressing the fundamental issues the deprived youngsters were at last becoming ready to recognize.

In our first Community Meetings everyone sat round on upright chairs arranged in two concentric circles and waited to see what would happen. The hour set for the Meeting seemed endless. It was explained that anyone could say anything they liked. But this freedom was only apparent for it resulted in nervous giggling, much uncomfortable shuffling, and long periods of anxious silence. As the clock struck ten the Meeting broke up with the force of an explosion. It soon became clear that sequential small group meetings were needed to help cope with the free-floating anxiety engendered by the Community Meeting. In these, people did hesitatingly express some of their feelings about bullying and similar social activity, but generally the House grew dirtier and the damage increased.

One night the food store behind the kitchen was broken into. No-one admitted to this in the morning Meeting. The locks were increased, but the door was broken down nightly; it was lined with steel, but was then totally removed – frame and all – from the wall itself. We then experienced one momentous Community Meeting. Someone hesitantly said that when he burgled houses he always cooked himself a meal. Apparently this was a common activity. He spoke of having wrecked the kitchen, excreted on the carpet. Yet, after a couple of Meetings of hysterically recounting such exploits the group began to sober up. They began to view their behaviour more realistically as bizarre and puzzling. The discussion moved forward. Boys began to talk of their own homes, of material hardship, of depressed mothers who did not cook, with stories of being packed off to buy chips, and then for the first time some expression of their sense of depression about the lack of comfort or standard of care implied by those poor feeding situations so many had experienced. This discussion could perhaps have been developed further than it was. After all, such depriving experiences can influence youngsters for the rest of their lives. The extent of their internal anxiety as to whether they could survive such a denying mother might thus have become more manifest; the relationship of this underlying anxiety to their compulsions to steal, their extreme aggression, their hatred of women, could have been verbalized, and therapeutically some long overdue experiencing of grief made more certain, because in the group the individuals could carry each other along. But even a group needs enough maturity to be able to tolerate painful insight. How could it obtain that pre-requisite skill? Fortunately, our experienced psychiatrist was able intuitively to suggest the answer. She proposed that we should set a table up at one end of the dining room. It would have bread and butter, jam, tea and milk, and sugar. It would have an electric kettle and mugs, and it would be available day and night. In exchange, it was agreed that the food store would be locked at night and it was not broken into again, not for several years.

(Rose, 1987: 149–62)

If, at the point when the boys had described their crazy behaviour, the psychiatrist had made various comments about the parallels between stealing from the food store and stealing from a withholding mother, only more rage would have ensued. Instead, a practical response was made to their implied cry for nurture by the most senior woman present that indicated they could change their delinquent and disturbed behaviour, and also take some responsibility for receiving good food.

The boys' behavioural message had – at its simplest – told us that they felt desperately deprived and also enraged. When they became able to verbalize and to consider the source of those feelings in the community meeting, they were undoubtedly heard with sympathy. However, the physical response of providing actual food and drink in a particular place was, most importantly, a symbol. Everyone knew that the issue was not physical hunger but emotional hunger. A symbolic response therefore allowed the boys to accept it at the level of either their adolescent or their infant selves. The symbolic response illuminated the real issue but allowed the youngsters the emotional choice of receiving an insight on their own terms. Furthermore, because their behaviour had been accorded the respect of a real communication once the boys had begun to seek more age-appropriate forms of expression, their relationship with the community as a whole began to change. They increasingly accepted that behaviour alone was no longer an appropriate language of communication. They no longer needed to break into the food store. The lighting of the fire in the front hall created a similar kind of symbolic message. That is why the frequent episodes of arson ceased at that point in time.

Nevertheless:

These youngsters always seemed hungry but, even when the most conscientious preparation of a meal was undertaken, much of it was wasted whoever had cooked it. Before every meal a hoard of savages invaded the kitchen and stuffed themselves with plain bread, wasting whatever had been prepared. They had craved milk, so we provided a churnful to be always available. Yet, in minutes it was always so misused as to be repulsive. Food and drink, the essential feature of their lives was undeniably a regular target for destruction.

(ibid: 156; see also Chapter nine, pp. 170–1)

Many of the youngsters referred to any meal, however well presented, as 'Shit! Poison!'. Food was regarded with considerable suspicion. We wondered how these problems, which stemmed from very early childhood, could be tackled. But it was difficult to confront the youngsters with the disparity between their infantile responses and the present reality that food now was actually good enough, at the same time as we recognized that the only cooking and dining facilities available to them were actually terrible.

We began to realize that the only way we could begin to tackle the problem was to start from scratch and begin by completely re-building and re-designing our kitchen and dining-room, and by re-designing the whole way in which food was provided. Committed to this expedient, we gutted one wing of the House and produced a large open-plan area, with views on both sides giving on to the green countryside. We divided one end into a space separated from the Dining area by a waist-high partition. This, in turn, was divided into a large central space which was the Kitchen area and, on one side of it, the Washing-up area and, on the other side, a permanently available Buttery. Our old table with the bread and kettle had come a long way. The floors of the Kitchen and the Buttery and Washing-up area on each side of it were raised to one level so that anyone in the Dining Room area could clearly see all that was going on. Beyond the Kitchen were foodstores and other systems, maximizing the efficiency of provisioning. The Kitchen contained a large cooking range, over which a beautiful copper hood extracted excessive smells. An integrated process was clearly visible. The food arrived in the Kitchen, was prepared, cooked, served, and then eaten. The cleared dishes were then removed to the Washing-up area. The Buttery's message that food would always be available was as constantly visible as the sequence of the regular meals.

We thought of the fortunate baby's experiences during the feeding process and imagined the specific ways in which all the senses are engaged, not simply his mouth, and we then tried by design and furnishing to fill the area with similar, pleasure-giving, sensual experiences. The floor was carpeted and the windows dressed in wool curtains which hung from ceiling to floor. The walls were covered with textile and the lighting arranged to be subdued and to highlight the different areas and particular features, like the food on the servery and the copper hood over the range. The colours were warm, though not strident. The height of the ceiling, as well as the carpeted floor, controlled the noise level so that even if seventy or eighty people were present it would be easy to hold a conversation. The Dining Room tables were discovered at the Yorkshire Show during the Summer Camp, by one of the residents. We chose tabletops in solid English oak, adzed with traditional skills a thousand years old, but we designed contemporary stainless steel plinths for them so that they would relate to the stainless steel of the modern kitchen equipment. The kitchen had to be efficient, rather than a quaint place of unremitting labour. Yet, it was important for pleasure to result from the cleaning process too. We designed benches to match the tables, with supports of oak and stainless steel. Though we chose benches so that people would have to sit together while eating, they were still intended to be comfortable and so were upholstered and covered with the same wool material as the curtains. While each item was to be significant in itself, it was necessary that the overall impression was an integrated one. The walls were hung with professionally framed pictures, painted and photographed by the residents themselves, and then we turned with equal care to each item of kitchen equipment and tableware.

(ibid: 156–7)

In the new kitchen and dining room was the abundant present. There were many therapeutic battles to be fought, for many youngsters were enormously threatened by this change. Here was an undeniably 'good mother', but 'she' demanded a 'good responding baby' and there were many complex reasons why that response was difficult to make. Attempts to damage the equipment, less than a perfectly completed task during cleaning, spilling coffee and tea that was not supposed to be taken outside the buttery, would be regarded as behaviour conveying a symbolic message rather than in simple legalistic terms. The kitchen, therefore, began to conduct a silent but immensely important symbolic relationship with all the youngsters.

At the same time, the old dining room, which was next to the new one, was now available for conversion into a new lounge. We realized that, if we moved the front-hall fire to this room, which backed onto the new dining room, we could at last form an integrated heart to the house. The new lounge needed furnishing and decorating above all and, if the fireplace with its beautiful country scene by Wilton in bas-relief marble was to be the symbolizing centre, the decoration would have to relate to it. The marble columns on either side of the chimney piece were of ochre-coloured Napoleon marble and that dictated the colours of the walls and ceiling and, in turn, the carpet and curtains.

The dado rail was carved with a Greek key pattern and its classic motif was echoed in the pattern of the carpet. The enormous curtains were related in their heavy, woven-wool material to those in the dining room beyond. The standard lamps and the low and high occasional tables, while designed in size to fit the lounge, were also made out of adzed oak and stainless steel, as were the tables in the dining room. Inevitably, this contrasted with the rest of the house, so eventually the carpet was extended from the new lounge throughout the ground floor, its colour and key pattern making a link between all the principal rooms.

The Gold Room was eventually recarpeted, its lighting and curtaining replaced, and the fine, moulded-plaster ceiling was again leafed in gold. The interwoven flower patterns in the ceiling above the daily community meeting were of painted blue and pink. This contrived humour was not lost either on the boys or on the girls when they began to arrive.

The old room, in which a few books had been kept and a few armchairs provided, was now needed as a library. By this time education was big news at last. It was felt that with seniority came the ability to achieve prodigious and dignified intellectual feats. The library was intended to symbolize this gravitas. Yet, it also needed to be experienced as exciting. To do this, we changed the scale of the room from a daunting one to one with an atmosphere that stimulated enquiry, by creating lots of private nooks and crannies inviting exploration. We erected a large gallery with a leather-bound rail and spiral staircase that invited one to ascend and view things from a different perspective. Green leather armchairs matched the stair rail, and the stainless steel plinths of the central oval mahogany table echoed those of the dining room and the lounge. Each public room was designedly individual but each was also recognizably part of an integrated whole. The rooms themselves thus paralleled the relationship of the individual to the whole group, or of any group to the whole community. The bookcases and carrels, which gave a sense of privacy to those who studied there, were of mahogany – the same material as the original doors in the house. However, they were designed to match the contemporary aspects of our new furnishings. Nor were they of oak. That was deliberately retained for the most basic, culturally symbolic roots. Therefore oak furniture was to be found predominantly in the dining room where the fundamental nurture of food was being addressed. Mahogany represented a further stage of sophistication both in the history of furniture and in the development of each individual – hence its choice for the library.

The final public room had been the rather battered staff room for some time. We were eventually able to obtain a grant from the Historic Buildings Council, and were therefore able to embark on its full restoration. It was to be a conference room. Staff would still be able to meet there, and many other meetings with parents, trustees, and outside agencies would also take place in this exquisite place. The restoration of this room's eighteenth- and nineteenth-century painted ceiling, its exceptionally fine woodwork, and classical plaques made it an obvious showcase. But we were proud of our heritage and added our own specially designed carpet to match the original ceiling.

At one local authority case conference someone sneeringly dismissed Peper Harow as 'wall-to-wall money!' This man's envious attack revealed his inability to comprehend why we had made such efforts and how we had managed to persuade so many people to contribute to the fund-raising that had been necessary to achieve all of this. All capital projects had to be funded from donations, so it can be imagined that the voluntary efforts to raise them were enormous. The most recalcitrant youngsters could not deny that what was theirs was valuable beyond their wildest imaginings and it called for a response from them that matched the building's implicit statement of their own worth. The community's self-esteem was significantly raised. When the arrival of the girls required a major development on the bedroom floor, we began with a much clearer understanding of the potential significance of our plans. The girls needed their own bathroom, shower, and lavatory area; they needed somewhere to wash their own clothes and, of course, having provided stunning facilities for the girls, it was imperative that the boys' bodies were then regarded with equal care.

There were many practical problems that caused our architects serious headaches. Bathrooms upstairs required special waterproofing to ensure that the listed ceilings beneath were not damaged by the watersports of teenage 'babies' splashing with unusual vigour! We wanted to ensure that the baths and showers offered privacy and yet allowed for a measure of staff supervision. Girls had been able to lock themselves into the temporarily converted bathrooms, holding everyone to ransom at night-time. If we needed to enter a bath cubicle in an emergency, we still had to find a way to make it feel secure to the user. Most of our youngsters had experienced a complete absence of security in their early childhood. The environment at Peper Harow was therefore especially designed to promote a sense of security. But it was also designed to promote good feelings within the individual youngster about himself. This is why we took great care to ensure that using the lavatories and the bathrooms would be positively enjoyable experiences.

The feeding infant, as well as discovering about warmth in his stomach and in his mother's cuddle, is also discovering about warmth in their relationship. If he rejects the breast but is then given room to find it again in his own easy time, he is being enabled to comprehend both his developing, autonomous self and his changing dependency in a safe way. Hopefully, a first successful experience will be reinforced by later successful experiences. An encouraging and individually enhancing mother will next see him comfortably through his potty training, for example. Perhaps what emerges as the most important consequence of their complex physical relationship while feeding, bathing, nappy changing, and potty training is what each of these experiences tells him and reiterates about his basic worth and his autonomy – as Erikson would put it. The lessons our adolescent youngsters learn must echo this message. Therefore, every meal-time, bath-time, and defecation must also reiterate the esteem in which the 'mother' community holds the resident. At best, we felt, we could ensure a truly new opportunity for our unfortunate youngsters. At Peper Harow, at least real safety and the confident expectation of a pleasurable experience could be built into the actual design of the lavatories and bathrooms.

This message of security and wellbeing was given by the texture, colour, and the quality of the materials. Lighting in the bathrooms was subdued and the heating raised slightly higher than in the surrounding corridors and bedrooms. The floor coverings were intended to be warm and comfortable for bare feet. We spent much time searching for noiseless and exceptionally effective air-extraction and waste-disposal systems. No detail was unimportant. The very shape of the mirrors offered some implied statement about masculinity or femininity as they were being used. The residents' self-interest was being encouraged and Peper Harow had placed great value and importance on their bodily functions and their worth.

Again, it must be stressed that maturation of the residents' self-image did not derive from one particular physical or material situation but from many. The total environment implied the same consistent message when they ate and received the nourishment that would grow their bodies, or when they were enjoying their bodily functioning within bathrooms and lavatories designed to imply respect and esteem for those very bathing and excretory activities.

These caringly designed resources were often perversely unappreciated. It was not surprising that, as a result of their traumatizing and depriving past experiences, they often felt disgusted with their bodies. They often damaged themselves with amateur tatoos or by cutting their arms, or by refusing to wash. Such behaviour indicated how much their experiences had undermined their sense of self-esteem, and to what extent those experiences had actually consisted of physical violence and sexual abuse. But the residents also derived an angry and perverse pleasure from shocking others with their physical demonstration of self-hate. In our kitchen, bathrooms, and lavatories the youngsters were being confronted with a completely different message about themselves. These real and new experiences implied that they should change their view of themselves. The physical situation, therefore, was the very essence of therapeutic confrontation.

Great trouble was taken to provide silent waste-disposal units for the girls' sanitary requirements. These units were built-in to be unobtrusive and easy to operate. Sometimes, however, they were blocked by the insertion of junk, requiring the male maintenance team to undertake a very unpleasant and awkward repair job. One can see that a machine for such an intimate purpose might be significant in many conflicting ways for girls with appalling histories of sexual abuse. The hostility that our maintenance team experienced when trying to repair the machines would only be one aspect of the girls' confused feelings about their bodies, their potential motherhood, and their own past vulnerability and current insecurity.

Generally, the residents treated the physical resources well. Most youngsters had previous experience of the more usual institutional provision. They also quickly understood the confirmatory, symbolic messages the materials and design expressed. They were also relieved to learn that so much could endure their depredations and could survive their destructive impulses. Only if there is somewhere for these impulses to be expressed safely can they begin the fearful and puzzling journey towards understanding what their behaviour reveals and then change it to something appropriate to current reality.

The fortunate child receives good messages from birth about his bodily functioning from a loving mother, until each caring activity can be undertaken personally. A mothers's physical communication is part of the language with which she is able to help the infant differentiate between herself and himself. It expresses the idea that the baby is entitled, able, and worthy of being an entity in his own right. When that experience is a good one, it is a good foundation for exploring the widening world with optimism. Managing disturbed behaviour and sharing emerging understanding of what our youngsters have missed, so that their damage can be healed, requires many community resources to provide a composite forum for their resolution. Yet, frequently, our youngsters are injured in the very core of their being. Restoration of the roots of self is perhaps the hardest psychotherapeutic task, and the most essential if our youngsters are to become effective parents themselves without having experienced effective parenting in their infancy. This is the issue to be tackled if the generational cycle of emotional, physical, and sexual abuse is to be halted.

It would seem to be impossible to provide an environment for our adolescents that recapitulates the succession of normal mother-and-child interactions that makes for healthy emotional development in normal children. To attempt to recapitulate these early relationships would risk confusing them with other feelings that are normal to adolescence. It requires great self-awareness and great skill for a member of staff to cuddle the 'baby' within a hunky 16-year-old boy or a nubile young woman. The member of staff has to be able to get the timing of his contact with that 'baby' exactly right and to be able to change their physical relation at exactly the right moment too. Otherwise, the value of that contact is lost and the adolescent becomes confused by the threat of later kinds of sexuality.

Someone who has been sexually abused within their family has been used as a plaything instead of being appropriately experienced as a vulnerable, individual human entitled to the protection of his vulnerable individuality. The abuser's fantasy life has spilled over into reality, indicating how very disturbed and incapable of reliably functioning as an adult the abuser is. The beginning of this disturbance in the adult may be as long ago as his own infancy or childhood. Often, family dynamics are still more complex: at one period the parents can function appropriately but at another time, destabilized by stress, endemic pathology becomes active. Thus, there are abused children who have also received good experiences from abusing parents and they might have partially begun to establish an autonomous sense of self. Their emotional growth may have become inhibited by the conflicts and confusions of their later experience. For such lost adolescents, it would be essential to find the child that used to exist before their premature sexualization (Winnicott, 1968: 69). The task of the community is to identify what it should provide so that the lost adolescent's childhood can be restored. At the same time, the development of an adult sexual identity requires different ingredients to be added at each developmental stage. The disturbed adolescent therefore really needs the resolution of his confusion at several developmental levels at once. And, if, as is more likely, the family's disturbance existed always, then to focus on one specific form of traumatization alone could prevent our seeing the essential issue of the resident's inadequate or distorted experience of primary care.

It is doubtful if any one adult, or even the entire group, could provide the many kinds of response needed by such young people through their personal interactions only. The symbolic physical provision, however, may play a stimulating or a confirmatory part that is just as important. There are, of course, many new therapies that enable the resolution of trauma through physical experiences. I have no personal experience of them but, even if we had developed our resources at Peper Harow by their inclusion, they would be an addition not an alternative to the symbolic physical environment.

We regularly need to remind ourselves of the continuing resistance to insight and to the demand for change throughout the psychotherapeutic process[1]. For me, it is an abnegation of the therapist's responsibility to place too much emphasis on the patient's or on the client's responsibility to choose. Choice is a luxury available to the healthy, the secure, and mature adult, who has grown the psychic ability to evaluate and make appropriate choices. Even normal adolescents are still in the process of developing such psychic strengths. Psychotherapy, in whatever form, should also be seen as a temporary crutch that the vulnerable individual needs to rely upon while he grows his own abilities to evaluate and choose. Thus, a major function of the psychotherapeutic process, and a major responsibility of the therapist, is the enabling of resistance to be overcome, albeit with objective and tender sensitivity. However, those particularly concerned with the recovery of disturbed adolescents have an adult as well as a psychotherapeutic responsibility for exercising authority. This will inevitably be resisted, and adolescents do need opportunities to exercise their own emerging authority, but the adult member of staff needs to be clear about his dual authoritative responsibilities.

The most ghastly irony about the present, well-intentioned 'care in the community' fashion, for people in psychic need, is the pretence that they actually have choice about whether or not to sleep in cardboard boxes, or whether or not to wander about in physical danger. Equally absurd are other supporters of the same well-intentioned, though under-resourced policy, who frequently delude themselves into believing that those who take appropriate responsibility for such derelicts are being oppressive and dictatorial. It must be acknowledged that disturbed youngsters are only able to cope with a certain amount of independence and choice, and that this amount depends on the 'emotional' rather than the chronological age of the adolescent.

The therapeutic community, it must be said, once more, needs every aspect of its experience correlated with the central, psychotherapeutic message. It is essential to circumvent the 'delinquent ego' as Redl and Wineman (1951) would put it. One should aim to deny any opportunity that might offer a collusive escape for such a delinquent ego by allowing it to say, 'It's all a con! You don't have to treat this experience seriously.' To avoid an unintended, collusive opportunity being spotted and seized, the physical experiences of everyday life, so potentially redolent with symbolic meaning, require the staff to illuminate and communicate the significance of these experiences. Hopefully, that continuously arbitrative experience, underlined by the manifold relationships within the community, and confirmed by experiences within the different kinds of groups, will coalesce to produce at least a kind of experience of the 'good enough' upbringing of the fortunate child.

We called a halt to deliberate environmental designing at the door of the youngsters' bedrooms – though the activity within continually attracted the staff's intervention. One argument for the exceptional material presentation of all the shared public rooms is that they symbolize something of the communal identity. They reflect undoubted quality in every respect - they reflect integration and design in colour and material that springs from the architectural source of the building with which the residents identify. Thus, it is the residents' communal responsibility to look after its 'good mother community'. 'We have to preserve this image for the next generation. We have to recognize and maintain the message "You are worth this much!"'On the other hand, there are different social psychotherapeutic opportunities that also need to be available. Our argument for letting the youngsters manage their rooms and individual bed-spaces was to provide them with the opportunity for individually expressed 'play', even if their expression was appallingly messy (see Chapter five, p. 90).

Some visitors complained that the emphasis on the group rather than on individual values and choice was socially oppressive. We are, indeed, less comfortable within our society with this kind of group. Despite our traditionally accepted family groups, we are currently placing a greater value on the rights and significance of the individual. It must be stressed that our youngsters are not in a therapeutic community for sociopolitical reasons. It is the provision and management of their psychotherapeutic needs that must dictate the community's functioning. Hopefully, when fully restored, our youngsters will have the internal strength to make the difficult transition to a more usual environment, or at least to an environment that is as much of their own choosing as it is for their more fortunate peers. Any relationship that is based on dependency, like the exceptional dependence on the group, can abuse the individual. Finding the correct balance between the special needs of our adolescents and normal human needs requires permanent monitoring and debate.

To what extent can a member of staff who chooses to help make the youngster's bed be described as colluding with the youngster's resistance to growing up? The demand is certainly there. Yet, the member of staff under pressure to be like a real parent can, in the twinkling of an unconscious association, be turned by the youngster into an oppressive persecutor and the loving contribution of the staff member can be rejected. Out of this scenario further opportunities could arise, enabling examination of the youngster's propensity to resist emotional nurture, or the recognition that the member of staff is actually real. What does arise depends on whether the intervention is predominantly creative, or whether it is predominantly self-gratificatory. The initiative must frequently come from the member of staff, as the youngster often operates with little regard for reality.

In the very early days of Peper Harow, a couple of youngsters staggered, helpless with hysterical laughter, to my door to announce that Marky was cooking eggs in his bedroom. Despite their amusement, I guessed they felt the situation was serious as we were all by now used to this particular young man's inconceivable, daily, dangerous activities. I flew to his room. Marky was nothing but ingenious, for his 'cooker' was constructed from a television cabinet and a series of wires of various thicknesses, two of which 'stripped bare' were jammed into a powerpoint. The fuse had been bypassed somehow and the whole contraption, along with a frying pan of eggs, was pouring smoke. I ripped the wires out, overriding electrification by miracle no doubt rather than by knowledge, but Marky was yet more outraged. 'I was going to eat those', he snarled, 'Why have you got to spoil everyone's fun?' He then cringed away as though he were going to be beaten.

Continued missions to sort out fire-risking contraptions inspired by fantasies were an essential part of staff supervision. The dangers of these fantasies arose partly from the youngsters' inability to realize how dangerous they were, but also from many other motivations. One motive was to see whether the staff would be able and willing to save them from themselves. As the community developed, the bedroom groupings were selected so that one or more senior residents shared a room with the most junior, and the senior resident encouraged the youngster to create his own living space.

Beds were surrounded with chests of drawers and wardrobes – often acquired for mere pence from the local auction – and were covered with pottery and paintings, books, and photographs. Beds were made and clothes looked after. Above all, the community values were still expressed in the bedroom, albeit in a way that looked significantly different from downstairs. The residents influenced each other a great deal, especially if a bedroom group consisted of people of different seniority. Most seniors would frown on posters of nudes, because of their pornographic implications. Others would tolerate 'a passing phase'. Musical, pictorial, and literary taste were thus passed on, along with the social culture.

The seniors prevented delinquent behaviour at night. They would rouse the 'sleeping-in' member of staff if necessary. A regular phenomenon was recognized in the community. It concerned the propensity towards a counterculture at night-time. It seemed to be at night that the delinquent impulses arose consistently. The senior residents usually ensured that the bedroom groups were self-aware and so did not give in to their impulses. Not that the senior people always lived up to such expectations. Their rivalry with younger siblings, their envy of 'baby brothers and sisters' produced much ambivalence. Sometimes it was easier for the seniors to pretend to be asleep, to sneer sarcastically at the newcomer's naivety, and even to threaten them physically as though their own reasonable personal rights arose, not out of normal social intercourse, but from a delinquent pecking order. Yet, these failures came to light often enough and frequently were raised in the community meeting by the failing senior himself. One could measure the climate of the community by a journey around the bedrooms during the daytime. A bed-space would be suddenly stripped of all its possessions, or wardrobes suddenly arranged to cut the individual off completely from the rest of his peers. Once more, a glib interpretation would be unhelpful. Nevertheless, if the state of a youngster's bed-space were compared with his behaviour in other community situations, it provided a very accurate reflection of his state of mind. Similarly, the general state of the bedrooms and bathrooms could be a guide to the feeling of the whole community.

It was important to know before a community meeting what the atmosphere had been like at getting-up time. Had most people been down in time for breakfast? Had the member of staff been assailed by curses and unsupported by the seniors? Was the fire lit first thing by the youngster who held that responsibility? Indeed, in good times, the seniors felt they should not require the member of staff to do more than simply be present; they would do the waking and see that the cooks got started on breakfast at the right time. Such an undertaking had usually resulted from debate in community meetings in which the residents had probably been challenged and confronted. At the meetings, they would have been exhorted to remember their original commitment and to renew it.

Surges of the resultant group awareness arising from catastrophe – a youngster's running away perhaps – frequently led to some physical expression. The cleaning of the house, the reactivation of community-meeting agreements about taking coffee out of the buttery, all were ways of symbolizing this renewed upholding of the values that eventually, when sufficiently experienced, would become internalized and so nourish the youngster's good self-image.

One small event seems to underline the importance of the physical surroundings to a youngster. Walking around the grounds one misty morning in conversation with a visitor, I noticed Alistair ahead of us wandering down to the river. Peper Harow is famous for its mature cedars of Lebanon, planted in the eighteenth century, tradition has it, by Capability Brown. Alistair seemed to be in a permanent state of profound depression that caused us great anxiety, as he had taken several serious overdoses before he arrived. Later we discovered the extent to which he lived in terror of becoming mad, as he had been told by his mother that her divorced husband had contracted a debilitating disease that caused their marriage to break up. Alistair would, in time, she said, develop its symptomatology. At other times Alistair's behaviour was dangerous to others – he had tried to derail a train. In his mind, Alistair toyed with other scenarios that would confirm him as powerful, but these fantasies were so excessive as to illustrate instead how helpless he truly felt himself to be.

The park had a dreamlike quality that morning, for the mist lay upon the river and wreathed in drifts between the trees nearby. Suddenly, as Alistair passed one of these great cedars of Lebanon, it dropped one of its largest branches to the ground with a crack as loud as an explosion. Alistair leapt, as we did at our greater distance. He gazed with an appalled expression, and we suddenly felt that he ascribed the bough's unexpected and sudden demise to his own mysterious, but unintended, power. For a time, he stared mesmerized at the branch and then slunk off along the river bank in as deep a gloom as ever. It was several years before that youngster could put his unremitting depression behind him and make a considerable success of his life. Then I was reminded of how like infants really disturbed people are with regard to their surrounding environment. They are not clear about what is inanimate, nor are they clear about the way the animate is the same as themselves and the way it is different from themselves. My eldest daughter as a toddler proclaimed with radiant delight that the newly opened wild flowers were 'smiling at me!' She half meant it.

The park, then, was another important feature at Peper Harow. It had the potential to be experienced in ways that youngsters who were too defended could not allow themselves to experience from other people. Other youngsters as insulated as Alistair built houses on stilts over the river, turned areas of the swamp into battlegrounds for their toy soldiers, and swung on a huge rope from an overhanging branch, to drop into the river and struggle up the muddy bank totally absorbed in the joy of their play. No-one could fail to appreciate these pleasure grounds – as they had been called in the eighteenth century – whether they were used for hide-and-seek, for fishing, or for seeking the imagined sympathy of nature. Many a depressed youngster could be seen gazing across the river at the eloquent sunset (see also Chapter seven, pp. 125–7).

The whole scenario at Peper Harow was as unlike the usual, inner-city, council-estate background of the child-in-care as it could possibly be. In fact, the background of our youngsters frequently defied rigid sociological categorization. Their parents often came from mixed social classes. The youngsters, as well as the parents, had often experienced very mixed material standards and educational experiences. Nevertheless, to find oneself in some kind of ownership of a stately home is almost like the enactment of a fantasy. Youngsters and staff were compelled by the shock of the new experience to be attentive to its messages. As far as the physical aspects of living were concerned, these were designed and developed to fulfil a symbolic task. There were also inborn qualities of physical experience that arose from the material provision at Peper Harow that had been too little experienced in earlier life. When people think of a psychotherapeutic experience, they usually imagine the patient expressing his predicament in some form, and that expression then being clarified by the therapist. In the residential community, therapy should actually arise from the transactions with every aspect of life and, of these, the physical and material aspects can be at least as important as any.

Chapter seven

Educating anew

*Adolescent identity crisis and emotional damage in early childhood
– major reasons for educational failure.*
*The roots of learning – fantasy and play and the management of
behaviour in the learning context.*
*The Peper Harow environment – a phaseological design for
rehabilitative education – from play to college.*
Learning disorders and therapeutic failure.
The essentiality of integrating education and therapy.

Most young people coming to Peper Harow have not found school
rewarding. The best schools can, of course, be an inspiration even for
someone with few personal resources. But our youngsters' failure was
almost predetermined, irrespective of the nature of their schooling.

There seemed to be two main reasons for this, both relating to the
extent and nature of our young people's particular problems. One arose
from their especially difficult, adolescent identity crises. This mostly
seemed to affect girls and boys whose families had particular educational
expectations for them. Lavinia, for instance, had achieved exceptional
instrumental music grades at an early age. She had managed her school
work to a similar standard until her life started to fall apart in early
adolescence. Lavinia threw away all those things that her divided parents
prized. Her parents had desperately hoped that her success would indicate
that their own failures had been less damaging than they feared. But her
education, music, speech, and appearance all disappeared into the drug-
orientated culture that swallowed her up. Lavinia's behaviour expressed a
plethora of conflicting feelings, both about who she was and how much she
had to reject in order to distance herself from her parents.

The other reason for our youngsters' failure was because most of them
had never reached a stage of psychological development that would
enable them to engage enthusiastically with educational opportunities.
Their early deprivation and traumatization had prevented them from being
able to use fantasy as a creative form of play in infancy: their use of fantasy

was predominantly defensive. In a sense, these children were pre-occupied and apathetic when they arrived at school. They were fearful and certainly had not yet learned how to react to new experiences with quickening interest and increasing concentration.

Bloch (1979) (see also Chapter eight, p. 149) illustrates the close relationship between the function of fantasy in our psychic development and the function of play as described by Erikson (see Chapter five, pp. 80–2). Erikson (1959) perceives play as the way an individual engages with problems he meets in the course of his development. Through play he discovers how to overcome these problems at many levels of being. The ability to play creatively does not arise by chance but as the result of successful development at earlier stages of life. Obviously, the physical activity of play is underpinned by imagination and indeed by fantasies that play represents in physical form.

Bloch (1979) considers children's psychic reactions to their life experiences. She concludes that small children continually fantasize in order to resolve how they should respond to their everyday, but frequently frightening, experiences. In the case of real trauma, fantasy alone cannot effect this resolution. The actual experiences of our children (and her patients) are so terrible that, however many times they attempt to defend themselves in fantasy, the attempts are ineffective. Invented monsters may represent the source of their terror, but, whether the character with whom the fantasizing child is identifying succeeds in containing the monsters or not, the reality of their danger cannot be disguised. Their parents are actually depriving, and dangerous, so these children can never use fantasy for its normal purpose, which is to reflect upon and work through anxiety, so reassuring them of continuity and of their ultimate survival. Because they remain in real danger, their search for a fantasy that will convincingly reassure them becomes increasingly desperate and even obsessional. Banging their heads against the wall of reality becomes habitual and often explains their apparently habitual, self-defeating, and self-destructive behaviour of later years. However, from early in life, these children are absorbed with fantasy as a desperate attempt to defend themselves, which thus prevents the normal consequences of fantasy which is to liberate their creative potential.

Of course the differences between these reasons for failure are not easily separated. An adolescent like Lavinia, who settles for such a negative identity, is only surrendering to the worst self-image she had feared would be inevitable. The roots of this fear lay in her early childhood. It was miraculous that she had held together for so long.

Alistair arrived with a grade A in his maths O level but he found it almost impossible to repeat this level of achievement in any other subject for a long time. The O level, therefore, only indicated a minimal level of potential and no more. Yet, for Alistair his grade A represented something in terms of self-image that he clung to desperately, because it contradicted his permanent sense of worthlessness and failure. It was his last ray of hope. Indeed, everyone has heard stories of undergraduates who have finally collapsed despite their success, no longer able to resist their encroaching sense of emptiness. Achievement, like anything else, can be a strategy of denial to avoid internal and unresolved anguish. As with all denial mechanisms, however, it cannot be maintained for long. There is a difference between, on the one hand, acquiring skills and techniques for pursuing an exam syllabus and, on the other hand, being able to use those skills thereafter in a way that encourages a sense of fulfilment, and indeed identity. Education, too often, is regarded as a process that concerns only the development of the intellect and has nothing to do with the development of the emotions. For our youngsters the development of the intellect is impossible until a psychic change has begun to occur.

Again, failure to work successfully through Erikson's (1959) three earliest stages of development almost certainly indicates the likelihood of later educational dysfunction. We hardly need to remind ourselves how, in Erikson's model, trusting, autonomous, and initiating personality conditions enable industriousness at school and an ability to identify with work and to anticipate achievements – all of which are constructive ingredients of the adolescent psychic identity. So many case histories of our particular youngsters reveal grim experiences that guarantee the opposite of this successful personality development. These youngsters' experience of early childhood had not merely been one of occasional trauma within an ideal family setting. Our youngsters' traumas had been frequent and they had originated from what should have been their primary experience of security and personal pleasure at each step of their exploration of their widening world.

The stress in a family group who have had to move from one substandard accommodation to another may only occasionally erupt into drunken violence and actual terror, but the general anxiety and misery are like a consistent background toothache. Each uncomprehended, fearful event – a series of sexual liaisons by the parents, a berserk physical attack by an unbalanced adult, the distancing taunts of siblings and other children – only reinforces the increasing emotional paralysis of such children. This emotional paralysis prevents the kind of play that is necessary for creative psychic development. Again, the physical activity of play, superficially similar to that of the fortunate child, is engaged in for obsessive and defensive reasons. We have seen that this kind of play embodies omnipotent fantasies, intended to bring some temporary relief from the child's state of emotional helplessness and fear.

But fantasies whose purpose it is to defend against reality do not enhance an increasingly enriching world. A child may be the giant slayer of flies in daytime reverie but this is dangerously self-deluding, and it practises compensatory, sadistic gratification rather than creative activity. It also tends to inhibit any learning. This kind of fantasy strives to resist and distort reality, rather than to encourage increasing clarification.

Perhaps for all children new situations tend to be daunting, especially to the toddler in his widening world – going to school, for instance. But as children become increasingly adept at solving each new problem, so they increasingly anticipate positive outcomes to the stress of each new situation. Each new challenge contributes to the child's sense of self and of self-confidence and adds to his internal store of positive associations. But for our youngsters any successful achievement will have been excessively hard-won and will be so out of tune with their negative self-image that it will add up to very little. Indeed, it may even be painful because it illuminates afresh the gulf that separates the youngster from where he would wish to be. Success for those who expect failure implicitly demands a less negative self-image, though the youngster often feels powerless to change his view despite the occasional social or educational achievement.

Recognizing that our youngsters' capacity to experience the world realistically has been injured emphasizes the complexity of reversing their way of functioning. Simply providing more individual classroom attention is not nearly the answer. Many teachers in ordinary schools go out of their way to help such youngsters. The demands on those teachers seem to increase in response to their extra effort until they begin to experience the youngster as insatiable. The rest of the class will probably resent the amount of their time being devoted to their unlovable peer. Furthermore, the youngster himself may be frightened by the personal attention and become impossibly disruptive, so, in the end, the teacher will have to give up.

Every infant, Erikson suggests (see Chapter five, pp. 80–2), needs to develop a recognition that his mother and he are two separate beings. His sense of his own autonomy is the beginning of a healthy sense of self. If the youngster has not been helped to germinate a sense of his individuality, then his capacity to distinguish between himself and others will be impaired. This obviously has many implications. One example would be that the youngster's uncertainty about the emotional boundaries between himself and others often leaves him overwhelmed and completely misunderstanding of his interactions with others. Starved of affection, the youngster cannot begin to evaluate, say, a teacher's praise or reasonable concern for him. He would be flooded by extremes of love and rage, for example, instead of simply being nourished by such a normal and needed relationship.

The teacher, unlike the psychotherapist, is not trained to recognize what he is caught up in. He is likely to be seriously stressed by finding himself perceived at one moment as the totally loving, perfect, longed-for 'mother' that never was and, in the next moment, as a sadistic, monstrous, and dangerous authoritarian figure. Not only is the teacher not trained to understand the constituents and functioning of the youngster's attention, but he is certainly not trained to manage it! To dispatch such a youngster to whatever 'time-out' situation is provided in the school will only make for temporary relief. Such a response cannot change the nature of the youngster's functioning. Indeed, the dilemma is very similiar to the one that makes for breakdown in fostering placements. The family unit, like the individual teacher, cannot cope with the impact of this kind of disturbed behaviour, for the focused attention of the one-to-one relationship of the intimate family unit may in itself actually arouse this profound level of internal need and chaos (see Chapter six, p. 97).

Indeed, specialist units, even as total as community homes with education on the premises or special schools, may also not be able to provide the special kind of resource that could cope with the impact of such disturbed young people.[1] These places may be well staffed; their class and group situations may be especially organized to allow for maximum personal attention. Nevertheless, an effective feeling of security in the classroom could only develop from the total context of an institution that has been geared towards integrating a similar sense of security overall. In the same way that even an exceptional member of staff's acutely perceptive relationship is not by itself likely to enable change to occur, except in the immediate behaviour pattern, so the most fortunate of circumstances in the classroom will not by itself promote full educational achievement. In a therapeutic community for adolescents, the therapeutic and educational programme has to be totally integrated.

A practical example of this is demonstrated in the Walker Home and School for Boys in Massachusetts. The late director's most famous book, *The Other Twenty-Three Hours* leaves no doubt that this school is about the enhancement and reinforcement of the therapeutic task. It envisages a total therapeutic experience and not one confined to the traditional psychotherapeutic interview (Trieschman, Whittaker, and Brendtro, 1969). Among the many excellent aspects of Walker's programme is the knowledge and management of specific learning disabilities. For example, specific rehabilitative programmes are individually designed for each child. Moreover, Walker is one of the very few establishments that sets out to integrate the staff tasks. There, teachers work under the jurisdiction of residential workers in the house unit. The residential workers, in turn, act as teaching aides in the classroom. Because the staff's task is so mutually understood, the youngsters' rehabilitative educational programmes are known to all. Even staff putting children to bed will ensure that bedtime reading will consist of prescribed rather than just any reading material.

Anyone who tries to teach a formal course to these youngsters actually requires considerable teaching skills. In an ordinary school the task is great enough. A teacher in any school would be responsible for several courses with many children in each class. Assembling material for each course and measuring each child's response is both time-consuming and exhausting. However, with each passing year, a teacher's prepared resources expand and his scope to bring to bear a variety of ways of understanding a subject increases. The teacher increasingly becomes able to respond to each child individually. At the same time, the management of the teacher's own department, and the resource banks available within the school or local authority, will all support and enhance the teacher's skills.

The teacher in a unit for seriously disturbed children is probably expected to cover a wider number of subjects, requiring individualized preparation and entailing at least as much work as for an ordinary class. The teacher may well lack the professional stimulus arising from the greater numbers of experienced staff and the variety of resources of the large day school. Yet, there can be little doubt that those least equipped to learn easily need the most skilled teaching of all. The pupils may well receive much good-will and patience from the greater amount of individual time, but the most appropriate material and presentation will be harder to ensure. It is not surprising, therefore, that a recent inspection of community homes by the inspectorate of the Department of Education and Science were appalled by the limited educational opportunities they offered.

However, as Redl and Wineman (1951) vividly suggested, the 'delinquent ego' is unimaginably skilful at defending its delinquent status quo and never more so than when a classroom is filled with a group of 'delinquent egos'! (see Chapter five, p. 78 and Chapter six, p.111). Teachers may think that they are teaching a history lesson, or discussing a poem. Nevertheless, they are also engaged in a complex group process, much of which is functioning at an unconscious level but which is therefore all the more powerful because of it.

A major component of delinquent pathology arises unconsciously from a need to defend oneself from acute anxiety. A classroom situation for delinquent adolescents would be particularly evocative of issues of dependency and of envy, in turn triggering unrecognized anxiety. It is easy to see how habitual behavioural consequences of anxiety might disrupt the class. However, powerful denial mechanisms, unconsciously intended to defend against anxiety, would also distract the student and, despite any conscious intention, also prevent learning. It is essential that a clear boundary be drawn between activities and discussions that would highlight personal problems – appropriate for group psychotherapy – and the specifically classroom task. This would be easier to ensure if the teacher were aware of the dynamic issues as well as the classroom task.

When I ceased teaching in ordinary schools after only a few years, it seemed that I had the potential at least to become a reasonable teacher. Nevertheless, my teaching skills did not develop in the world of the approved school. As an ordinary member of staff at Park House School, it was part of my job to teach English and a variety of other subjects each afternoon. I also taught a special English class designated to take O level English, and all its members were certainly bright enough to do so.

We enjoyed ourselves together. I was a popular member of staff, and my class actually had a waiting list. Several of the boys wrote fine poetry and, although one was startled at the illiterate colloquialisms that crept into written English generally, it looked as though they would all pass the O level examination easily. Not one of them did, however, and I was severely taken to task by the headmaster. He could have left the wigging to my own conscience as I felt very shocked by the results. I could have done with some teaching myself about the structuring of lessons, and about organizing a sequence of factual presentations, but there was no-one to offer that sort of help, nor was there anyone to explain the need for carefully managed boundaries between the kind of discussion necessary in the personal interview and what was required to further learning in the classroom.

In the individual interview it was essential that the youngster felt you were on his side. In the classroom there were other priorities. The head, whose class had all passed O level maths, told me that he offered financial prizes to everyone in his class, every week.

'Never mind the morality', he replied to my petulant response.
'Look at my results!'

Try though I did, I could not really understand what had gone wrong. Perhaps I was a far worse teacher than I had thought I was. Yet, having thought this over for so many years since, I am inclined rather to think that my relationship with that class was delinquent and collusive. Yes, we 'had a laugh' together, but I was accepted almost like a gang leader and the kind of different attitude towards work and towards themselves that should have been promoted unknowingly took a back seat. The delinquent ego triumphed. At the time, under the anxiety, I remember casting around for someone other than myself to blame and then found that there was no-one – not even me on whom I felt the responsibility really lay and that baffled me even more.

Now the lesson is clearer. Peper Harow had to function for three or four years before the youngsters were seriously able to undertake and pass examination work. This was because it took that length of time for a new culture to have evolved. Thus, the youngsters taking exams had been there for four or five years, the first two or three of which had been spent in developing the personality qualities that could sustain their commitment to work. By that time, theirs was not a false commitment to a false image that defended them against their negative, internal world, but a commitment that gave expression to their partially changed and still changing internal world.

No boy in Park House Approved School seriously saw himself going to university. The boys were being trained as plumbers, bricklayers, tailors, and so forth, but by and large they did not take those opportunities seriously. Almost no-one remained in the job for which they had been trained for longer than a year. Approved schools professed that they trained people to lead competent, useful, and honest lives. In reality, the boys were patronized and punished by a staff who unconsciously reflected the views of the general public towards emotionally disturbed children. Most youngsters were badly let down by a sham system and were therefore guarded about engaging enthusiastically with anything that the approved school offered.

The classroom behaviour, in their ordinary state schools, of the youngsters who eventually went to the approved school had probably not differed much from that of the later boys, and eventually girls, who went to Peper Harow Community. The same motivations underlay the potential behaviour of most of them. All the youngsters were frequently argumentative. Many of them had been described as excessively attention-seeking. Both sets of youngsters frequently experienced not knowing something as public humiliation - which they then construed as an attack by the teacher on them! In Peper Harow, feelings about the teacher's knowledge were frequently discussed by the youngsters. The teacher's knowledge, they felt, gave him 'superior' authority, to which the boys in particular responded by feeling powerless. Their early and sometimes life-threatening experiences had often created their underlying sense of powerlessness. For such very injured young people, the normal classroom situation almost inevitably provoked issues about authority and power, thus triggering the youngsters' unresolved fantasies about their terrorized early childhood.

The teaching situation might also arouse envious fantasies from the youngsters' earliest infancy. After all, the small teaching group, too, can be perceived as an intimate, nurturing experience. That such an intimate and dependent interaction might create problems derived from much earlier experiences is not surprising if we recall the anxiety that must have dominated so many mother–infant relationships; an anxiety, moreover, perhaps most experienced during the intimate moments of the feeding, nurturing process. With anxiety raised, the baby might become voracious, thus making the frightened mother anxious about whether she could meet those astonishingly excessive needs. But the baby is completely dependent upon his mother. Within her reside all the resources the baby needs. The baby's intense envy of his mother's power over him and the good food that she possesses is not easily soothed away.

If mother, in turn, was envious of her baby's entitlement to receive goodness, because she may have been a deprived baby herself, she might be quite ambivalent about actually wanting to reassure an anxious baby, despite his need for a constantly reassuring response. In a symbolic sense, the teacher, too, is filled with the knowledge that the youngster is supposed to consume. Yet, the envy of the teacher's possessed knowledge is often so extreme as to prevent the receiving, let alone the ingesting, of his good milk of knowledge.

These issues cannot, of course, be resolved the moment the youngster enters a therapeutic community like Peper Harow. They arise from attitudes that were likely to have formed a reinforcing and self-defeating pattern throughout the youngster's school career. For such youngsters it is better to concentrate on integrating them within the dynamic, overall community environment and to avoid personal confrontation. The dynamic environment would confront the reality base of their disturbed emotions and contain the youngsters while, at the same time, assuaging their emotional hunger. In due course, spending time with an adult, acknowledging one's ignorance, and acknowledging one's need to learn would not feel too dangerous and so a more normal education programme could then be begun. At Peper Harow, therefore, we played a game of pretence:

> 'You are not here to be educated. This is not a school, it's a
> therapeutic community. Well, if you do the things you are supposed
> to do here, we may let you do some work later. For now, however,
> you are not allowed to work!'
> 'Well, what am I supposed to do then?' the startled youngster might
> reply.
> His tone of voice might suggest delinquent delight that he had
> found an adult willing to collude against the usual adult demands; he
> might sound extremely suspicious that he was being tricked. But, if
> as was likely, his habitual resistance to learning and his habitual
> defensiveness against a situation in which he would fail were
> defused by this approach, his response was also bound to include an
> element of anxiety. If there was nothing to fight, what was there left
> to do? He would also be that much more aware of the enormous
> emptiness he sensed within him.
> 'Well... what am I supposed to do all day?'
> 'I don't know. It's up to you. You could rest for a bit.'
> 'Rest!' the youngster would expostulate, baffled and uncertain as to
> what the smiling adult really meant.'I don't need no rest. I'm
> young!'
> 'Well, you could always play instead then.'
> 'Play!' he'd snort. 'What sort of play?'
> 'Oh, I don't know. Cops and robbers?'
> 'Do you think I'm a bloody kid or something?'
> 'Well, I'm terribly sorry', said with a smile. 'Please, do accept my

humble apologies. The trouble is that I am so very old that I am not
sure what games are appropriate when you are fifteen, but I expect
you will find something to do. Everyone else seems able to.'
And as he turns to leave the room, he usually realizes that he has just
been 'playing a game'. It's not one that he understands the rules of,
but it really feels unhurtful, albeit very puzzling.
'You're all mad here', he mutters, shaking his head at the nodding
and smiling acceptance of his last sally. Wandering down the
corridor his brain would be working overtime!

Robbed of the opportunity to fight against being compelled to do
something he did not want to do, he would then be struggling to do what
he had probably never done in all the lessons of his life. He would be
struggling to think of something he wanted to do. In that frame of mind he
would see the many 'educational' wares that surrounded him. On the
journey to the buttery to obtain a drink to comfort him in his uncertainty,
he would almost certainly pass a member of staff and one or two residents
engaged in a maths lesson, perhaps in the dining room. Whatever the
reasons for that venue, the oddness of it, especially in face of his own recent
conversation barring him from 'work', would certainly cause him to notice
the activity. Wandering elsewhere, he might put his head round the door
into the hushed and beautiful library. Someone else, as junior as he, might
be curled up in the huge leather armchair by the fireplace, absorbing the
studious atmosphere generated by the wise, old members of the community
working away at their examination courses. Eventually, feeling uncomfortably out of place, he and his junior peer might both leave the house
itself to run out into the park. Half an hour later they could be found up a
tree, or exploring the river bank, but in either case engaged in what had
been recommended to them – the experience of play.

The grounds at Peper Harow were ideal for use as a 'play' studio by
older adolescents (see Chapter six, p. 114). The park had been developed
out of the river valley. Advantage had been taken of its looping course, so
that some views from the house, halfway up the northerly side of the
valley, were projected along a length of water, as well as across the river
to hills that rose several miles away beyond the Surrey Commons. Because
of the carefully tree-framed vistas, contrasted with sweeping panoramas,
it was difficult not to be aware of the park's exceptional beauty. It was
presented to them at a time of life when adolescents are capable of being
intensely sensitive towards natural beauty. Many of our residents come
from areas of inner cities where there is little encouragement to sense the
beauty of one's surroundings! Nevertheless, our newcomers' first response
was not usually to the beauty of the eighteenth-century cedars of Lebanon,
and the great oriental planes that had been planted especially as an
inheritance for our own century; for them the park was a place to explore.

At a distance from the house was an elegant bridge leading to our neighbour's land. You were not supposed to but you could explore underneath it and cross it to see dangerous cattle – all fierce bulls of course!

You could almost fly – especially if you closed your eyes - by swinging on the huge rope that was tied to a cedar branch that overhung the river. Sometimes four of you could swing together to drop by accident, on purpose, into the river itself! You would be covered with mud as you crawled up the bank. Nobody minded the mess you got yourself into; only if you crossed the front hall dripping with mud and leaving a trail of footprints would you annoy other people. You could wallow in the mud yourself to your heart's delight.

Along the bank of the river Terence had converted 50 yards of mud into a battlefield of gun-emplacements, trenches, and various military redoubts for his army of toy soldiers. Terence was aged 16 at the time, but there was at Peper Harow both social and physical space for him to play like a child. At the proper time for this kind of play, the misery of his family's collapse obliterated the desire to play. Terry was weighed down for years with suicidal depression. Another loner, Howard, who had been locked in an attic for several of his childhood years, built himself a cabin on stilts in the river itself. In both cases, their play was an expression of profound importance. In both cases, this expression was part of a transitional process whereby Terence and Howard had each begun to move from an emotional state of shock and paralysis to the sublimation of their traumatic experiences into creativity.

Youngsters could help themselves to fruit in the orchards, or anything else that grew in the walled kitchen garden, and they explored the barn and greenhouses, not always with the most fortunate of results. Yet, these forays enabled them to express and experience many of their internal conflicts in a 'language' for which the predominantly verbal activity of group meetings, or of discussions with senior peers, or with members of staff, were not adequate on their own.

When trouble arose from the youngsters' activities in the grounds, they were often called to account in the community meeting, and it was then that the link between the way the youngsters functioned when freed from the constraints that a more obvious programme would impose and the disordered way they perceived themselves and their surroundings were made more plain. I certainly would not want to romanticize this too much. The issues were often extremely serious, as was the behaviour that had made them manifest. At one time the chickens were sexually assaulted; at another a puppy disappeared without trace; the cat was thrown from a third-floor window; a goat died from neglect; the geese had their wings broken and were found trailing in the parish churchyard as worshippers arrived for Sunday morning Communion! Liam, who kept pigeons with tenderness, also transfixed them with a stake in some diabolic ritual. Mickey kept squirrels and a jackdaw in his bedroom, where the jackdaw covered the furniture and bedding with excrement. He, at least, was persuaded to build a superb and more appropriate aviary in the grounds!

Our attempts to encourage these youngsters to relate with live creatures were not successful. These incidents were not daily events but we concluded that, irrespective of the benefits arising from the presence of animals, their suffering in the interests of the youngsters' development was too heavy a price for them to pay. The neighbouring church, itself, also received the dubious honour of enabling the expression of certain youngsters' disturbance. They broke into the underground boiler house, sometimes apparently only to smoke a surreptitious cigarette, but at other times there were stories of their fantasies concerning the desire to dig up graves and to engage in rituals to frighten themselves with at night-time. Not surprisingly what often lay behind the surreptitious cigarette, that could actually be smoked openly anywhere, turned out to be related to past death or separation experiences.

After one such incident, the boy concerned was being questioned in the community meeting. Everyone was puzzled as to why Ronnie went to the effort of breaking into the church boiler house simply to smoke a cigarette. He could offer no explanation. Then Max, who shared a bedroom with Ronnie suddenly blurted out 'When did your Dad die?' It turned out that the night of the break-in was the anniversary of his death. Ronnie had forgotten. Though he had some months earlier told Max that his father was dead, he had not been specific about the date. In the dynamically alive context of the community meeting Max had suddenly got a hunch that the events were connected.

For several years the number of youngsters who had seriously attempted suicide before they came approximated 65 per cent of the total number! One such attempt had been made by a youngster when he was only 9 years old. By a miracle he had been found and recovered consciousness in hospital without even any apparent brain damage. Such serious destructiveness, whether directed towards self or another, was obviously critically important to understand and resolve. So was the cruel or callous attitude to weaker, living pets or farmyard animals. Unless the springs of such attitudes were resolved, one trembles to think of the abuse their own children would receive in the future.

In therapeutic terms, the grounds were a dynamic location in which fantasy could be enacted and so contribute to the stimulating of verbal exploration. At the same time, the grounds were very much a nurturing resource, in which the nourishment took the form of play in line with Erikson's model of childhood development. It is this aspect of the experience that relates especially to the youngster's later educational programme. It took some time for this possibility to become clear to us so that we could actively promote the process that potentially existed.

Following the closure of the approved school's trade-training departments, the consequent departure of the vocational instructors, and the physical conversion of these workshops into studios and study rooms, a period of about two years elapsed before an educational programme was developed that was deliberately related to the overall purpose of the community. As new staff arrived, so the youngsters who had been selected as suitable for the new regime were increasingly reaching a stage where they were able to invest energy and motivation into more formal learning. During this period new staff exercised their own initiative and various experiments began to develop.

One member of staff was responsible for a frightened and speechless newcomer. For some intuitive reason he thought the new boy would respond to electronics, and so he did. An old, abandoned room was soon filled with the entrails of television sets and Lennie was soon absorbed, at first getting things to work and later converting the wreckage into sculptures. He eventually obtained some welding equipment and began to create sculpture from images within him, rather than from the preformed *objets trouvés*. Indeed, during this process, Lennie found his tongue, too!

How another member of staff persuaded 'Bootsie' of the importance of Greek literature, I never understood. Recorded on film, though, is an epic performance of the Oedipus trilogy over the member of staff's kitchen table. In the case of Oedipus, 'He who came seeing, went forth blind', whereas 'Bootsie' reversed the experience. His new insight, stimulated by his studies, gave 'Bootsie' a wider perspective of Peper Harow as a community whose collective and therapeutic nature of itself encouraged the clarificatory enactment of personal dramas. These cathartic revelations, in a similar way to classic Greek drama, then liberated the maturation of qualities that had previously been inhibited. Although 'Bootsie' eventually decided to return home instead of going to university, he took with him a very different self-image to the culturally barren one with which he had arrived.

Another member of staff began to teach the history of art. She and her husband often worked together, their Oxbridge accents and academic backgrounds contrasting with the less couth contributions of their Gothic admirers. Asked if he had some idea of what the pursuit of Orestes by the Eumenides must have felt like to him, 'Bootsie' replied, 'The Eu'oo? Oh, the Furies ... them barstids ... this is what 'appens when the fuckin' Furies comes ter get yer.' His disquisition left one in little doubt of his understanding of Orestes' dilemma, yet his expression would certainly have made examining dons anxious about his educational progenitors.

We encouraged another brilliant youngster, Trevor, to paint on the wall of his room, as he would not commit himself to anything further from his bed. Trev drew an eye of unimaginable power. Blake might have conceived of such a penetrating glance. Craftsmanlike the skill may have been, but the visual statement made by the wordless eye was staggering. Month by month Trevor was encouraged and coaxed to draw more. By the time he left Peper Harow he had still only managed half a face. We never got further than speculation as to why he found the completion of anything so impossible. Years later he had a complete folio and was persuaded to reveal it to an astounded London art dealer, who immediately offered him a one-man show. The same night Trev tore all his work to shreds!

A studio was opened as more and more youngsters, impressed by their senior peers' status-gaining achievements, put brush to paper. We were fortunate to have a succession of quite outstanding art teachers. Their aim was to create the wish in the youngster to express himself. It was only after the youngsters recognized the need themselves that the teachers introduced the techniques that would better facilitate expression. Much later this policy produced difficulties for youngsters attempting O and A level fine art exams. Many achieved only mediocre passes. However, when they presented portfolios for admission to art college, the authorities were utterly astonished, for they recognized the touch of powerful originality in all they saw.

So many youngsters wanted to do something that we decided to open a second studio, for those who could not yet concentrate for more than 5 minutes and for those who only wanted to watch others making things. This studio became known as the foundation studio. Because it introduced activities relating to very early or pre-school learning, its grand title was devised to save the sensitive face of a 17-year-old. It was essential for our youngsters to experience success despite their incompetence and sense of inadequacy. Thus, staff began to teach photography. Given carefully contrived situations, the youngsters could always produce something. It was magic for which they, somehow, could take legitimate credit. A photographic dark room was opened in the main house and, by the time the first public exhibition was held, some amazingly original and talented work was being displayed. A pottery studio, consistently producing exceptionally creative work, had existed in the approved school and was one of the very few traditions that bridged the transition. A sculpture studio was also developed from one of the original workshops in the coachyard. So was a humanities studio. This enigmatic and adult title was also intended to sugar the major learning deficiencies of many of our youngsters. The humanities studio paralleled the early learning activities of the foundation studio but its special purpose was to reconstruct the roots of verbal and numerical ability.

After two or three years it was obvious that the hour-long community meetings that we held every day also made a significant impact on the language development of our youngsters. About one-third of the membership of the community meeting consisted of staff, whose linguistic competence often impressed the youngsters. However, what most effectively promoted language development was how urgently it was needed for the sophisticated communication that the meetings were about.

Many of the residents picked up half-digested bits of psychological jargon that they then used to impress visitors. The youngsters would start to do this after they had been at Peper Harow a few months – and they did so partly as an attempt to identify with the community. With hindsight it appears that they were also playing with the words and their meanings. Again, this underlines the function of play as the way by which learning skills first become established. After about eighteen months at the community, the residents ceased playing with technical terms. Three or four years later, if they used words like projection, defensive mechanism, and transference, they were used correctly and only in order to describe therapeutic processes.

The subject matter of community meetings always was complex. Trying to make sense of relationships, trying to describe feelings, and trying to describe their origins required the youngsters to develop new ways of thinking as well as speaking. Frequently, the adults used words in the community meeting that the youngsters did not understand. This was partly because the adults were caught up in the group drama themselves, or were struggling themselves to clarify issues. Sometimes staff lost their teacher's objectivity that enabled information to be presented professionally to the youngsters, and in the most easily assimilable way Instead, staff had been drawn into the ranks of emotional explorers. This change of role both taught another kind of lesson about adults by implication and also helped to develop a different style of teaching. Fairly often someone would ask what a particular word meant, and a halt had to be called to explain it. In terms of language development, therefore, the community meeting was always seen as educational, however much its prime purpose was also therapeutic. It was also an inherently dramatic situation, which therefore provided a context for communal play, both with ideas and with language. This context above all emphasized the close relationship between intellectual and emotional learning.

The staff themselves designed the humanities room, which was situated in the old coach house and stables building, built by William Chambers in the same year as his orangery in Kew Gardens. They look very similar. The foundation studio was put next to the 2–D studio quite deliberately. The kind of learning in the 2–D studio arose naturally from the kind of learning made possible within the foundation studio. It therefore seemed essential that the humanities studio should also be juxtaposed, with activities in the coachyard that could follow on naturally.

The humanities studio looked as unlike a classroom as possible; it was carpeted and curtained, and the staff decided to put in leather furniture in order to associate the room in the minds of the youngsters with the flagship, educational room – the library – in the main house. There were no blackboards, and equipment like overhead projectors were all provided with cupboards designed to contribute to an atmosphere as little like a classroom as possible. A house magazine was composed and published from the humanities studio called 'Uz', which, while the title reflected the sixties background of many of the staff, was not a magazine of the 'underground'.[2] Almost everyone was persuaded to contribute something to it. The magazine was filled with poetry of the widest content and quality, with crossword puzzles and drawings.

An edition of the magazine was usually produced at the annual public exhibition. This exhibition took place in the front hall where the neighbours were invited to share a glass of sherry with the youngsters, who conducted them around a display of paintings and writing and sculpture and photography of amazing quality. A carousel on the projector displayed the slides of the year's expeditions and summer camps. There was always a wonderful standard of pottery. The pottery had been established next to the photography and music rooms in the main house.

Music was a later development. There had always been one or two youngsters who played the guitar and who demanded electronic opportunities. We had numerous 'groups' who brought all other activity to a standstill with their powerful amplifiers. Competition between heavy rock and folk musicians extended into competition between the best drummers and so forth. In the service of the power-wielding competitors, amplifiers burst their membranes and twitchers and tweeters lay down and died daily. The cost rose higher and higher until even the musicians were glad when I cried 'Enough!'. We were very fortunate in obtaining the part-time teaching of a famous rock guitarist from an internationally starring group. Thereafter everyone wanted to learn the guitar – but classical guitar was what he insisted on teaching them. As older residents rose up the musical grades, so they were able to encourage newcomers. Several of the staff were also able instrumentalists and, eventually, every special community event, like the Christmas and Summer Feasts, was followed by a musical concert, often of a movingly high standard. Initially, classical music was heard politely, but with the passing years with rapt attention. The community knew all too well the years of daily practice that had gone into a Chopin étude that was now being so tentatively presented. The significance of a quartet of flautists actually capable of co-operation was certainly as important on these celebratory occasions as the most virtuoso performance or sophisticated composition.

In the late seventies, youngsters who left Peper Harow were beginning to go to university, art college, and music college. It was astonishing to think that many had been educationally retarded when they had arrived, some being hardly able to read and write. One springtime, a heartening confirmation arose of our view that youngsters could devote phenomenal energies to their studies once they had been set free and been imbued with a sense of worthwhile group identity. I came into the house early, about six o'clock, to find a group of senior boys who were taking various exams in the summer, on which their futures would depend. They had been working in the library for about an hour. I expressed my astonishment when, at about half past seven, they came out to get breakfast going before getting the rest of the house out of bed. 'Well, there's little choice', they said, 'It's no use us spending all day in the Library. We need to be out influencing others in the Community when they are around. Then there's all the meetings so, unless we can get a couple of hours in when everyone is still in bed, ...' I thought it must be hard to get up every morning like that, but they explained they had a pact. If anyone could not get up, then the rest saw to it that he did and got down to work with the rest of them. Here, indeed, was peer-group pressure put to a good cause, and it is gratifying to relate that they were all successful in their academic aspirations.

Indeed, two of these boys, after taking degrees and qualifying, are now members of staff at our new community, Thornby Hall. It is fascinating to see their influence and that of the one or two ex-Peper Harow members of staff on the rest of the staff, who are new to that particular way of working. The programme is necessarily different because Thornby Hall is for a younger age group, but the style is similar, as is the recognition of the need for the practising of creativity through play, as a precursor to formalized education.

Thornby Hall does not have a foundation studio. Its pubescent youngsters go to a place called Garfield. Apparently, there is a cuddly, animal-like, television creation called Garfield and somehow this became the name the children called the room. Garfield contains all the toys and equipment one might expect to see provided for much younger children. These pubescent and early adolescent children are increasingly able to play uninhibitedly as though they actually were much younger. It is an experience many of them missed when they were younger. The staff who play with them clearly understand the significance of this playing time as the foundation for more age-appropriate learning. At Thornby Hall, as at Peper Harow, the physical relationship between the studios, classrooms, and laboratories reinforces the message that disturbed and deprived children need to be part of an educational process that contains psychotherapeutic as well as intellectual and social influences.

The laboratories came much later at Peper Harow. For years we struggled to establish maths and the sciences, as well as languages, but these were subjects that required you to be right or wrong in fairly stark terms. Basic maths and sciences do not allow one to exercise one's ability to be self-aware or tolerant, or to turn an elegant phrase, or to propose an ingenious view of history. It is not possible for a right-angle to be other than 90°! The question of two plus two requires to be faced four-square.

Our youngsters' uncertain and therefore anxious response to such an unequivocal question was likely to produce the wrong answer even to the simplest numerical problem. It took a great deal of rebuilding of a sense of self-worth before mistakes were no longer automatically seen as evidence of their abject failure.

Even those who finally left Peper Harow to go to university were still sometimes assailed by such self-doubt. Their sense of personal worth and their academic ability were almost totally intertwined. It was bound to take still more years before they could accept themselves as fully equal with others. Without the pre-learning opportunities and the freedom from what in their earliest days at Peper Harow would have felt like persecuting academic demands, they could never have arrived at a situation where they could be eager and thirsty for knowledge, and where they could delight in their achievements.

The requirements of the new General Certificate of Secondary Education examination will be very hard to meet for our youngsters as so much depends on continuous assessment. That has advantages for the ordinary youngster who may not cope at his best with examinations. The examiner can receive a much wider perspective of an individual's ability than can be provided in the old General Certificate of Education Examination. Our youngsters at the ages of 16 or 18 could not possibly have the same wide knowledge base of their peers. They have to spend most of the time, which the normal youngster following his school course can devote to a wider understanding of the subject, in developing a basic ability to learn. By the time they are capable of consistent study, little time remains in which to prepare for an examination. Skilled teaching and careful subject choice gave our past students the basic entrance qualifications they needed. The opportunity to extend their knowledge and catch up with their peers was preserved. It is a dilemma our current staff are engaged with, and no doubt further understanding will arise from having to resolve it.

The other problem never fully recognized when I was director of Peper Harow concerned the management of youngsters with specific learning disorders. Walker Home and School in Massachussetts, which I visited after leaving Peper Harow, underlined this issue. Because of its reputation, two out of every ten children who arrived there had been diagnosed as suffering from a learning disability but, after further testing on arrival, I was told that actually eight out of those ten showed some learning dysfunction. There were many reasons why minimal dysfunction might be overlooked. Walker's view was that, unless the disability was remedied, then the child would not be able to achieve his own proper educational level. Walker recognized that many of their pupils were also emotionally disturbed. However, their future depended on educational as much as on emotional rehabilitation. This set me thinking anew about the youngsters who had 'failed' at Peper Harow and the consistency of their pattern of failure. Of all those who came, about one-third never completed the 'course' of four or five years. We tried to comfort ourselves by saying that, if we took only youngsters who had failed everywhere else, we were doing very well if only one youngster stayed the course. However, so many of those leavers had a real relationship with the community. Staff felt deeply committed to them, and their premature departure was almost too painful to consider. It seemed that approximately half of those who left inappropriately did so around the time they had been in the community for two years. Another quarter of all those who left the community before we judged they were ready to go tended to go in their first six months. They had not been able to make the initial attachment.

The two-year point, therefore, seemed to have a particular significance. In fact it was when formal education usually began. Those who stayed would at last begin their commitment to regular classes, with exams beginning perhaps only a year later. With hindsight, one wonders how many of the premature leavers felt that they could never achieve this kind of success. All the youngsters who stayed beyond the initial six months had struggled on equal terms with the culture shock of a therapeutic lifestyle. Did youngsters who had an inner sense that they suffered from an unrecognized, specific learning disorder realize that they would not cope with the next stage? If this were so, they would 'know' that, compared with their peers, failure inevitably awaited them. After their rekindled hopes, such a conclusion would feel devastating. It was easier to create a conflict than to face the bitter failure of their hopes. They would become desperate to avoid peer-group expectation to begin formal education if they sensed that this confrontation would leave them humiliated as their peers advanced. It is difficult to find another explanation for the regularity with which youngsters worked quite hard at the therapeutic task and then suddenly appeared to change course at that specific point in their development.

What we did learn from our experiences was that the therapeutic and educational processes should be interdependent and should provide an opportunity for a regressive life experience. These processes should reach back to a time in their early life when they were unable to play creatively. The initial aim of this regressive experience was to teach the youngster how to play and to widen his capacity to do so in several forms. Once the youngster could engage in the verbal and experiental life of the community, he would automatically become increasingly adept at exploratory play. We were increasingly able to refine the overall therapeutic environment. We were also increasingly clear about the experiences the youngster required if his sophisticated play was to develop.

Anxious newcomers almost looked as though they were shrinking into a corner of the lounge at Peper Harow. Everything was so huge and he was so small, and so exposed and vulnerable. Gradually, it became possible to sit comfortably in front of the fire, and then progress to an exploration of the grounds. In the process of this exploration, he would find the coach-yard, where various exciting things seemed to be going on. No-one minded if you wandered in to look. In one or two places, like the foundation studio and the humanities room, you could stay and do things. You could stay and have a cup of coffee, and you could play with clay and finger paints and with messy materials similar to those that you had already messed about with in the grounds. You could look in next door, where older people did brilliant things, though you were not encouraged to talk or ask too many questions there, because everyone seemed to concentrate so hard on their work. Eventually, instead of only being a peripheral member of the humanities room, or foundation studio, you would spend quite a lot of time over there. When you were not in your group, or doing your household job, or taking your turn at cooking, it was likely to be open. Sometimes the staff who were regularly in one studio or the other would be meeting together and they might even discuss what might be fun for you to do. After a while you would want to do things that required much more skill than you had, but you were told that, if you were going to be taught, then you would have to promise to stick to the lessons and not simply leave when things got difficult, because they required patience and concentration. Then you could come to realize the obvious fact that the next step would be to take an examination course. By then you would already be formulating larger goals and would have a very different conception of yourself than the one you arrived with.

The juxtaposition of park and coachyard and house; the overlap of learning and arts repeated and reflected qualities that unified the signifi-cance of the separate places. All this produced a programme that educated as it nourished and healed, and in which all the community's experiences became increasingly integrated and, accordingly, enabled consistent strengths to be internalized.

Chapter eight

The treatment process of a total approach

Residents' normal adolescent problems are amplified by inadequate psychological development in infancy and childhood. Resultant destructive behaviour needs containment in psychodynamically orientated, socially age-appropriate peer group.

Psychodynamic processes in the large group - focus of the total community.

Issues of authority, control, pathological functioning like scapegoating and therapeutic qualities like containment, play, differentiation between fantasy and reality, and the formation of identity.

Small groups – their historical and organic development. The multifunctioning 'guru'. His therapeutic task and his integrative task.

George Lyward used to say that the Roman God, Janus, should have been the symbolic deity of adolescence. In the same way as January was felt to be looking back to the past and forward to the future at the same time, so by its transitional nature does adolescence. Nor is it easy for any adolescent to assess how well he is managing his conflicting feelings. In his struggle towards balanced independence, he is increasingly unable to depend as in childhood on his reassuring parents.

In the struggle to escape the dependency of childhood, adolescents often look for models of adulthood other than their parents'. Yet, in usual circumstances, no-one would have provided greater security in the past than their loving parents. Therefore, even normal adolescence is likely to be experienced as a time of loss, as well as a time for the excitement of increasing independence. The parents of adolescents must now change their identity too and they may not find such an upheaval much easier to cope with than their children. For many years the predominant self-image of these adults has been that of parents. They can hardly now become the kind of people they were before they were parents; that role is now for their children to take up. It is small wonder that the family security of earlier years often seems lost when both parents and children are struggling with their separate identity crises. It is therefore unsurprising that the adolescent, whose predicament is acknowledged by society, and particularly by his peers, often falls into seemingly stereotypical ways of answering the question, 'Who am I?' His dress, his mood swings, and his iconoclastic declarations, present him as a typical adolescent, but it takes a remarkably well-balanced parent to cope comfortably with someone so alien to the child he fondly remembers.

Unlike normal adolescents, ours have an additional handicap. Our adolescents have not had the good, early life experiences that come to the rescue of even the most chaotic boy or girl. Normal adolescents know who they basically are; for them adolescence is only the final mountain range – however difficult – between dependent and independent identity. Erikson suggests that normal children of whatever age always know both who they are and in which direction they should travel. Our adolescents, who have experienced only insecurity, inevitably become distrustful, self-doubting, guilty, and fantasy-ridden. They literally do not know who they are.

The inner world of our adolescent is so sore that he can hardly bear to be touched even by the tenderest therapeutic concern. At the root of all his disturbance is the fear of unmanageable impulses, like rage or insatiable hunger, or the terrified panic arising from his memory of horrific scenes of incomprehensible violence that he has repeatedly experienced. At Peper Harow we have had children who, as babies, were held to be 'not capable of understanding what was going on'. For all that parental denial, they still suffered violence stunning to their development. These children were unable to differentiate between the violence meted out to their vulnerable mothers and the assaults inflicted on themselves. Sometimes such quarrels broke out over them, leaving them feeling guilty and anxious that the ensuing violence was in some way their fault or perhaps even deserved. An abused child is further confused by the inability to separate aspects of assaults that might have involved excitement or pleasure from those parts that were agonizing, endless, and terrifying. As a consequence, they find it impossible to identify with adults and adulthood, as we might expect them to begin to do as adolescence progresses (see Chapter nine, pp. 176–7).

There are other disturbed youngsters who have not experienced physical or sexual abuse in the past. Yet they, too, have been deprived of the emotional ingredients for growth and so their motivation towards identifying with adulthood has also been undermined, even though the reasons for this do not appear in as stark a form. In fact, their parents may not have loved them. Yet, babies need parents who do actively and positively love them. They need continual reassurance of this love whether they have sleep problems or tantrums or even if father perhaps resents his displacement by a new infant. Babies often have explosive impulses. They have no sense of boundaries or control and they absolutely need the parents' reassuring love, or they never fully learn how to manage their impulses. Such children grow up with insecurity gnawing away at the foundation of their being. On occasions, their ill-managed impulses will produce appalling behaviour, leaving them with an increasing psychosocial anxiety that they are totally bad, worthless, and so deserving of the neglect and ill treatment they have received. Pines' (1988) description of 'borderline patients' in a recent paper illustrates the treatment dilemma that a particular kind of adult patient poses, but the description is relevant to many of the youngsters at Peper Harow. Like the borderline adult, the borderline adolescent becomes overwhelmed by his feelings at times and becomes unable to differentiate between fantasy and reality. His behaviour, therefore, often seems to others to be quite mad and frightening.

> The principal affect with which the borderline patient has to cope is that of primitive rage. This is either a constant background to the patient's awareness of his own feelings, or else emerges with great intensity when provoked by disturbances in interpersonal relationships. Disappointment and frustration almost invariably lead to rage, to projection, to blaming, and then to withdrawal and self-punishment. Because of the unrealistic capacity for idealization that the patient displays, based upon the use of splitting as a predominant ego-mechanism, these patients ... often display a capacity for rapid and engulfing relationships with others. Primitive, powerful, dependent relationships are quickly formed, and invariably lead to either clinging, exhausting, emptying dependency, or else to rapid break up of relationships with blame, recrimination, and anger. Very often, devaluation of the therapist (Community) [my parentheses], and of all attempts to help, is used by the patient either to defend themselves from entering into threatening and close relationships, to protect themselves from overwhelming envy, or from fantasized attacks of a dangerous nature from the fantastically powerful therapist.
>
> (Pines, 1988)

In an adolescent community, whether of mixed sexes or not, the youngsters often display similar behaviour. The relationships Pines describes are often exemplified within what Lyward called 'pairing off' relationships. He saw 'pairing off' by two youngsters as resistance to the community's confrontation with their defensive position. There is often a delinquent collusiveness about the pairing that not only cuts the two youngsters off from the reassuring nourishment of the community, but also arouses the hostility of the rest of the group.

Sam and Charlene were individually very ambivalent about their necessary involvement with the values of the community . Both espoused 'punk' lifestyles that had alienated them from their respective families. Sam had been at Peper Harow for over a year and had been beginning to respond to the affection he received from older residents and staff. He had been starved of affection in his adoptive family, leaving him frightened, confused, and angry about why this had been so. It was clear that he would have to talk about these feelings that made him feel extremely helpless and vulnerable. Charlene's personal history explained her own need to flirt with self-degradation, and the two rapidly became absorbed in each other. Though sexual attraction was involved in their 'pairing off', their predominant activity consisted of endless talk about punk clothes and dress. They would sit next next to each other in community meetings, disruptively drawing attention to themselves but refusing to respond to the attention except with curses. Time and again they aroused the community's hostility and thereupon felt justified in getting drunk or running off to squats in London, blaming the community for their sense of alienation.

When Sam and Charlene made their final, inappropriate departure, the community was left to feel guilty, angry, and depressed at their failure. The peer group mostly consists of youngsters whose sense of integration and worth is equally fragile. Only by their combination does the group acquire the self-confidence to feel that it has something profoundly worthwhile to offer to the 'mad, bad' individual. When even the group self-esteem is rejected by the contemptuous, sneering pair who insist that they do not need the community because they have got each other, everyone is left feeling devastated.

Attempts to establish a taboo on sexual intercourse, for instance, are hard to maintain. After much bitter experience, senior members of the community will explain that this would be too much like the abuse in the family so many have experienced. Sexual intercourse is thus bound to detract from the sense of security fundamental to the community's therapeutic functioning and it is essential that it should not occur. Senior residents would also be conscious, perhaps overconscious, of the community's image in wider society, and of how eager the Press might be to focus on such a 'scandal' and how it could lead to serious consequences. But above all these seniors would be intensely frustrated by the difficulty of reassuring their peer, not only that they have no need to take flight but also that such behaviour is dangerously self-destructive. Those residents with less seniority, however, despite their generous attempts to endorse their seniors, will suddenly change from adult, integrated, and caring behaviour to the self-same behaviour of those they were trying to help. The underlying reason for this change is similar to the underlying reason for the pair's delinquency. Usually the *amour propre* of such youngsters – fragile to say the least – is not strong enough to withstand the projected badness. At one moment the resident would be saying 'We don't allow drugs here' and in the next he would either be sharing the 'smoke' himself, or else ending up in a fight with one of the pair in an attempt to distance himself from their behaviour.

It is pathology like this that requires the main therapeutic context to function as much within the peer group throughout the twenty-four hour day as it does within the formal large group. Before considering how the large group actually exerts its managerial control over the therapeutic task, it is important to recall that the peer group generally has extra-ordinary sociopsychological significance in the therapeutic community and especially for adolescents (see Chapter three, pp. 35–6).

The young person in a leather jacket draped with chains is surely enacting many personal problems at the same time. Is his dress a commentary on himself, or society, or does it reflect what he would like to do to parts of himself? Is the youngster more concerned to express his problems, or to frighten the staid adult? He may feel exceptionally isolated, and his swastikas and demon motorbike may therefore be an attempt to shock others into acknowledging him. If he joins some kind of peer group like a Hell's Angels gang, he will feel that his isolation is both confirmed by the gang's distance from the larger society, but also he will be relieved by his sense of belonging inside the gang. The peer group may thus be both helpful but also confirmatory of some of his deeper problems.

A therapeutic community group will understand self-destructive fantasies but it will also take the individual from a nurturing beginning through to changed internal attitudes. In the therapeutic community you can almost see the fantasized identity when, at a musical evening, a half-naked drummer thunders out inaccurate rhythms. The ill-practised and highly amplified musicians are a group that acts something out about fantasized pop-star identity for their peers in the audience. The music does not matter, but the image certainly does. But those same youngsters will similarly share an emotion in a community meeting. Indeed, the youngsters will identify with the individual who is being taken to task about abusive behaviour, for instance, and who ends up by sobbing as though forever; and who, between tears, pours out another appalling tale from the past, of impotent vulnerability in the face of abuse. Those who have been in such situations are close to tears themselves. Others squirm as they try to forget the sudden memories flooding back towards them. In a moment all the youngsters are caught in the arms of their mutual recognition and understanding. The group has become the mother and the father that never was.

Awareness and insight unlock the defences more than the shared tears and sympathy. Another therapeutic brick has been laid for the individual and for the whole group of individuals. When the arrhythmic drummer is beating hell out of his drums, his audience is aware of the wider identificatory statement and of the beating he has taken and occasionally tries to give. The musical evening not only symbolizes the residents' life together as a group, and that life includes their need for grief and mourning, but it also engages them in normal adolescent joy.

Whether the peer group is functioning as a large group – as in the daily community meeting – or whether as an audience and performers at a musical soirée, its same members are able to share their integrative strength and to share their needed psychotherapeutic experiences, whether ego-building, or insight-achieving. Members of this kind of peer group are able to share, despite the various kinds of resistance their un-coping and inadequate personalities have hitherto created.

One of the characteristic features of a therapeutic community (see Rapoport, 1960) is the flattening of the hierarchy and the democratiza-tion of the whole interactive process of the residential institution. Rapoport was particularly describing a therapeutic community in a hospital setting and at a time when a new generation of psychiatrists were challenging the incarcerating regimes of the huge Victorian asylums. Since then we have realized that a dogmatic disposal of organizational structure – including a hierarchy of authority – may sometimes increase stress rather than relieve it. For all that, it is essential that patients them-selves feel they have a stake in their own treatment; that they have power; that their motivation will enable them to regain an entitled independence of opinion and social position. It is recognized that you cannot pour treatment down someone's throat, only exercise the manifold encourage-ments for the patient to seek and use treatment for himself.

Hypersensitive and fragile adults often need to be handled with kid gloves by the therapist if they are to stay in treatment. Similarly, making contact with the disturbed inner world of adolescents is indeed walking on eggshells. However, relationships with adolescents cannot be on an equal basis. In a therapeutic community the adolescents are certainly not independent. Nevertheless, residents often demand greater independence than they can cope with but they then swing to a dependency reminiscent of their childhood. It is the adults's responsibility not to pretend sycophantically to some spurious notion of equality, but to accept responsibility for maintaining secure boundaries and for standing by adult standards. Some staff can cope with this more easily than others. However, acknowledging and exercising one's proper authority often produces problems for staff who identify passionately with the adolescent and against adult authority.

In Chapter four (pp. 58–9), the director was described in an early community meeting ordering a delivery boy to get out of the meeting he was disturbing. It was indeed the director who regularly stated uncompromisingly that a meeting would not start until everyone was present, and insisted if necessary that any 'mutineers' would be carried in.

Direct orders to sit down, or to sit up, were frequently given, and sometimes I would even harangue the community authoritatively about its behaviour. There was no doubt that ultimate authority lay with the director, yet, in another sense, the youngsters were perceived as having the ultimate therapeutic authority and having the responsibility to exercise that authority. Without the youngsters' own sense of authoritative significance, the community could not function.

Bedtime was ten o'clock and the lights were to be out half an hour later. This was very early for the older adolescents and often difficult to accept for the newer youngsters, who became increasingly anxious as bedtime approached. On one occasion it was raised as an issue in the community meeting with considerable anger. I was concerned to draw the community's attention to the timing of when this had become an important issue, in order to clarify how the complaint was being used to avoid the real problem. We attached significant meaning to the way the nights were managed. You often learned more about the significance of the daytime's apparent activity as the result of night-time activity than from anything else. The youngsters simply wanted a later bedtime and did not want to consider the problem their proposal would pose for staff on duty, and they certainly did not consider my enquiry as to whether their demand's apparently spontaneous emergence was a clue to some disturbance at night-times.

I said that I was not prepared to change such a carefully thought-out routine unless I felt that we had become sufficiently aware of all the implications. The community became angry. Several sessions were almost silent. While the angry trial of strength took place, the seniors did not raise issues that came to their notice. The community values were not being supported by the residents, and a significant increase in negative behaviour occurred. Eventually other issues overtook this one, which was never talked through.

In some meetings, shameless appeals were made to the youngsters' better nature. In others, their guilt was played upon to remind them of the rare opportunity they were participating in, and to which they were responding without appreciation.

In adult settings the large group is usually managed in a less focused way. Usually there is no agenda, the principle being that, if the staff resist the pressure to organize, ostensibly on the patients' behalf, then the patients will have to contribute increasingly themselves. The patients will thus also come to see that they really do have authority, competence, and a significant identity.

This was certainly not my view as to how the large group should function in the adolescent community. This is because it is ultimately the adults' responsibility to maintain boundaries. Getting the balance right is very difficult. The adolescents eventually have to become responsible for their own lives. They need practice, even if this leads to serious mistakes. Frequently there are long periods of silence. The forum becomes a hushed battleground while staff and residents resentfully feel that it is up to the other group to lead the way. All large psychotherapeutic groups at times tend to pressurize the staff into making decisions and so be seen as carrying all authority. When the staff give in to this pressure, even if their decisions are based upon accurate insight, their contributions will be rejected unconsidered. In our case, the youngsters were not interested in debating the particular issue and taking their appropriate share of authority, but only in denigrating the staff. However, if the staff can withstand this for long enough, then eventually the youngsters can begin to express and then explore their anger with the staff. If the meeting ends not with such exploration but with denigration, then a difficult day is fairly inevitable. The youngsters' sense of destructiveness would then be mobilized as a defence against their anxiety, and then later in the day it would be turned on themselves or others. Afterwards, they would be left feeling unchangeably empty and hopeless. On the other hand, one community meeting, even if it ends with these immediate results, should still be seen as only a part of a process. Sometimes the real dynamic issue may take weeks to become clear enough for change to occur.

However wilful and stubborn such resistant group behaviour felt, it actually expressed the residents' confusion about what they really wanted. The large group offered the opportunity to consider feelings and behaviour in a mode appropriate to adulthood. At the same time, the reality of such an implicitly adult expectation terrified the youngsters because they felt like helpless children. That they were enmeshed in so pervading a sense of helplessness was immensely frustrating for them. What the large group might actually be expressing, albeit in a bizarre behavioural fashion, was a demonstration of some lost emotional battle of long ago. The specific ingredients were different in each case but the overall group reaction expressed the general hurt and unhappiness that each individual had carried for years. Whatever defences each youngster had adopted in response to his ill treatment, they had proved inadequate. The youngsters' sense of self had been seriously injured, leaving them with an inescapable sense of utter vulnerability and helplessness whenever challenged to take on a new experience and new responsibility. In the community meeting a general sense of chaos would often emerge. Sometimes individuals would represent different aspects of the complex feelings of chaos through their roles of compulsive scapegoat, or bully, or clown. They would usually have a history of such behaviour, which can be seen as attempts to escape from the anxiety engendered once again by the community meeting. Whatever the individual variations – whether delinquent or self-destructive – the Large Group would frequently cause this major emotional area of pathological vulnerability and helplessness to emerge. Sometimes, as in the series of meetings referred to earlier (see Chapter six, pp. 101–3), they did not surface immediately.

The group was not immediately able to reflect on an individual's problems. Instead, it created some issue of conflict that related to the current life of the whole community. The meetings that eventually led to our recognition of the significance of food provides such an example. To begin with, the eighty people in the room all felt intensely uncomfortable. I was anxious as to whether the boys could be controlled if they were as uncomfortable as they seemed. Their sighs, sniggers, farts, and guffaws of hysterical laughter indicated their anxiety.

Occasionally someone would blurt out an angry curse. Staff would mutter encouragements or accusatory challenges about behaviour. In fact, there never was a riot in the community meeting setting, though the outburst at the end of the meeting seemed to remind everyone of the theoretical possibility. Outside the meeting, the food store was broken into. Inside, only silence greeted adult enquiries. The conflict between adult attempts to prevent break-ins and the boys' determination to do so became more determined. Perhaps we should have seen the encounter as an indicator, not only that the unknown issue was reaching a climax, but that it was going to allow expression to begin. The next stage was the bravado expression of how much damage and how much hatred had been expressed during their supposed past burglaries, and therefore we were being given an indication of what the current break-ins were trying to enact. I do remember feeling shocked and frightened by such crude hostility, and repelled by their delighted descriptions of what they had done to innocent people! Though daunted, the staff did not attempt to condemn this expression, which perhaps was the key to the next development. This consisted of individuals' personal descriptions of how they had actually been deprived in childhood and of their anger with actual parents. Thus, over two or three months, the simplest of questions actually emerged, 'Will you, the staff, look after us better than our real experience in the past?' This was the real issue hidden behind an artificially created community issue that in fact was the response to being invited to join with the adult staff instead of being institutionalized by them as hitherto.

Sometimes the large group process was not handled well and the basic issue did not emerge (see p. 142). But, whenever it did, what was revealed was the residents' tenuous ability to believe in themselves. This was the real significance of their emotional injury. The anger, eventually expressed after another series of community meetings (see Chapter three, pp. 43–4) about the discovery of drug-taking at a member of staff's house, was actually about the betrayal of their fragile trust in the staff's ability to look after them. The community meeting in which that anger was expressed had also been preceded by weeks of resentful silence and uncooperativeness in the residents' group.

Over the years there was frequent debate about the centrality of the director in the community meeting. Originally, it seemed essential to control this very volatile group. But, after considerable insecurity about my own motivations for insisting on maintaining primary authority in the large group, I eventually concluded that it was actually essential to do so. It had become clearer that the need for security was so real that some symbolizing ritual authority was required as a therapeutic crutch. When the youngsters demanded that the staff be authoritative, and then turned them into ogre figures, they were actually representing a hitherto inexpressible issue. It seemed to me that this therapeutic requirement should be focused through the director and not generalized to other staff. This might often mean that he would be locked in a raging confrontation with some recalcitrant youngster. Then the mythical tribal rite, irres- pective of the other youngsters' identification with the recalcitrant, would absolutely require the director to win.

Any situation of conflict seemed to trigger unreasonable and destructive primitive impulses into life. It did not matter that the conflict was sometimes justified – perhaps an argument about bedtime, or an argument about the time to be back after a weekend away – all normal hassle for adolescents and their families. But our youngsters' limited development caused them to react as though they were either totally omnipotent and dangerous, or totally helpless and vulnerable. If, however, the director could be ascribed omnipotent power instead of them, this then freed the meeting to consider other matters. The certainty of that authority boundary, as with a small child's consistently loving parental authority, defused panic and rage and enabled others to begin a process of reflection.

The reason that everybody had to attend the community meeting was the same reason that nobody was allowed to walk out. Residents some- times tried to. The exit was at one corner of the rectangular room. I used to sit in the centre of the short side nearest to the door. Most people would have to pass in front of me to get to the door but, if they started to do so, I was quite prepared to leap in front of them. I am less than average height and many of the youngsters were considerably bigger and stronger, yet they always backed away from such a confrontation and went back to their seats. In the rare situations where violence broke out, I was renowned for having a magical wrestling grip called a wrist lock, that even brought giants back to their seats! So, while the picture of my physical challenge was absurd, I am sure the youngsters needed to ascribe such powers to someone. The whole staff group could not be made into such a myth in the same way at all. When staff leapt to defend the door, this was understood in the same way as when a senior resident did it. It was a sign of seniority, of common sense, of upholding the community values, and of not allow- ing someone to injure themselves by their behaviour (even if this meant risking one's own nose in the process). Their behaviour related to the sane and conscious; mine could be said to speak directly to the internal chaos and pain.

Occasionally, other staff were able to borrow this mythical cloak. An Australian assistant director, with a turn of 'Strine' that was relished, got into a blazing row with a very delinquent 15-year-old. Mattie, who had been much cared for by this member of staff, poured out the most venomous language in response to every attempt to defuse his wrath. Finally, in a moment of desperation to find language adequate to curse back, the assistant director yelled with antipodean inventiveness, 'Go...' splutter ... 'stick your head up a dead bear's bum!' After a moment of astounded silence, the room collapsed in laughter, the miscreant swept along with it, and at last so, too, was the exasperated adult. The adult, having got through his genuine rage that erupted into humour, from then on fully reassured the community of the reality and purpose of his authority.

From very early days it was established that, if a situation got out of control, the responsibility for re-establishing control would be that of the entire community. And this control would be exercised at an emergency community meeting. Anyone could call such a meeting if they obtained fifteen signatures. The director could also call one. Sometimes, if such a meeting was late at night, it would simply attempt to calm things down and defer until morning any attempt to get to grips with what lay beneath the delinquent behaviour. Sometimes it was not easy to calm things down and in that case the accepted authority of whichever senior member of staff in charge became still more essential. There might only be one or two members of staff at such a meeting. In these circumstances the senior residents would all the more quickly order others to 'Do what he says!'. The atmosphere in a night-time community meeting, when only the gold room was illuminated, was often more intimate. The issues of authority were constant. Seemingly unmanageable and damaging impulses expressed in behaviour arose almost instantly. It required the director to carry a power beyond one individual, or even beyond the Group's combined authority, to demand and obtain order with ultimate reliability.

Despite the director's being ascribed a kind of tongue-in-cheek magical authority, it was not always easy to exercise. A certain ritual had to be fulfilled. The director would have to demonstrate, often in exaggerated terms, yet somehow with credibility, that the issue of the moment was enormously important. Sometimes, by implication, the community's very existence could be in doubt! Often, I would do this by roaring with rage at the behaviour. Sitting bolt upright and on the edge of my seat, and in deliberate contrast to everyone else, I would literally express enough rage to make everyone else's bad temper rather irrelevant. Sometimes I would take the opposite, histrionic path and whisper with icy fury. The quality of acting might have embarrassed the professional, bu t the youngsters were playing out a process that enabled 'controls from without' to be established, so that 'controls from within' could thereafter be exercised (Redl and Wineman, 1952).

My role was not an easy one. If my role were as consciously contrived as I have described, it would not have worked. My 'performance' also had to engage with whatever was the unspoken issue of the moment for the group. For instance, one night-time emergency meeting in the mid-1970s was caused by a disturbance in one of the bedrooms. A senior resident woke me up. The noise of the disturbance had already wakened some others so I called a community meeting. I assumed that, after I had put the miscreants in their place in a forthright manner, and supported by the senior residents, we could all have trooped back, safe until morning. However, I had misread the situation. The miscreants were not being delinquent simply because they were new and unsophisticated.

Throughout the week the senior residents had seemed unwilling either to reiterate or to explain the importance of the therapeutically orientated values whenever these had been challenged by newer residents. The daily community meetings had been desultory and, when the boundaries on behaviour had been broken, they had not been repaired. Whatever was disturbing the senior, informal subgroup, these two youngsters were acting out the seniors' resistance in the middle of the night.

When we eventually got into the Gold Room for our meeting that night, the mood was desultory. I tried every ploy to provoke a positive response, but an hour later I began to feel defeated. I then decided to call in some of the debts. I acted as though I were astonished at the seniors' withdrawal of their support for the community's values. Where would they have been without my commitment to building the community? What did they owe me at least?

The sullen mood became uncomfortable in a different way as a result of this personalizing of the struggle. Eventually Fergus said, 'OK! OK! What's the guy supposed to do for us, bleed?' The desultory mood broke and the old order was re-established, to the youngsters' relief as much as to mine. For a while it had seemed as though the group's delinquent alliance would triumph, and our ritual way of dealing with the endless conflict with authority would have to be discarded as empty. At the end of the day, we were still able to hang on to our relationships.

There was no doubt in anyone's mind how much I did care for the youngsters. There may have been all sorts of complex and contradictory motivations underlying my concern for them. Nevertheless, I must have communicated a consistency of concern. Perhaps it was this ingredient that allowed all the other positive adolescent processes in the youngsters to function. Idealistic qualities, the desire to identify with a parent figure

147

gave rise to the half-acknowledged rituals by which the youngsters avoided their usual pathological sense of inadequacy. Instead, they could use the group to enable themselves to function in an adult fashion until such time as they had really changed and could feel really in command of themselves.

Perhaps my apparently idiosyncratic and dramatic procedure is what people perceive as charismatic leadership. However, it is clear to me that this activity was not merely inexplicable and maverick magic. Experience suggests that, however hurt and inadequate these youngsters are, there is a spark of hope that still awaits the encouragement of genuine care. If this care can be provided in a group setting, then the youngster can find the resources within him to respond. The individual may hitherto have only been able to repeat inappropriate behaviour, despite being offered genuine concern. The group setting enables the individuals to use this concern to motivate them as a group. As individuals, they would take flight or worse.

Conflicts within the adult group instantly raise the anxiety of the residents' group, whose forward-shuffle then slows to an uncertain huddle on the edge of a stampede. There are bound to be these conflicts. Each member of staff will have been appointed for his creativity and for his significant personality. Adolescents respond to 'personalities', but 'personalities' often find it is hard to work together, especially when they are subject to the unconscious group pressures that push them into ways of feeling and behaving to which they are not used.

It is clear that the community meeting continually expresses both the main feelings that arise from the communal life and those that arise from the residents' psychopathology. Nevertheless, unless behaviour is contained, there will be no security for a youngster and, without this, therapeutic work is impossible. The community meeting exercises various forms of containment, from the authority with which it invests the caring leader to its regular rehearsing of agreed communal values. On occasions, the large group demonstrates the actual therapeutic process undeniably. A youngster's attempts to explain his behaviour stimulates others to relate similar feelings. One may cry at the sudden contact with buried feelings. Something lost is grieved and the mourning is felt by all. The group ends with a sense of growth and joy. However, the individual's personal problems are rarely worked through in a community meeting, though they are often partly considered. The group's fundamental belief in its worth and strength is what contains the inadequate individual's ego and that frees him to undertake a more personal journey in other settings.

When the community meeting has demonstrated containment, but also a shared emotional experience like the sharing of grief for a lost family perhaps, everyone leaves the room in high good humour, buoyant, and optimistic about their life together. Life is infrequently this good, however, and it is a mistake to look at the content of only a single meeting and judge it as a success or failure. But, if one looks at the development of the large group over a longer period – two or three weeks, or two or three months even – then it is possible to discern the germination of insight and the changing of attitude.

Another way of construing the community meeting is to see it as yet another form of 'play'. Indeed, Henry Maier, commenting on Erikson's view of play as a major ego function, tells us that:

> Play deals with life experience, which the child attempts to repeat, to master, or to negate in order to organize his inner world in relation to his outer. Further, play involves self-teaching and self-healing; 'The child uses play to make up for defeats, sufferings and frustrations, especially those resulting from a technically and culturally limited use of language' (Erikson, 1940: 557–671). 'Playing it out' is a common expression for this form of behaviour. In childhood, play activity becomes the child's means of reasoning and permits the child to free himself from the ego boundaries of time, space, and reality and yet to maintain a reality orientation, because he and others know that it is 'just play'. In other words, play is the ego's acceptable tool for self-expression, just as dreams afford expression for the id.
>
> (Maier, 1968: 24–5)

While Maier and Erikson seem to be discussing children particularly, it was clear that our adolescents at Peper Harow had also missed out on play at a crucial developmental stage. The therapeutic environment at Peper Harow was designed to encourage regression, so that adolescents can find ways to play that are child-orientated, as well as ways to play that are adolescent-orientated. For the adolescent, the ego is not so much concerned with making sense of the family and its environment as young children are but rather with the development of identity towards adulthood. The activities of adolescence and childhood are both forms of 'play'. For instance, the adolescent identifies with and then rejects different kinds of music, styles of dress, and so forth. By doing so, the adolescent gradually becomes clearer as to his own identity.

If the normal child 'plays through' the problems he encounters until they become manageable in his mind, we have to remember Dorothy Bloch's important contention that fantasy makes this growth-promoting play possible, but fantasy becomes ineffective for children who are severely deprived and traumatized (Bloch, 1979). Their fantasy play only repeats endlessly, perhaps obsessively, but little gets 'played through' (see Chapter seven, p. 117).

Everyone recognizes that the kind of unconscious drama enacted by the community meetings is in a sense unreal. Ordinary people do not conduct daily large groups to assess their lives. Yet, the community meeting, in a way, freed the participants as a group 'from the ego boundaries of . . . reality, because they know it is "just play"'. There are real dangers if this kind of play makes the participants forget the reality of the world beyond and encourages them to see everything only in terms of unconscious dynamics. (Baron, 1987. Here it appears that the community's collapse was brought about when even the patients' attempts to collect their social security money was interpreted psychodynamically, rather than realistically).

At Peper Harow, 'reality' was often discussed in the community meeting. Sometimes, as we have seen, reality was often the outside enemy in the shape of the Press or the Department of Education and Science who, in their various ways, might threaten the community. Their apparent threat may have been partly realistic, but it is often easier to blame outsiders for limiting what can be done than to address one's own limitations.

Generally, the youngsters were reminded endlessly about the reality of who was paying for them and why, or what attitude a court might properly take to any of their behaviour that overstepped the boundaries of the community. If the community as a whole required a conscious effort – especially by the director – to see itself in a realistic societal context, so the community meeting needed to reflect that perception by being clear about its own relationship to the rest of the community life.The meeting appropriately aroused crazy feelings that the youngsters struggled to keep buried. The meeting also needed to clarify that there were boundaries to the expression of craziness. It achieved this by clarity about the boundaries of the meeting. It took place in a special room – the Gold room – with symbolism of the importance of the meeting expressed in its furnishing and decoration. Attendance was compulsory. It was the first item on the daily programme. Its beginning and end were specific. No-one was allowed to leave before the end, or go to sleep, or be disruptive.

It is significant that at Thornby Hall the community meeting for children who are just pubescent is being developed at a very measured pace. There are daily meetings, some of which are much shorter and in which the emphasis is on factual events. In the longer meetings, it is evident how difficult it is for the youngest children to express themselves in words, though they obviously recognize the worth of the discussion of the older boys and girls. Any discussion that threatens them, they react to with singing, or giggling, or farts, or other forms of immature behaviour. An adult's responsiblity for holding the boundaries is even more crucial here, as these children are even more incapable of holding them and are even more entitled to have the staff acknowledge their adult responsibility.

If staff disagree with each other, the consequences can be very serious. The unrealistic, but understandable, anxiety becomes magnified by the meeting. The feared catastrophe of adults clashing is too terrible for immediate expression. So, alternative explosions brought about by the youngsters may occur all day. Days, or weeks, can be spent mopping up the consequences of consequences without ever getting near the situation that originated it all.

If such groups are so difficult to manage, one might ask whether the effort of providing an opportunity for verbal and fantasy play is worthwhile or even responsible. My view is that the large group in the residential treatment context is what makes sense of the whole process.[1] We have seen how both adolescent play and childhood play are essential parts of the treatment process. The specific aspects of the total life experience – such as therapy groups, expeditions, and art studios – or the less specific experiences, like the feelings around in the kitchen and the grounds, have all been conceived so as to stimulate the expression of fantasy that can reveal the inner world. Groups can also provide an opportunity once more for exercising the process of fantasy and ego-functioning through play. Physical play begins in the grounds. Its physical significance is acknowledged in the foundation studio. This physical expression is widened to include verbal and numerical play in the humanities room and it is thereafter developed into intellectual expression in the studios, library, and classrooms. At the same time, the youngster increasingly sees himself as a member of the group that 'owns' all this activity for the purpose of furthering the therapeutic objectives.

Above all, the large group is the focus where the experiences of the grounds and coachyard, the music room, and the feast can also be expressed. The community meeting's form of play is an adult one, reaching out for self-awareness, insight, generosity of emotion. It will be more difficult for our youngsters to leave this sheltered community for the outside world than for ordinary adolescents to leave their home. All youngsters engaged in that transition to real independence particularly need to be able to apply their internal resources to sustain themselves. Strength to tolerate separation, loneliness, anxiety arising from work, finding a home, friends, a place in the world, arises from a clear sense of personal worth and confidence in one's ability to succeed. The application of this inner security, once it has begun to develop, to the task of coping with stress is regularly practised in the community meeting. New situations are raised in the community meeting, like the need for a day conference. This will require a response by the residents. Not surprisingly, the initial group reaction is resistant to making an enthusiastic response. After some fantasies about the proposal have been explored, awareness of reality can develop. The youngsters can then develop enthusiasm about the day conference. The senior residents will recognize that they have passed through this process many times before and so be able to encourage others while re-establishing their own realistic response comparatively quickly, precisely as they will need to do when facing the stresses of the real world when they leave.

While the community meeting may practise its residents' ability to apply their new-found internal strengths, it must first help them to internalize the good experiences of their therapeutic life. The daily meeting is bound to be the focus of everyone's experiences and for the community's history and culture. And, because he is a part of the community meeting, even a newcomer will increasingly identify with the community identity. Every resident, therefore, is experiencing what it is like to have a sense of identity and this is an essential preliminary to the development of their own. Thus, when they leave they can the more easily carry within them the good nurturing experiences that they may have been receiving consistently for the first time in their lives.

The community meeting has many different functions (see Chapter four, p. 60). One of its functions is therapeutic change. Sometimes the form of its therapy is in adolescent play and sometimes it converts that play into a realistic appraisal and management of community issues. Above all, the community meeting expresses an integrated sense of the community identity.

These modes of functioning can also be recognized in the small groups, though they varied considerably from each other in their functioning. The small groups were established in 1970 because it was recognized that the large group produced enormous anxiety over which there was little control. This was still the time of Park House School, and identification of the mutual task for the individual and the community had not been established. Many youngsters had not chosen to come to what was still an approved school and many staff wanted the venture to fail. It was hoped that, by holding small groups immediately after the community meeting, the build-up of psychodynamic steam could be released more gradually and so avoid too much disruptive behaviour.

These initial groups, formed in the transition from approved school to therapeutic community, each consisted of eight or nine youngsters. Each group originally met twice weekly. A visiting consultant pyschiatrist and the director co-conducted the Monday, Tuesday, and Wednesday small groups, and another visiting consultant psychiatrist and the director co-conducted the Thursday small group. The Friday small group was co-conducted by an assistant director and the director. Another member of staff also joined each group to learn about group processes. At first we had intuitively wanted to experiment by not constructing our groups on formal and traditional lines. We noted that when significant members of the community sat down simply to be available, a core of youngsters always gathered round them. How much, we wondered, was this also affected by the location? If, for instance, one of our psychiatrists sat in an armchair by the fire at the same time each week, would the same group gather? Could such a way of providing groups be managed so that psychotherapy emerged organically from the overall context? Would groups like this form around other members of staff in the kitchen or the library, or the gardens, for example?

In the event, we ran out of thinking time to engineer such an experiment. Even the formally established ten small-group meetings per week were too demanding of the senior staff's time. Within a year, we reduced the groups to one meeting per week each, and it stayed that way for many years. Detailed records were originally kept, and the co-conductors met after each group in an attempt to clarify their experiences whenever time could be snatched.

The content and operation of the groups changed over the years. When the small groups first started, the numbers of residents in the community had fallen to below thirty. This allowed some selection as to which residents would best fit together in a group. We hoped that the group members would gradually establish a warm relationship that would provide the security to express and share their traumatized past experiences.

Our predominant experience of small groups in those very early Peper Harow times had been of groups gathered around campfires in the Sussex Downs, or in high valleys in Snowdonia, or Lakeland, and we expected an atmosphere that promoted the same kind of expression. On those occasions during expeditions the boys had sensed their freedom from the persecutory institution. Yet, those groups from the approved school and from Peper Harow's earliest expeditions were separated in every way from the normal task, programme, and location. So, the campfire represented an escape from reality to a focus of warmth and beauty in a rare and time-limited situation. Darkening twilight concentrated the group's experience still more closely. The contrast enabled an idealization of the experience that for those brief moments felt wondrously secure.

In the hurly-burly of an emergent community that had yet to define its direction, purpose, and mode of travel, the new groups were often experienced by boys and staff as yet another crazy and dangerous threat. They would feel dangerous in the sense that the community meeting felt intrusive, slightly mad, and occasionally persecutory. The separation from the rest of the community was only the door to whatever room the group occupied. Beyond the door, devilment and disruptions took the form of screams and arguments, enabling those within to be distracted. Undoubtedly, freely associating thoughts, freely expressed, felt highly dangerous, so there was also much silence and discomfort.

In one group, one member was eventually challenged about his long-standing bullying in the community. It was even revealed that he had threatened to beat up anyone who raised this in the group. The adults were angered at this threat to the cosy, anticipated intimacy of the group. Furthermore, the director was not primarily concerned to understand how the bully had now become the scapegoat, or that the bully or the bullied represented both sides of a single coin of human functioning! Instead, disclosure was recognized by the group members as a social compact that would thus gain control over bullying, which had hitherto flourished in secrecy. This could have been seen as representing a way to unlock the barred entrance to understanding the internal past and, because that opportunity was neglected, serious consequences developed concerning the groups' functioning. They tended to become judgemental and persecutory, with an overactive concern with righteous behaviour that seriously slowed their development.

In a way this limitation was understandable, and perhaps unavoidable. Unless one has experienced the insidiously undermining power of a subculture, it is difficult to believe how powerful it could actually be. For instance, some youngsters arriving at the approved school actually lost weight because they were deprived of even their carefully measured rations by the voracious underground 'barons'. They lived in fear until they were sufficiently senior to function in a similar fashion. We were so properly anxious to get rid of this evil that perhaps we were not too aware of the repressive potential of what we were trying to replace it with.

Nevertheless, over the first three or four years, the small groups did change their character. This was made manifest in two ways: one was the changing of the general content of the groups' deliberations and the second related to the importance the general community ascribed to the small-group opportunity. After two or three years, a group of residents usually gathered informally around the exit to the group room, or in the buttery, specifically in order to enquire how the group had gone. This informal group was concerned to see if anyone had been particularly distressed. Sometimes one of them had been engaged, in the darkness of the bedroom the previous night, in a discussion that caused him to encourage his partner to 'Talk about this in the group'. Had he done so? Once this sort of commitment to the small groups had become established, any disturbances outside the group room were immediately stopped by other members of the community. A reluctant newcomer was looked for and brought to the group by other members of the community.

But as well as the different valuation being placed on the groups by the rest of the community, the content also changed a great deal. Initially, as we have seen, the content was predominantly about behaviour in the community. Inevitably, it took in the individual's more personally related behaviour. Non-return from a weekend at home, for example, would end with discussion in the group, as in the community meeting, trying to clarify exactly what had happened. The small group had more time to move from discussion of facts to focus on the significance of the backgrounds of the individual members of the group. Eventually, we heard, often expressed over several weeks and with great suffering, the story of one boy's early hospital experiences over much of his early childhood; of another's setting fire to his father's clothes in a wardrobe before he could speak; of exasperated mothers, who in a moment had become an archetypal witch chasing the children with the inevitable carving knife.

The sensitive and gradual clarification of what they had actually felt at the time of these events, and how they had tried to cope with those feelings, and how that was reflected in current functioning, was much harder to achieve. It always is, of course, especially as the other youngsters, whilst somehow sanctioning the release of this material, could hardly tolerate the pain of such revelation. So many of them had endured similar or worse experiences. Yet, their defensive disruption often felt just as intolerable as the exposure. In the middle of such a story another youngster would pretend to sleep, snoring loudly. Others would protest angrily. Attempts to perceive scapegoating as an avoidance ploy could hardly be considered, for the original sufferer would by now be threatening to leave the group or the community, or threatening to kill himself or the disrupter. In a second, time and again, the room had become like the mad and drowning internal world of the individuals.

The nature of admissions had changed since the previous approved-school days. There had always been a handful of apparently borderline youngsters, who were sneeringly dismissed as 'the nutters'. Not only did they express in their behaviour the hidden fears of those whose different, angry behaviour conformed to the delinquent group culture and was therefore accepted, but they were easy scapegoats and so had a role to play of temporary value in that particular scheme of things. Not only was the defensive effectiveness of the delinquent, attitudinal formulation removed when the therapeutic community had begun to function, but an increasing number of youngsters were referred who were, in fact, hardly able to maintain any kind of personal integration. They were volatile, labile, often on the edges of breakdown, and requiring much greater management by the adults in the group than had originally been envisaged. Later, when staff leading the groups had begun to go on courses, and when a proper supervisory system had been established, the groups' tolerance levels increased with their more specifically skilled and resourced management.

Another set of difficulties arose when the community had become co-educational in its tenth year. The effects of the often sexually provocative, unlimitedly volatile, and vitriolic girls on the ostensibly stable and caring group of boys were conflagratory! Such an outburst occurred in the 'good mother' kitchen, as it had become, one evening. In an instant, the 'fatherly' approach of the respected senior resident was rejected by a shrieking, foul-mouthed harpy. No pretty, innocent newcomer only calling up male protective concern – or even sexual excitement – here! Suddenly, a terrifying, unmanageable hell-cat and the respectable senior young man cowering in speechless collapse. To an onlooker, the light of intuition said, 'So this is what his kitchen at home is really like!' In such disturbed families these incidents were frequent and the boys had been protected from having to deal with this reality, or indeed from the extremity of their own attitude towards their own mothers and women in general. Being denigrated and robbed of identity by 'protective' patronization was the least assault the girls themselves had experienced.

It is very difficult not to be a creature of one's engendering society, but the backgrounds of our residents made the worst of the male–female struggle. Their mothers had actually been horrifically beaten by berserk thugs, and had actually endured the nightmare of rape. Indeed, the girls themselves had experienced such things. What are only many people's shameful fantasies were actual experiences in their background and the compulsions to re-enact, rather than deal with them in some other way, were very powerfully present.

The girls coped with their originally overwhelmingly, male groups by passivity and by silent refusal to contribute. The splits in the staff group were often re-enacted there. Until the community experienced women as appropriately significant in their own right, these issues did not begin to ameliorate. It was perhaps the clearest reminder that, not only has one to keep in mind how both individual and group dynamics are components of group functioning, but also organizational dynamics that relate to organizational status and power are equally significant, and they are very much influenced by the wider social ethos of the time. If they cannot be successfully managed, then the potential for psychic healing is almost bound to be reduced.

Because the groups were limited in what they could achieve, there were needs that could only be fulfilled through the resident's relationship with his special individual member of staff. In the approved-school days the building had been approximately divided into four areas, delineated as houses, and each house was in the care of a housemaster. His role inevitably derived from the way that kind of institution saw itself. The role was intendedly benign and therefore the boys were expected to have a relationship with their housemaster, by which they would be morally influenced. The title was borrowed from the approved school's attempts to model itself on what it perceived as good, public school principles. But the title is important for it communicates a great deal about the institution's perception of the task.

Because they each promoted inappropriate messages about the individual relationship, such titles as caseworker, counsellor and, above all, key worker were avoided in 1970 when, despite the recognition that individual adult responsibility for each resident was required, we also looked for a relationship that stemmed from the individuals, rather than from some institutionally perceived task. Mahareeshi Yoga and the 'All You Need is Love' Beatles were still close memories at that time so, as a joke that could be understood and shared by the youngsters, I referred to staff as gurus. Images of their personal member of staff looking like Mahareeshi Yoga appealed to them mightily! Since then the term has become embarrassing, yet, as so often occurs, it seems to have stuck despite the forgotten origins.

Very few staff have any training as psychotherapists when they arrive, yet they are quickly subjected to overwhelming transference phenomena that would provide difficulty for the experienced psychoanalyst (see Chapter nine, pp. 161–4). By and large though, the individual resident requires a special kind of companion rather than a psychotherapist. The guru's therapeutic role is to be a listener, a person with whom the resident can increasingly practise his ability to trust. He will be someone who is continually tested to see whether if in the end he will be rejecting in the way that all other relationships seem to the youngster to have ended. The experience with the guru has to enable an increasing reality to be accepted. He cannot love the youngster unconditionally, but frequently has ended up by becoming a real friend.

The guru would also be responsible for two or three other residents, and the difficulty in sharing and being shared are very real ones to be worked through. It is obvious how important this is. It can be seen that the better the relationship with the guru, the easier it is to compare him symbolically with the youngster's real family. It is important that, by developing a nonjudgemental relationship with such a family, if it still exists, the guru will fulfil a valuable therapeutic task of countering the tendency to lapse into disturbed and polarized relationships. Instead, relationships with such a family can be retained on a realistic level and, at its rare best, enable its functioning to be integrated with that of the community.

The guru, then, will be involved in apparently normal staff activities, such as teaching and possibly leading a small group. He will clean and cook, and go on camp. In short, the usual professionally differentiated tasks of care worker and teacher – to name but two – are fully integrated for all staff engaged with the professional task. They are all paid on one pay scale, irrespective of professional origins.

This undoubtedly complicates the member of staff's task. He may have been engaged in a long wrangle as to why his youngster should not go home for the next weekend. The youngster knows his guru is probably right, that, with the home situation as it is, a visit now would be as big a disaster as ever. However, he cannot bear not to be at home when goodness knows which of his fantasies are being enacted there. Moreover, at his age he is bound to chafe at the control that his guru is exercising.

Irrespective of their wrangle about the guru's authority to prevent his going home, if his member of staff is also a maths or an English teacher, he would have to put his resentment aside when part of a group of four or five other youngsters whose task was to learn maths or English. How are the boundaries to be maintained? The next day the guru will be around when the youngster is supposed to be cooking. It will be quite easy to disrupt the class, the community's meals, the small group, and hassle the guru into anything but the issue in hand.

On the other hand, the awkward resistance in the kitchen to providing others with good food, when he feels he is being deprived himself, makes crystal clear sense to the guru, who would have debated this as much as anyone. He knows what is going on at home; he can see clearly how the educational development can become disrupted in response. Nevertheless, it is only the guru's task to share the management of such a youngster. Central he may be, and of prime importance at times, but so, in their turn, are other members of staff, the small group, the bedroom group, and many others. The guru will also need personal supervision to enable objective evaluation of the differences between what he feels and what he thinks the youngster feels. The guru will want to see emotional growth, but can recognize that this will occur, not because of his Messiah-like relationship with the youngster, but because of the multiple presentations of the community's therapeutic messages. The guru will be keen to help the youngster relate experience in the group to his individual experience. He will encourage the youngster to talk in the group, to express commit-ment to the community in the large group, to participate in the annual exhibi-tion, the musical evening after the feast, and in the manifold experiences that, as an integrated whole, provides the nurture and the understanding that makes for real psychotherapy within the overall context.

Chapter nine

The limits of hope and inspiration

*Initiating awareness in youngsters of unconscious processes as a
potential pathway to understanding behaviour and becoming
happier.*
*The transference phenomenon as it arises in the community and its
significance in individual psychotherapy. Complex issues for groups
and for individual adults arising from transference relationships.*
The scapegoating process and ways to control it.
The nightmare scenario and the failure of control.
*Importance of focusing the positive community experiences and
identity on the director.*
Issues arising from damaged psychosexual development.
*Understanding the psychic processes and managing sexual
behaviour.*

Disturbed young people are aware that their life is going increasingly
wrong. They see their peers getting on with each other, while they feel
isolated. Compulsions to steal or to be aggressive overcome them, despite
all struggles to resist. Time and again, delinquent youngsters seek punishment, swear they will try again, yet, with a sinking feeling, recognize that
their remorse and good intentions will come to nothing. Forces exist
beyond their control and their understanding, and that realization is the
nearest they come to a recognition of the existence of their internal,
unconscious world.

Adolescents arriving for interview had already been told that the
community could help them (see Chapter two, pp. 20–1; Chapter five, pp.
91–4). Peper Harow would be able to help them to understand their
problems and to achieve things, but very few had an inkling of how this
could happen. During their initial visit and interview they would be
struck by the different atmosphere, activities, and functioning of this
rather awesome place, and the seeds of hope would once more stir in
them. Perhaps what they had been told was true; they could be helped after
all. I would go to great lengths in their formal interview to nurture

159

their sense of hope, and that interview often became something like a demonstration of the process at Peper Harow that would enable their lives to change. I would ask the youngsters about family relationships, and very quickly they would encounter a fundamental dilemma. 'But if you imagine that your Mum never really wanted things to go this way, how do you suppose they came about?'

One of the two representatives of the residents might say, 'My Mum's like yours, but she doesn't know why she does it. Now I tell her what she's doing, but she still can't see. Mind you, she had a hell of a life when she was a kid'. Further discussion with the resident will clarify how his mother's behaviour reflects that 'hell of a life'. The discussion will enable the interviewee to share the recognition of the more experienced participants that distressing behaviour need not be wilful and that it is often prompted by unconscious feelings. Thus, implicitly, the participating interviewee would have perceived a new non-judgemental way of thinking about his life. Perhaps, after all, he could develop a sense of control and so avoid behaviour that acts out his own 'hell of a life'! Perhaps he might even be able to choose to behave in ways that would allow him to realize the aspirations that other youngsters of his age have. Indeed, the residents talking so sensibly in the interview, and those people playing guitars so beautifully by the lounge fire, might be demonstrating just that possibility!

The interviewee leaves to think about the offer of a place just made to him, excited at his glimpse of a new world and of himself in the cloak of a new identity within it. Now he will have to think about his experience and write to confirm his personal acceptance of the place offered. When he finally arrives at the community after all the arrangements with his local authority have been completed, he will feel like someone who in desperation has finally acknowledged the need for psychotherapy. Such new residents have overcome the anxiety that expressing their worst fantasies will only confirm how mad and bad they are. They have risked the ultimate rejection; instead, they have been accepted as worth working with, and their sense of relief may be considerable. The adolescent feels totally grateful to the adult in the adolescent community who threw him this lifeline. Imagine then his shock when speedy change of mood leaves him feeling suspicious and extremely hostile to the one who had so recently rescued him.

Perhaps a first experience of this reversal of mood might occur in a community meeting when the director presents a completely different image compared with the warm, humorous, and understanding member of the interviewing panel. If the newcomer's hope is not dashed by this ogre-like metamorphosis, then perhaps the desultory quality of the meeting might undermine it, especially if the tone of the meeting is actually expressing the residents' hostility. In such circumstances, the resentment that each individual resident carries within him will suddenly be aroused. Like everyone else, the newcomer too would inexplicably find his buried resentment and hostility aroused because of his unwitting involvement in the group attitude of the residents. Only the most senior resident would recognize the ground they had crossed so many times before. Perhaps in the darkness of the bedroom an eloquent though unfamiliar fellow resident might have been scornfully destroying the treasured image of hope in this good parental figure for the newcomer. So the next day, without a moment's uncertainty, he would feel convinced that he had again been betrayed by an adult whom he had foolishly trusted.

In reality the adult need hardly exist for this loss of hope to occur. Supposing that the director had played the part of a tyrant in the community meeting, the newcomer would be unlikely to consider that there might be reason for such a demonstration of authority. The youngsters are frequently bound to experience group life in much the same way as they have experienced family life. They will then perceive adults as though they were their actual parents. This transference is, of course, an unconscious process. Fortunately, the group, as well as being a significant setting for arousing unconscious fantasy, can equally provide exceptional control over group behaviour. Its variations are like the individual's, even if written somewhat large. Thus, it can demonstrate the craziness within the group at one time, and the group's exceptional maturity at another.

Transference is a psychic phenomenon whereby a patient experiences his therapist in the same way as he experienced a parental figure in the long-buried past. Someone who becomes trapped at an early stage of development often fails to differentiate between people outside the family and people within the family. Even those of us who are not actually trapped will find that our relationships today resonate with those relationships in the past that we had with our parents and siblings. But our very damaged youngsters are frequently unable to differentiate between the adults they encounter today and their very first experience of adults who were their frequently exploitative parents. As a result, these youngsters tend to perceive significant adults now either in the same way as they saw their parents in the past or as the compensatorily longed-for, idealized beings that never exist in reality.

In individual therapy, the therapist will quickly feel that he is feared and hated by the patient. This is because the patient has submitted himself to a relationship that makes transference possible; that is, to a relationship where those feelings and thoughts that had their roots in the patient's earliest connections with others can now become played out. As a consequence, the patient will behave in ways that seem to defy logic, though the unconscious purpose of those ways is to defend against something fearful while at the same time trying to express what is so troubling. Thus, the patient may be oversubmissive when there are matters to be debated; he may accuse the therapist of aggressive attacks, and he may try to present his actions in a way that will gain the therapist's approval, though they may not merit it. The patient in a transference relationship reacts to the therapist in the same way that he found necessary to respond to his parents at a much earlier stage of life. Hence the patient is compulsively likely to assume that the therapist has to be placated, appeased, and defended against.

As suggested in earlier chapters, the terror was in actuality beyond definition and so extreme as to cause the defences to be exceptionally massive. Therefore, while it may be easy for an uninvolved observer to conclude that these transactions between the patient and therapist are unrealistic, the patient will resist recognizing that his feelings are unrealistic. As soon as the patient accepts that his feelings are not based on reality, he must conclude that they are based on fantasy. Exploring his reawakening consciousness of his fantasies will put him closely in touch with long-buried feelings that originally gave rise to those fantasies, often in order to protect him from that painful reality of long ago.

The human therapist may momentarily tire of wandering through the self-defeating maze of the patient's attempts to remain without insight. The patient's instant recognition of such boredom will instantly confirm, not that his desperate manipulations are boring, but that he himself must be bad! Even the most skilled therapist cannot avoid this situation. Neither can the most skilful therapist entirely conceal his own feelings about the patient. And this counter-transference in turn springs from the therapist's own formative relationships in the past that have made him the person that he is. Thus, the therapist must inevitably experience both positive and negative counter-transferential feelings. But the object of the therapist's training is to alert him to what is occurring in individual therapy, even if he cannot immediately understand what is happening. The therapist will be evaluating continuously why he has come to feel this or that at a particular time, what emanates from himself, and what emanates from his patient.

Transference and counter-transference processes in group therapy are more difficult to manage in some respects, and in other respects more easy to manage than in individual therapy. The group's identity is complex in its own fashion, for it includes each individual's personal problems as well as their shifting relationships with one another, and with the group as a totality. Yet, each individual is helped by each other's encouragement to press on with their mutual journey. Unrealistic responses to the conductor of the group may not inevitably cause wasted hours of wrangling because they may be balanced by the different perceptions of other group members. Sometimes the group does become united in defence of a crazy stance, but, at other times, it can very much enhance the therapeutic endeavour. The preoccupations of individuals may also more accurately pinpoint the less obvious group concerns faster than might occur in the one-to-one situation.

For instance, in one group, Alistair talked tonelessly about his mother's recent visit. He was a senior member of the group, as were Roddy and Terry. They offered a series of apparently helpful questions, to which Alistair contrived to respond with little apparent emotion. Suddenly, Howard, who had recently joined the group, began to cackle and shriek with laughter. The group's first reaction was to be angry about the disruption to the apparently caring discussion. The members then assumed that Howard's disruption was defensive, as the discussion was 'too close to home'. Howard, whose mother was indeed persecutory, merely said that he was bored! What Howard's behaviour eventually revealed was that the seniors were being defensive rather than he. They were identifying with Alistair but were also unconsciously intent on keeping their feelings about their own individual mothers at bay with their apparently thoughtful questions. Howard was not conscious of the denial process in which the others were engaged either, but his unconscious awareness compulsively forced him to act out his anxiety that had been intensified by the older boys' defensive denial. To what extent were the man and woman co-conductors of the group also colluding with the denial because of their own anxieties, both about being and about fearing persecuting mothers? In this example, therefore, we see the group being both supportive and collusive. Yet, we also see that the group could derive insight into the meaning of its functioning from examining what at first sight was apparently disruptive behaviour. Part of the impulse towards denial arose from transference relationships in the group between Alistair, Roddy, and Terry, and the woman co-conductor, but, because of both co-conductors' individual counter-transference responses, this was not recognized at first.

Many of the ways in which the psychotherapy group functions are also observable in the informal groupings as they occur throughout the wider community. My basic tenet is that psychotherapeutic understanding should inform all aspects of the community's functioning, so that all experiences, whether social or educational, become mutually reinforcing. Successfully achieving a general level of age-appropriate maturation depends on the integration of these experiences within the culture of the total community group. Of course the particular content, whether psycho-therapeutic, or social, or educational varies in emphasis from situation to situation. Though discussion about the youngsters' fantasies would be seen as specifically appropriate to the individual or group-therapy situation, the therapeutic worth of those fantasies would not be ignored, even if the discussion arose in a totally informal group of youngsters in the buttery.

In the individual therapeutic relationship between a member of staff and his particular youngster, positive counter-transference that generates a powerful concern for the youngster must surely be valuable if it resources the member of staff's essential commitment, for example, to a person whose depression feels wearing and whose suicidal ruminations cause much anxiety. Of course, the member of staff himself must continuously assess the significance of his own feelings: at which point, do they reflect his own gratification and perhaps begin to make him dependent on the youngster? To what extent is a youngster's depression and suicidal threat unconsciously intended to generate and manipulate the member of staff's counter-transferential concern? The youngster may feel that such manipulation was essential in his family, or it would not have offered even minimal concern for him. While this may not be realistic, the youngster's despairing feelings about his family must inevitably become manifest, in one way or another, in the one-to-one treatment setting.

Additionally, it should be remembered that adults and adolescents are often engaged together in community activities that are not necessarily aimed at psychotherapy. It is essential for a member of staff functioning as a teacher to be able to share the delight of his pupils at the fusion of responses that a poem creates, and for that teacher to develop the discipline of methodical study. The adult should surely be able to share the wonder and creative pleasure of the Christmas Feast with the youngster. It is the total group's rich humanity that reassures and nourishes the youngster once he has become an integrated part of it. The staff make available to the young people rich and varied opportunities for healthy relationships with adults; in turn, the young people's therapeutic endeavours also put the adults in touch with much of their own unresolved adolescent experience. The excitements and crises of everyday life in the community provide essential learning experiences for the youngsters, and through these experiences, as much as through group therapy, or the individual relationships, opportunities are provided for the young person to re-evaluate and acknowledge his changing psychic relationship with the world. However, sharing in the youngsters' development also offers a similar psychic experience to the members of staff. Many ex-staff acknowledged the radical changes in their lives that had been generated by their experience at Peper Harow.

Although a psychotherapeutic experience is not the only requirement for our disturbed adolescents, it must certainly be of the highest priority, especially when it arises – as it should – out of the general life of the community. However, though something of the enriching experience is bound to rub off, and while practice in verbal communication and in conceptualization, in the partially regressed community meeting for instance, must improve psychosocial competence, unless the insights and other emotional nourishment are finally internalized, the individual cannot make the eventual transition to independence. Ensuring that internalization takes place requires those with therapeutic responsibility to ensure that the individual is actually recognizing the significance of what the experiences of the community mean for him, how and why his recognition and responses are changing, and thus how his psychic competence is strengthening. Sometimes this will require the member of staff positively to encourage his youngster, for example, to stay for a holiday, join an expedition, continue with the Grade V music exam, in order to practise experiences of special significance for him. Sometimes it might mean examining the nature of a relationship with another youngster and perhaps combining with that other young person's member of staff, so that they can examine this relationship in a group context.

Not only are there a myriad of psychotherapeutic opportunities towards which the member of staff needs to be alert, but often these same possibilities frequently arise – as it were – spontaneously in the studio, or library, or over the kitchen stove. It seems an impossible task for the one member of staff to be able to encompass so many skills at all, and, even more, to know at which point to change professional hats. As well as being alive to the everyday transactions of the community, the member of staff's emotional position in the organization also varies. For instance, every member of staff is both a follower and a leader. In the former, dependent position the member of staff relies on his leader, with all the conflicting feelings this entails. But when in the leadership position himself, the member of staff has to develop a special kind of sensitivity, both to the youngster's feelings, his psychic needs, and all his resistance. Staff must be leaders and guides for their adolescents. While psychotherapy is specifically relevant to their task, it is mostly so in the way that its formulation of human experience can clarify and promote healing through everyday experience in the community.

I suppose that my absurd, though seriously intended, statement that defined the kind of staff we needed as those who were 'expert in broom handling' illustrates this (see Chapter four, pp. 53–5). The staff's university education denotes their ability to learn new concepts. Nevertheless, they need to develop a special instinct if the broom is to be valued so as to 'make drudgery divine!' In the approved school it often seemed we were obsessed with cleaning. Scrubbing floors with gritted teeth seemed almost flagellatory and therefore was 'good for you'. The member of the therapeutic staff, who saw the community not so much as 'doctor' but as 'mother', could also communicate to his adolescent cleaning colleague the need to treat the house as a valued object, to care greatly about the task because of its symbolic meaning. Thus, an activity as ordinary as cleaning the house could potentially raise important issues and feelings through its physical and material language.

In the first year or two of the community's existence, and before its legal status had changed, many governmental pressures were directing

Park House School, as it still was, towards becoming one of the new community homes. The trustees of Park House School, who on change of legal status would change the name of the Trust to Peper Harow Community, felt very sure that the risky, innovative work they wished to see undertaken at Peper Harow would not be possible under the aegis of a local authority (see Chronology, p. xviii). When we became a special school we were fortunate (see Chapter one, p. 6 and Chapter two, p.23) in encountering Michael Walker as the civil servant with responsibility for the Special Schools Division of the Department of Education and Science. It certainly seemed that, although his inspectorate disapproved of our apparent lack of good order, he grasped the principle of what we were striving to achieve, and so we obtained his department's support when we most needed it.

The Children's Department of the Department of Health and Social Security was particularly anxious to fulfil the intention of the 1969 Children and Young Person's Act and see all the approved schools consigned to their latest bureaucratic slot. The Children's Department seemed little concerned about, or able to judge realistically, the kind of work we were trying to develop. The government-supported community home schools, albeit having millions of pounds spent on rebuilding in order to be the flagships of the changed provisions resulting from the 1969 Children and Young Persons Act, allowed little insight from developmental psychology or psychotherapy to affect their programmes. The same old attitudes practised by the same staff in new buildings still provided the value-judged resources they assumed the youngsters would need. Various directors of social services tried to persuade us that we would be free to do our own work under their aegis, but, at a conference some four years later, they sadly acknowledged that they had been wrong to do so. We needed maximum independence to have done what we had intended and what by then were achieving.

It can be imagined though that, against these politics of survival, finding an outside enemy on which to focus aggression was easy. There were authorities with real power anxious to prevent our following our chosen course. Whether or not our prejudice was justifiable, the fact of its existence made an unhealthy attitude towards the real world beyond the therapeutic community very easy to develop, with the long-term consequences that arose from it.

In those early 1970s we were very anxious that we would be closed down, for so we had been threatened. When we arranged our first day conference it was to confound our critics with the number and status of our supporters. All through the night staff and youngsters had worked to ensure we would be seen as efficient, despite our apparent lack of good order. An old film made in 1973 illustrates, through some of the comments of the youngsters themselves, the expectation that 'they' would be negative, that 'they' were hostile and needed to be guarded against.

And how well the community worked together at that day conference. Similarly, with what solidarity was the director supported when he set off for court – a frequent occurrence then – to persuade the judiciary to give our miscreant one more chance! I fear we shared too much paranoid pathology in the supposed service of our therapeutic opportunity. In a sense our youngsters were especially prone to deal with their own painful sense of badness, not by a realistic evaluation of this feeling and its excruciating origins, but by blaming outside agencies. To the extent that people outside themselves had actually damaged them, it was an exceptionally convincing defence – except that using it led only to more personal alienation and to no alleviation of the corrosive, internal assumption of worthlessness.

Closely related to this sense of being persecuted is the psychic mechanism whereby one ascribes to others the negative intentions of one's own fantasies. Believing those others to be hostile, the whole variety of defensive behaviour can then be mobilized in support of the paranoid delusion, once more further entrenching a self-defeating rather than a growthful way of functioning. Other unrealistic projections equally fall into this purposeless line, though they effectively bar only healing and growth.

Scapegoating is one example of these projections and is a major problem in therapeutic communities. I suspect it is made worse when the staff set the lead by blaming the outside enemy and call on the youngsters to unite against it. A most serious consequence of scapegoating among suicidal, dangerously self-destructive youngsters arises from the fact that each is partly eager for punishment. They misguidedly imagine that their badness can be expiated with enough pain, degradation, and punishment, so there is always a volunteer for the role of scapegoat. That 'badness', of course, is rooted in unconscious fantasy that their bad behaviour also partly expresses. What remains more deeply unconscious, and thus unexpressed, feels even more dangerous. Such youngsters have such a poorly developed sense of psychic self-control that unimaginable horror frequently feels imminent and even severe self-punishment provides only very short-term relief. The person whose behaviour frightens or creates immense hostility is very difficult to tolerate. Other residents demand that this person should leave; the staff who have been kept up night after night also feel this. 'If they cannot fulfil minimum standards of behaviour then they must go! Otherwise, other innocent people will not be able to stay.' This may be true, but when that youngster is expelled, his departure can hardly be talked about. There are fears that the worst, omnipotent fantasies have become true. The residents actually have the power to kill off rivals! The residents become angry, feeling that the incident should have been prevented somehow and that now they are all that much more insecure. Polarized splitting is another unconscious group consequence. If the staff are not all-powerful and able to defend themselves and others against the worst the residents can do in their omnipotent fantasy, then perhaps the staff themselves become perceived diametrically, as powerless and inadequate, and therefore dangerous for a different reason. The youngsters cannot make up their minds, as it were, whether they want the staff to feel dangerous or not. Another surge in incomprehensible anxiety occurs causing yet another desperate 'volunteer' to test the process out. Once more, after much frustration with the new scapegoat candidate, the old community hue and cry is raised and another victim adds to the emptiness of the sacrifice.

When youngsters are being abused, they are undeniably aware of the pain, confusion, and anxiety they are experiencing. While they may respond angrily to their parents, they frequently suspect that they deserve their suffering because they themselves are fundamentally bad. Even if they were vaguely aware that the abuse reflects their parents' disturbance, this only increases their anxiety. Their straightforward, angry fantasies could be seen as a logical response to being abused, but uncertainty about the consequences of their own hostility becomes turned back on themselves to protect their parents who might otherwise be destroyed by their fantasies or who might cease to offer even a crumb of parental affection.[1] In foster homes and children's homes they act out their fear of incipient badness until what seems to them like confirmatory rejection becomes inevitable. The community's task is to ride out this compulsive demonstration of what the individual unconsciously feels. Instead, the community often colludes in the self-destructive compulsion. Someone who lights fires, who breaches the community's agreements about unacceptable sexual activity, or who robs the neighbours, does indeed jeopardize the rest of the community. Such behaviour, however, is often compulsive and not simply callous. Therefore, it cannot be halted quickly and finally. For the youngster to be able to change such behaviour requires the clear growth of insight to have occurred. Instead of recognizing this, the outraged community often demands the expulsion of the infuriating offender.

While no-one has yet found a pefect method of managing this self-destructive and scapegoating interaction, its worst consequences can often be avoided if the adults remain steadfast. It may be necessary to deal with an arousal of the scapegoating drive with increased structure and containment. One example would be the temporary holding of extra community meetings.

In an ordinary community meeting, Brad complained bitterly that Albert had broken three bedroom windows the previous evening, and the room had been freezing all night. It turned out that this was the fourth or fifth day in which Albert had broken a total of eighty or ninety windows! The maintenance staff could not keep up with replacing them.

Eventually, Mickey cried out, 'If he can't stop smashing our home, he should leave!' Albert's recalcitrant response was to spit a mouthful of obscenities at little Mickey. After a totally frustrating hour, everyone turned to the director to await his ultimatum, which, of course, everyone knew Albert would immediately break. Scapegoating was about to become an inevitable ritual.

Instead, an extra meeting was called. The director announced there would be continuous meetings, with breaks for meals, until the issue was resolved. He was not prepared to expel Albert. The residents had not come to be expelled but to help each other find another way. However difficult, however hurtful, and however long, he expected all the residents to help him save Albert from his self-destruction. 'It's us he's destroying!' shouted Brad angrily. But the appeal had been to the group's adolescent idealism, so the meeting quickly became absorbed in debating the relationship between breaking the community's windows – its eyes perhaps – and self-destruction. It took a whole day of meetings to bring Albert's behaviour under control, and yet another meeting before clarification of what Albert's behaviour was actually expressing occurred. However, as soon as the group became absorbed in the issue of the relationship between destructive and self-destructive behaviour, the headlong drive to scapegoat and to become a scapegoat had been turned aside.

Structure, rather than sacrifice, may sometimes produce conflict between the adults. The staff group suddenly feel that they can no longer tolerate the consequences of the youngsters' dangerous behaviour. After a series of minor fires, and no certainty as to the culprit, the residents indicated such a need for reassurance that the staff agreed to take turns to stay up all night, in addition to their normal day's work. Not surprisingly, after a week of this, various members of staff attacked the director in a staff meeting. 'What right do you have to volunteer us to stay up all night? Why can't we at least have the day off? Why can't we employ some night staff? If we actually find the kid that did it, will you guarantee to throw him out?'

The general sense of impotent rage at the secret fire-raiser is beginning to be projected from subgroup to subgroup. Perhaps the staff or the director could play the role of scapegoat. In such an anxious situation, the two parental groups engaging in mutual conflict can produce quite extraordinary fear in the residents' group. A sense of either adult group's absent attention arouses the spectres of loss, deprivation, and separation, as so many members of the residents' group are haunted by such unresolved experiences in their actual past lives. They are then likely to become even more destructive because, in a state of exceptional anxiety, waiting for the anticipated, inevitable catastrophe feels intolerable. Acting-out behaviour, followed by excessive guilt, again provokes the desire for sacrifice.

In fact, the conflict was taken to the community meeting, though not

169

as conflict.

'Wasn't it right', enquired the director, 'that staff had to have compensatory time off? We'll have to cancel some small groups, visits home, lessons, trips out, and perhaps your special sessions with your guru'.

'This is ridiculous! It's not our fault that they're staying up all night.'

'That's true, but they're doing it so that you can sleep securely. Can't you give up something for them?'

'Well, what if we share the night watch with them?' asked Fred.

So it turned out that the staff obligation was halved as an increasing number of senior residents volunteered to share the wearing task. It was not long before an urgency to 'get the place feeling secure again' developed, so that the sleepless nights for senior residents and staff could end. If the task had been left to the staff, we would have continued until we dropped. Instead, the whole sense of endeavour by the residents was rejuvenated. The community needs all of its subgroups to be at least represented in the task of containment if it is not to become overwhelmed by the craziness it must carry on behalf of its members. Suddenly, youngsters were able to return from weekends, having better managed the family relationships. They returned on time. Stealing and damage in the community declined. A much greater level of spontaneity became apparent in the community meeting and in the small groups. The house was better cleaned. The obliterating noise of radios declined and more musical instruments were played around the house. Lessons seemed to go better and people arrived on time. Most noticeably, that overall barometer – the amount of milk consumed in a day - declined by as much as a half!

When George Lyward first told me about the milk barometer being an unfailing measure of communal anxiety, I was amazed at the simplicity of such an indicator. Yet, at Peper Harow too we found it to be surprisingly accurate. At Finchden, however, their churnful of milk was often ruined before it could be drunk and provide its 'maternal' relief. When we created our specially designed buttery, we concluded that we would no longer leave the responsibility for looking after the 'good mother' so completely in the hands of so many mother-hating youngsters. Instead of an open churn and ladle we instituted a refrigerated milk container such as is seen in cafés. It was loaded with two five-gallon packs of milk that were attached to two taps. Despite its unromantic cuboid shape, there was no doubt as to what it represented; various curvaceous motifs often were added by our artists' ingenuity and the occasional one word of poetic appreciation, 'Mother!' It was also bashed and vitriolically cursed at times, especially when the packs were found to be empty. There were always spare packs kept in the main refrigerator in the food store, so there was always a constant supply of milk in perfect condition available.

At Peper Harow, as at Finchden Manor, in times of the greatest stress we found that as many as six packs would be consumed in a day compared with the usual two. This is another example, of course, of the active and flexible response built into the living experience that produced behavioural control, and, at the same time, met a therapeutic need. We had no doubt that, without this symbolic experience being immediately available, the behaviour at times would have been intolerable.

Nevertheless, the panic that overcame youngsters had sometimes in the past been met by a frightened and thus an unresponsive mother, or child-care worker. In early life it would have been normal to respond with such oral love on demand at certain times. The opportunity for this to be experienced, albeit in surrogate form, was essential if the youngsters' future positive parenting was to be addressed. Thus the psychic experience of the provision of milk related to infancy while the form in which it was provided related to adolescence. That is why it fulfilled a complexity of needs that otherwise could only have been expressed by frustrated temper tantrums – though of adolescent proportions! (See Chapter six, p. 103).

The importance of providing milk on tap in order to meet volatile need would not be appreciated by most visitors. Indeed, when the various mechanisms for satisfying primitive and basic needs were working well, the community would appear to be functioning on its own without staff having to do much. The senior residents, having been up early working, would wake the rest of the house. Staff in community meetings made fewer contributions, the youngsters the most. The meals were prepared with no apparent adult involvement and were cleared away conscientiously. Staff reported that trips out were a pleasure! Bedtime occurred on time and spontaneously. It was all rather like a good family in which there is no need for carefully negotiated legalities in its relationships.

Unlike a good family, however, it cannot last for long. The residents, in the face of such warmth, comfort, and security will divide into two groups. One group will be amazedly relieved that, after their own years of struggle, they are at last capable of resourcing such a group and of being resourced by it. The less senior group, still caged within its members' lifelong defences, shows a reluctance to accept such a peer-group 'family'. Its members have longed to be part of one for years – but they are now most afraid of losing it. They know even by the tolerance accorded to them by senior residents that they will progress to a similar relationship with the community if they stay, but that, if they do stay, they will also inevitably have to give up the community 'family' in time. From their existing, unnourished position, the recognition of having to give up such an embrace, at the same time as they are considering taking the risk of finding out whether it really is what they have longed for, creates an extreme anxiety of indecision.

It is easier for them to strike out at the community, to force it to withdraw its implicit offer, to reinforce their bitter sense of exclusion. Thus, behaviour that strikes at the heart of the community begins to challenge its functioning at those times when its functioning is going really well. Staff and physically weaker members of the community are threatened with violence. Tantrums embarrass a group in the local town, and often the more understanding the community the worse the behaviour seems to become. 'Despite all our efforts...', staff write wearily in reports, and sadly too – and even despairingly.

At such times, problems of leadership increase within all the community's groups, so that maintaining a fundamental sense of purpose and hope becomes more difficult. Staff must often feel bewildered and overwhelmed. The extraordinary commitment required by this kind of residential work is emotionally draining. Nevertheless, the emotional hurly-burly in which staff are also engaged personally, either through the reworking of their own internal world, or through coping with and managing the feelings that the youngsters off-load on to them, makes the adults' task especially challenging to their own emotional stability. So many of the various interactions in which the staff are engaged have no clear meaning – not immediately at least – or are beyond their power to relieve. Staff are inevitably rendered helpless again and again in the face of the human hurt and damage with which they struggle. Long, long experience accustoms one to the inevitability of being rendered helpless without accepting it resignedly, and that same experience reminds one how more often than not the impossible does resolve itself and thus that which is most feared evaporates. But the average member of staff, while possessing the youthful energy and physical resilience needed for this work, cannot also have had that long experience and so he must rely upon those more senior and especially the director.

The emotional conflict for staff, between a sense of grateful dependency and an infantilized resentment at finding oneself once more the 'child' in the 'family', is bound to become alive yet again. Nor is the situation any easier for most people who lead, for, despite their role and their experience, they, too, may have no certainty as to how a crisis is to be handled, beyond the knowledge that they have come through before, and that they must do so again because so much depends on their doing so. The director is likely to be muttering to himself, 'Why can't they just get on with the job and stop wittering like so many kids!' Of course, the staff are likely to be grumbling, 'He doesn't seem to care about us at all. It's all right for him, he just leaves the community meeting and goes off to hob-nob with all those people outside the community.' The senior residents will very quickly reflect this scenario themselves, wondering why 'Everything in this community gets left to us!'. They will immediately go 'on strike', to which the staff might respond by becoming more punitive through critical and sometimes sadistic comments in meetings, or they will start grumbling about inadequate salaries, or the need to timetable their commitment 'more realistically'.

Inevitably, then, when a youngster, partially in response to the community's atmosphere, broke the agreed boundaries of behaviour – smoked dope, or had sexual intercourse perhaps – almost everyone would righteously begin to demand their exclusion. The temptations to reject the offender are powerful, for all the youngsters are, at best, vulnerable ex-addicts to the delinquent, emotionally self-defeating way of functioning in the face of stress. They know how helpless everyone in the community is rendered if one of them refuses to acknowledge the rational and adult-orientated boundaries of behaviour that support the community's culture. These boundaries of behaviour, mutually agreed at times when the community had been functioning more positively, seem to be the only boundaries that exist, the majority feel. They are, therefore, clung to desperately. If individuals treat the community values with contempt, then the rage in response is murderous.

If the director attempts to buy time and wait for a calmer opportunity for a more caring appraisal to occur, he is likely to be obliquely attacked himself. He will be seen as inadequate, disorganized, emotionally exhausted. The demands to exclude the offender may drive the director, too, into extreme behaviour. A young member of staff may have been attacked. Frequently this member of staff will have unconsciously provoked the attack, having become caught up in a process that might, in fact, pertain to generalized feelings by the youngsters as a group about the whole staff group. Nevertheless, if the director is aware of the possibility of being similarly caught up in the conflict, and if he then makes special efforts to resist verbal attacks on him, and does not respond in like manner, he is likely to be castigated as being unable to cope, and certainly as being uncaring about the staff.

These situations are extremely dangerous. This is when youngsters run away and may indeed endanger their lives. Those youngsters prone to suicidal compulsions become quite desperate. Arsonists set fires. The community's functioning collapses.

This is the nightmare scenario of a therapeutic community, for the residents, the staff, and the trustees. Once the nightmare has occurred, it is extremely difficult and expensive in human terms to bring the community back to balance. However, when it is in a state of balance, it is extremely difficult to convince people that the nightmare really is always only just around the corner. All adults concerned with the community, most of whom will not have a sense of being in control of it, and the youngsters, because of their fragile sense of personal security, will powerfully deny the possibility of collapse. It is extremely difficult for the director to persuade everyone to treat the possibility realistically, without exaggeration, or without mobilizing the scapegoating process. Staff and trustees often interpret statements about such dangers as if they are being politically manipulated, especially if they are made with requests for increased resources that seem very difficult to find, be they time, or money. 'The director really does make very wild statements. He is just trying to off-load his anxiety onto us. He is just trying to protect his back, in case he can't manage the situation!'

Obviously, even in the face of such denials that the nightmare is always close, the director must try and maintain even an unappreciated balance within the community. It is not easy to describe the series of interventions that will counter the powerful group pressure for him to do his hatchet job on its behalf and sacrifice a line of willing scapegoats. If witch-hunts are possible in much larger social and national communities, then it can be seen how powerful such tendencies are in an intense therapeutic community.

In principle, the director needs to be aware of where a current inter-group conflict is likely to end long before anyone else can imagine that possibility. He can then introduce clarifying reality in the largegroup, before everyone else has become so anxious that destructive events start to occur even faster than the opportunity to consider each of them. He can do so in ways that are appropriate to the community's culture, and in ways that would enhance the community's experience that it is capable of controlling wild feelings and behaviour.

The general interchange between the small groups, the community meetings, and work between individuals solves the issues of confidentiality. Discretion is always important of course – the priority of disclosure being that it would be in the youngster's interest. However, when a resident is able to talk about the similarity between his family situation and the community in the here and now, this encourages others to talk about their experiences, and to examine their behaviour realistically. This is especially so if the youngster is not involved personally at the time of such discussion in some kind of shocking behaviour. As the result of such contributions, someone, who is at that moment overwhelmed by difficulties, and who may be overwhelming everyone else with their behaviour, can more easily come to recognize that they are not alone but that they are part of the whole community in which everyone runs into similar difficulties from time to time. This is an example of how the process of one individual's flight into behaviour can become 'owned' by many, re-establishing a secure sense within that individual that his behaviour is actually under control. Everyone else, too, can see that their individually inadequate control can be sufficiently supplemented by a united community. Anxiety then reduces, and the opportunity to reflect and to receive others' caring increases.

Humour, especially when allied with stark truth, often provides a simple way to defuse the runaway sequence of feelings and behaviour. It is up to the director to describe the processes that are occurring in the community, in clear, non-persecutory terms and 'to play a straight bat' in the face of those activities, personal attacks, or derision of the community's values, for instance, whose object is to deny what the director is not afraid to state openly.

The director needs to cope with the sense of betrayal he may experience, or with his anxiety, in the face of such united resistance, that perhaps his perceptions may not be correct: he may doubt his previously confident ability to manage this enterprise after all. He will be privately confronted by these doubts even if he is convinced that he does recognize the process that is occurring. There will also be many times when he does not. Will the community then benefit most from the true acknowledgement that no-one knows what is going on, or from his apparent but false self-confidence in the face of everyone else's behaviour?

Herein lies a great problem for such communities. It is easy to make the case for outside support for the director, that would enable him to remain objective and emotionally resilient and fresh, but there are very few consultants who can combine the knowledge of the residential situation in a sufficiently sophisticated way with their general consultant 'know-how'. In the end, the director is on his own with the hatred generated from his willingness to demand from the staff and youngsters more than they have assumed they could endure, in order to control the uncontrollable. If the staff and the youngsters are united, and their 'enemy' has temporarily become the director, then at least that enemy exists within the safety of the community. As a consequence, there is a chance that they will all be able to address the real problem. If the problem arose from a significant number of the residents feeling threatened by the undeniable caring of the community, then the residents will have to find a way of considering the significance of the community's nurture without having to reject it. Alternatively, the staff once more will have to cope with rejection by those they love, without either feeling destroyed, or having to destroy them. The director must stand as best he can for the therapeutic resolution of these states of affairs, and he must do so consistently, so that his position can be clearly recognized at times of real crisis.

Some people would say that, in a democratically and maturely organized community, the director should not need to carry so much responsibility. Its weight could be shared. Indeed, they might add, such focused authority encourages the staff to become dependent and so inhibits their own professional development that would enable them to take increasingly important decisions. Responsibility focused so much on the director does pose real dangers. I am sure that on occasions my decisions were based on grandiose rather than realistically assessed assumptions as to what I could achieve. Staff and youngsters are often forced by the dynamics of such focused, structural authority to collude with the director, so that they all march off in the wrong direction. Nevertheless, the staff have a very special psychotherapeutic potential in the therapeutic community, but it is of a kind that requires them to engage personally in a very special experience if that potential is to become maximally effective. They must constantly be aware of what it feels like to be vulnerable and dependent if they, in turn, are to handle the youngsters' necessary dependency on them therapeutically. As well as being aware of the youngster's emotional situation, staff will also need to manage their tendency to identify with the youngsters' sense of vulnerability. Through their own experience of their relationship with the authority of the director, they will need to help the youngsters move from resistance, to dependence, and on to independence.

The youngsters also absolutely need to have a sense of their dependence on the community. To bring this about, that relationship needs to be personalized in the director, who most represents what the community stands for. The staff have to understand that need, and they also have to know what such an experience would be like for the youngsters, or they will not be able to help the residents make that essential identification. Of course, both youngsters and staff would rather avoid the personification of the symbolic representation of the community in the director, for it is acutely uncomfortable to be aware of hating an actual person whom all reason tells you you should appreciate – or indeed to experience such overwhelming emotions at all. However, a therapeutic community is not like a product-producing organization. Its task is to exist between the unconscious world of its residents and the reality of where they should psychologically exist at their age. The central task for staff, therefore, is to co-exist in that partly regressed world alongside the youngsters. It is through their experience of being part of the psychodynamic melting pot of the community that the staff's intuition and creativity will be sharpened, thus enabling them to communicate increasingly effectively with the youngsters, while simultaneously helping to keep the therapeutic experience within the behavioural boundaries of its residents. The community as a total entity manages this most successfully by engaging with the residents' tortured, unconscious lives, not by commandment, but by providing symbolic communications with those lives that answer the questions they are barely aware they are asking. The staff's own psychodynamic relationship with the director actually provides part of the therapeutic learning experience as a result of its own development. The staff, as a result of their own emotional sharing of a similar psychodynamic relationship, are then able to facilitate the youngsters' learning.[2]

Obviously, the manifold issues of sexuality are of major significance to such a group. Many of the youngsters have been abused in ways that affect their ability to develop a clear sense of their sexual identity. An adult who had achieved some perfect ideal would be clear about his gender preference, and therefore would not be personally threatened by others. He would be able to differentiate between the different kinds of loving experience that could be enjoyed – as a child, or as a parent, or as a husband, or wife, or intimate friend. Perhaps their sense of ease with intimacy, and with their own masculinity and femininity, are what allow emotionally mature adults to express themselves creatively in sexual activity.

Our youngsters are even further from such notional maturity than the majority of their peers. Someone who, at the same time as they were being tormented in childhood by sadistic, physical violence, had also experienced some excitement may eventually re-enact that mixture compulsively (see Chapter eight, p. 137). Someone who had become genitally aroused, at the same time as having been physically hurt, frightened, and left with a corroding sense of shame, may also become very promiscuous in early adolescence. Several of our girls and a few boys had been involved in prostitution. But such continual re-enactment of those youngsters' predominantly hateful experiences is not the way whereby they will come to a separation of the different feelings that they retain about having been abused. It seems likely that such youngsters will be increasingly distanced from being able to enjoy intimacy and that their hatred of a sexual partner may become a serious problem. Moreover, they are most likely to relate to partners who are equally troubled. They may understand each other but they are likely to be too immersed in their own needs to be able to fulfil each other's. The community was frequently disrupted by individual youngsters whose sexual behaviour re-enacted their past experience – or rather their past experience as they supposed it had been. A girl seduced by a stepfather, or mother's boyfriend, might mistakenly feel very guilty that she had seduced the supposedly responsible adult. She may not be aware of how hostile she felt towards her mother's relationship with anyone else. The girl's understandable jealousy may have been exacerbated by her own loss of a secure relationship within a normal family. Consequently, such a girl might be exceptionally competitive with mother, or wish to destroy mother's relationship and so, years later, as well as feeling deprived, she might also have retained the guilty feelings and the feelings that she both deserved the abuse and also that it had all somehow been her own fault.

There are two broad issues concerning sexuality in a therapeutic community for adolescents. The first issue relates to behaviour control. Without control, the whole work of the community will be jeopardized by secret activity based upon exclusive relationships, by jealousy, by mutual exploitation rather than mutual support, quite apart from matters like pregnancy (and by the predominant discussion in community meetings revolving around legalistic arguments about boundaries rather than about therapeutic considerations). The second issue relates both to control and to treatment.

The treatment situation requires the youngsters to disclose what they feel, talk about their anxieties, and trust the staff. There is always a problem about overcoming resistance to psychotherapeutic treatment, especially for adolescents, because they anticipate they will be unable to bear the resurrection of their traumatic experiences and feelings. By all possible means, the therapeutic community reassuringly tries to overcome this resistance, to obtain full participation in the group process. This requirement for participation is close to a demand for compliance. Yet, one of the major factors Lorraine Fox (1988), in her work with sexually abused children, has defined is that it is the child who was originally passive and compliant who was the target of abuse, and not the aggressive one. Demands for trust and for co-operation offer a particularly insidious threat to such children. What these children demonstrate, Fox tells us, is their sense of impotence. They feel betrayed by adults who should have protected them. Yet, they remain likely to be enslaved by the threats that have been made to them 'if they tell' and which thus prevent their being able to tackle their feelings. The result of their experiences may not be the sense of anger that others feel, but instead a state of ambivalence. The identification with the community, which they need temporarily while their own missing strengths are developed, requires considerable commitment, so abused youngsters' pathological ambivalence will inevitably create a serious treatment problem.

We are a long way from resolving this dilemma. It may be that some exceptional therapeutic intervention is necessary prior to the youngsters' actually joining the community, in order to free such sexually abused youngsters from a condition that at least inhibits their participation. Nevertheless, they will still need the same symbolic experience of nurture that life in the community offers. It must be very rare that sexual abuse or serious physical abuse occurs in an otherwise normal background. Usually, the youngster's background will not have provided anyway the ingredients that would enable a confident sense of self to develop through adolescence, irrespective of the additional confusion caused to a youngster's sexual identity by specifically sexual abuse. Thus, it will not only be self-destructive behaviour, acting-out traumatic sexual experiences, that will cause such children to feel profoundly disparaging about themselves, but also their fundamental emotional deprivation.

Sexual issues provoke enormous anxiety in staff. Yet, the adults must address these issues if the youngsters are not to be sold short. It is difficult to imagine that any adult always feels secure about the all-pervading sexual aspects of their own life. It takes an exceptional adult who does not have to be repressive about their occasional personal discomfiture. Great insecurity is aroused when young staff's normal, psychosexual development is interrupted by confrontation with adolescent, bizarre behaviour. Despite their own needs for continuing growth, the adults will consciously need to distance themselves, in order to consider disturbed sexual behaviour in an objective manner, despite the fact that it may also be disturbing.

Yet, even the apparently bizarre behaviour can eventually make sense if objectivity can be brought to bear. So much promiscuous behaviour, for instance, is a bizarre attempt to be lovable. It is not easy to see how that promiscuous behaviour originated as an infant's desperate need to be cuddled. Those simple beginnings have now evolved into something more complex. If the promiscuous behaviour at one level speaks of a desperation to be nourished with loving interactions, at another level that same promiscuity has also led to a dependency on pleasurable and exciting, physical feelings for their own sake. These feelings would be a lively contrast to the inner sense of deadness by which so many deprived youngsters are weighed down. Nevertheless, that kind of physical dependency is different from the regenerating, fulfilling sexual activity that derives from a secure sense of self. A secure sense of self would best enable partnership and parenthood too in the future. Our youngsters' sexual excitement is often detached from emotional relationships, except in so far as they may act out some past experience or confusion. These youngsters seek disturbed partners in the hope of gaining understanding, but such partners are the least likely source. After such liaisons they are frequently left with shame, and with further reinforcement of their sense of being unlovable and deserving of punishment and rejection.

The baby whose parents beat each other in front of him, without consideration of his presence, and certainly without considering his feelings, finds it difficult to discriminate between his parents' physical engagement with each other and their sexual intercourse. Either would be frightening and incomprehensible. Though the parents apparently totally deny the baby's presence, he cannot help but share what is for him a traumatizing experience. Again, the child who has been genitally stimulated, and then hurt, and then threatened, and then blackmailed by an abusing parent's threat that they will lose that parent's affection altogether if they tell, cannot but be full of confused feeling that is impossible to put into words. How can they, several years later, with a physically different body, and with so many consequentially traumatic experiences having happened, begin to express their conflicting emotions?

It is not surprising that youngsters who have these experiences have begun to behave in ways that worry adults as being grossly unusual. Twelve-year-olds do not normally engage in prostitution, or sexually assault strangers in the street. Many such youngsters have learnt that they can excite adults by their flirtatiousness, though they are as likely to end up as a victim of such bizarre expression of their own sexualized sense of worthlessness, inadequacy, and of the sexual traumatization they have actually experienced.

Staff are very frightened if they themselves are in any way excited by some of this behaviour. Many youngsters have been rapidly dispatched from children's home to children's home because it has been so difficult for staff to acknowledge and then consider their own reactions. It is difficult enough to retain a sense of integrity in a society that has only recently been trying to come to terms at all with the politics of sexuality. For our staff it is a very tough task indeed to have to cope with questions, not only regarding their own exploitative, sociosexual attitudes, but with questions that challenge their own sexual orientation, or their still more unexpected feelings about children. When a youngster's personal boundaries are so fragmentary, he is likely to express his feelings for adults in ways that are barely tolerable.

Yet, when an adolescent arrives in the community and steals unremittingly for months, however much distress it causes, everyone knows he cannot just stop. His behaviour gives a rough indication of both where and what its roots are. A therapeutic community, however, proclaims the child's right to behave badly and yet feel accepted, for as long as it takes to unearth the roots of that behaviour. It is much harder to tolerate such early pain and the related sense of chaos when it is demonstrated in overtly sexual behaviour. For the adult, such behaviour often seems like a reflection of normality in a distorted mirror, except that the youngster's distorted behaviour is actually real.

Once more, the real world outside the community might be even less understanding and certainly less tolerant. Why do the staff not control this behaviour – simply not allow it?! The outside world's supposed condemnation makes repressive interdiction seem like an easier and safer way to deal with this but, of course, this would be bound to be self-defeating in the end.

When these are live and central issues, as they are for all abused children, the advantage of the functioning therapeutic community is that no one person has to carry the youngsters' volcanic behaviour alone and no one person has to manage his own feelings on his own. It is possible to instil within the group culture a real recognition of the injury promiscuous behaviour does to the community 'family', and a recognition of why that very image of a family might itself stimulate promiscuous behaviour. When this recognition is clear then these issues can at least be acknowledged in the large and small groups. The demand to be sexually exploited, and the desire to exploit sexually, occurs in society generally of course, and it is easier to tackle an individual's problems on a personal basis when the wider sociosexual attitudes can be differentiated from those arising from an individual's exceptional experience of abuse. To this end, the politics of sexuality really have to be tackled in the staff group. It is important that the staff is equally male and female numerically. The same applies in terms of senior staff. This is extremely difficult as there are fewer women able to make a career in residential work than men. Yet, these well-recognized difficulties may be as much excuse as reason, and it is essential that a genuine wish to escape the stereotyping is nurtured.

There is certainly a need for female status, respected female power, and similar matters to be developed. A girls' group could lend the strength of its sisterhood to the individual girl; a boys' group could avoid the prurient complication of parading its sense of inadequacy in public. If the politics of sexual power are acknowledged, and can be legitimately explored somewhere, then a greater sense that there is room elsewhere for the exploration of sexual dilemmas and their consequent behaviour is also possible. Very careful boundaries need to be drawn between groups such as these dealing with psychosocial issues and groups that might be created specifically to counter the emotional damage of sexual abuse. Similar clarity would need to be established as far as the different small group tasks also.

As ever, the greatest struggle is to sort out the eternal entanglement of feelings and behaviour within the community and within each individual fast enough to make most of the acting out expression of such feelings redundant. This requires, not only very courageous staff, who begin with a clear recognition of how essential it is to deal with the youngsters' sexual problems; but it also requires that these staff be properly resourced so that they can separate themselves from the different issues. They need supervision, not as an adjunct to their work, but as of equal importance. Staff members' work in groups and with individual children, and the work's impact upon themselves, needs continual consideration. It is essential that this supervision feels nonjudgemental to the member of staff, and that it is totally confidential, and that it is given by someone with great skill and experience. It is also an advantage if the staff supervision can be conducted in small groups so that the nourishment of supervision does not take place in a different world from the general world of the staff.

When professional, ongoing supervision and the community's programme has been organized to provide a counterbalance to the potential maelstrom of confused sexual feeling and behaviour, then the community as a whole, by its other symbolic transactions, can start to fulfil some of the earlier, unmet roots of mature sexual behaviour. For example, the kitchen provides and legitimizes oral stimulation – through its context of sound and light levels, textural, and olfactory experience. It makes the eating experience a safe and pleasurable one that symbolically feeds the earliest kind of sexual experience the infant enjoys with his mother. We can suppose that this form of sexuality was often not successfully developed beyond infancy. Development at best was partial and inadequately experienced: some symbolic, positive communication of the relationship between anal experience and self needs to be made. If these primary experiences of sexuality arising from oral and anal activity in infancy can be detached from past shame and guilt and anger, there is hope that subsequent sexual expression can develop towards an intimately orientated adult sexuality.

Thus, the carefully constructed lavatories, designed to make manifest a sense of being greatly cared about, particularly in the privacy of defecation, are also validating early, anal, sexual experience as intrinsically good experience. In many youngsters' original experience, of course, their sexual self was not further validated and confirmed by parental approval when engaged in potty training. The cuddling between people, the manifold opportunity to express affection between people; these are likewise examples of the ways in which the transactions of everyday community life fulfil a nourishing function for the appropriate and earliest sexual experience of life. At the same time, the proper resourcing of staff enables the boundaries of behaviour to be addressed by the community in a non-scapegoating fashion.

Once more, it must be suggested that the many, many experiences of everyday life in the community each have manifold meaning, though, as within a kaleidoscope, these are constantly changing their patterns of relationship and significance. To suggest that, even if the community is alive with so rich a content, the issues of the rehabilitation of sexual identity are ever totally met would be foolish. Human resources – even their practical and material resources – have limitations. We ran out of the necessary energy even to complete the refurbishment of the boys' downstairs lavatories, for instance, despite our recognition of its importance. Each time we undertook such a physical project, we had to initiate a significant, fund-raising exercise. An enormous amount of thinking and debate had to take place in order to design an atmosphere that implied a particular symbolic message to the user. If only the importance of consistency, of communication with staff and trustees, of defining the boys' downstairs lavatories' symbolic significance had been raised to another level of effort, then no doubt the energy to raise the necessary money and to plan the appropriate design would have been achieved. And, of course, there are many psychological issues concerning our youngsters' damaged sexuality that we had not begun to address.

Against the manifold, complex difficulties, even our best efforts at times seem somewhat ingenuous, but perhaps it is only possible to be at the earliest stages of exploring the therapeutic mountain of community life. The general topography can only be unclear so far, but at least the main features are beginning to be recognizable.

Chapter ten

Conclusions

The complexity of the healing provision.
A developmental case-study – Tara McLaughlin – the resident's experience.
The stress on staff and their capacity to manage the process.
A developmental view of Peper Harow in six phases.
A summary of the Peper Harow process.

It is clear that the task of creating and operating a residential treatment facility like Peper Harow is immensely complex. It is not surprising that few such communities exist, or that those attempting to manage such a facility so often find themselves embroiled in one problem or another. The community needs to be seen as an organic system – a process of many forces and requirements, continually shifting in their relationships and in their individual significance. Many of those forces are intangible, like the excitement that can change the mood of the group of residents from a boisterous one into an ugly one; or the way in which staff disputes filter unspoken into the subliminal awareness of the residents, and thus create intense anxiety with its consequential behaviour.

Youngsters at Peper Harow require the fullest educational provision, since some individuals may need both remedial programmes and external examination syllabuses at the same time. Despite the small numbers, a full range of subjects must be covered. In addition to understanding, tolerance, and security, the examination syllabuses require extraordinary commitment from aspirant residents because so much 'educational' time has been used earlier in unravelling profound resistances to learning. Furthermore, undeveloped learning abilities have had to be regenerated before examination work can be undertaken.

Enabling youngsters to reach a level of psychological maturity, from whence they can engage in relationships without visiting on others their own deprivation and suffering is, at best, a tentative task. Perforce it must take years. Imperfect and immature as any normal teenager must be, those responsible for the rehabilitation of those with extraordinary problems

183

Conclusions

must always be left with a sense of uncertainty as to the completeness of their task. It could equally be said that the staff's task is to reach a profound understanding of their own group and individual functioning, as well as that of the youngsters'. How could the staff help a youngster to consider his sexual fantasies if, for instance, they were only able to deny anxiety-provoking feelings arising within themselves? Recognizing and even sympathizing with the youngster's discomfort is not the same as addressing its source objectively and without self-deception.

The capacity for self-examination depends as much on the staff as a group as on the individual. Much of a resident's psychological change and growth arises from the dynamic group life. Perhaps no change could occur except in a context that is able to acknowledge the mad, the bad, and the shameful feelings and fantasies of the individual. The staff group both contributes to this and sets an example, not so much by some kind of confessional honesty, but by its style. That style depends on a group attitude towards its own functioning by which its individual members are encouraged to participate in the group process. Redl and Wineman observe that the 'delinquent ego's' final defensive manoeuvre is to present 'apparent change' (Redl and Wineman, 1951). This, they tell us, is the most deceptive ploy of all. And so it must be. Individual staff and the staff group, for many reasons, need to feel that they have succeeded in enabling change (see Chapter five, p. 78). It is very tempting therefore to accept changed behaviour at face value, and to rejoice at examination successes and at the wise comments the senior adolescents make in meetings. It is hard to resist being captivated by the euphoria of celebratory leaving ceremonies. It may take years, however, before it becomes clear whether the individual is able to manage his life as successfully as others with a more fortunate upbringing. The staff undoubtedly need to be optimistic, but what the youngsters need from them is their clear-sighted objectivity.

It might be illuminating to examine the Peper Harow process from a resident's viewpoint. Thus, although the following history of Tara McLaughlin is wholly fictional, and her experience in this fictional process ends in a somewhat ideal fashion, her story is typical.

Tara was born fourteen and a half years earlier, in Glasgow, at a time when that city contained large communities with many social problems and many damaged families. Her parents were typically young – Father twenty-two and Mother only nineteen. There were already two older sisters and a brother, and Father had been in care himself. Following Tara's birth, Mother was hospitalized for severe post-puerperal depression and from that time the children were shifted from one children's home to another. The parents divorced. Father removed the children from care and moved with them to London, with a girlfriend, whom he then married.

Not surprisingly, this second marriage was threatened by the disturbed behaviour of the children, and, as a consequence, they were once more placed in care. That also meant another succession of children's homes that were unable to contain their increasingly disturbing and disturbed behaviour. Tara ended in a remandlike setting with an anxious social services department looking for a 'very special placement that could handle her'.

In order to imagine what would happen to such a girl at a place like Peper Harow, we shall examine her development under eight categories, as follows: (a) social, (b) psychological/psychotherapeutic, (c) educational, (d) the kind of treatment experiences being received, (e) her anticipated responses, (f) Tara's relationships with her family, (g) relationships between community and family, (h) relationships between community and the referring social services department. Obviously there could be others but these should give a broad perspective of Tara's developing experiences in the community. In a chart, those eight categories would head corresponding columns, with parallel entries, each of which would relate to the same point in time from Tara's arrival to her departure four years later. The parallel timing of these entries would reveal the complementary and sometimes contradictory experiences which at any moment in time make the objective consideration of one adolescent life alone very complex. Some experiences affect others very considerably. For instance, a change in social worker creates a situation of conflict between the social services department and the community. One can then speculate whether, and how, this conflict between adults affects the parallel conflicts that Tara might be actively promoting over the telephone between the father and the community.

Many conflicts can be demonstrated by such a chart, that considers an individual from separate viewpoints at one point in time. For instance, while Tara is shown to be telephoning her father to accuse her peers of bullying and stealing, and to complain of boredom, you would expect that this would in some way reflect her own confusion about who is the truly caring, responsible 'parent'. Turning to Father could at first sight seem a declaration that 'blood is thicker than water' after all. Indeed, Father can then be seen to be phoning the community and accusing staff of not protecting his daughter, or depriving her of her education, and generally supporting her 'hard-done-by' stories. Yet, in our picture he also complains to staff that her sojourn is causing still worse behaviour whenever she returns home. Additionally, in contrast to their apparent alliance, both father and daughter break promises to each other by 'forgetting' to make telephone calls. Visits to the community demonstrate little ability to communicate between them, and visits home seem to indicate that Tara spends almost no time with the family. Therefore, from early in Tara's stay we can see that there are many mixed messages to reflect upon concerning the real issues in this family.

However, our imaginary chart shows the first four or five categories broadly describing what is occurring in the community, which seem, initially, totally unconnected with the family.

In Tara's first six months in the community, heading (a) describes her predominant activity as engaging with her personal 'environment'. Tara is developing the way in which she arranges her own bed-space, displays her cosmetics and other possessions, arranges pictures, and the way her bed-space varies from comfortable tidiness to chaos. She seems very concerned about the laundering and repair of her clothes, and of her own body, managing her own personal hygiene somewhat obsessively, and requiring to see the doctor and dentist perhaps unnecessarily.

The next heading, (b) psychological/psychotherapeutic, begins by describing Tara's response to the 'initial culture shock' and thus throws some light on the significance of her social behaviour. It suggests that Tara is in a state of subdued anxiety, and that she tends to 'hide' in the corner of the public rooms in the house, and that this defensive presentation is an attempt to mask her sense of loss and isolation.

Tara's development then indicates an increasing involvement in play and recreation with her peers. She builds camps in the grounds, plays table-tennis, spends time in the foundation studio, and volunteers to join in group excursions to the cinema. Although in parallel to her increased relaxedness, we can see that she is also fulfilling the expectations of the educational programmes under heading (c), exactly as expected. Though her initial uncertainty has changed to 'childlike play in the grounds', with her greater relaxedness comes the re-emergence of some of the behaviour reported in her preadmission history. It is suggested that this is being presented as a 'testing-out process'. For instance, she abuses the library arrangements by being noisy and leaving magazines strewn around; she disappears at bedtime; refuses to help to clear up the foundation studio when it is time to close. Tara is becoming more aggressive towards the adults who confront her behaviour and is flirtatiously provocative to the boys.

Nevertheless, all this antisocial behaviour is still occurring in a context that engages Tara in the routine of the community's day. She must still get up, go to the community meeting, attend meals, and go to bed with the rest of the residents. She still continues to participate in the routine of the community's week, attending the Friday night session, taking her turn in the house-cleaning team and in the cooking team, joining in the different weekend programmes, and, as time passes, so the routine of the community's year – Bonfire Night, Christmas Feast, Summer Camp, and so forth – unfolds and still includes Tara.

Again, at the same time that Tara is involved in the community's manifold activities, and as well as her often negative behaviour, Tara is also engaged in a new people's group, with her regular small group, with the daily large group, and in a regular, weekly, individual meeting with her member of staff, making a total of eight 'therapeutic hours' per week. In addition, her many informal discussions – after cooking and cleaning groups, and in her bedroom with specially selected seniors – enable Tara both to clarify what is occurring and to become increasingly open.

After about six months, Tara's defensiveness against the criticism her behaviour receives illustrates her increasingly desperate attempts to subdue the surfacing anxiety. Tara seems to be getting up at night and engaging in sexually promiscuous behaviour. She leaves the grounds without permission, tries to avoid attending groups, or, when forced to attend them, refuses to speak and becomes aggressive and disruptive, or weeps angrily.

Tara is also becoming increasingly depressed. The community transactions around her all the time inevitably make her aware of the issues of loss and separation, and of the deprivation in her own life, and of her isolation from her peer group because of her aggressive and delinquent attitude to others. None of this is surprising, for the relationship with her peer group is beginning to reflect a great deal of her feelings about her elder siblings and her general familial situation, though still with little awareness of the parallel between life in the community and in her family as far as Tara is concerned.

In addition to her depression, Tara's anxieties are increasingly revealed. She refers to her aggressive fantasies, which frighten her. She wakes very early, and occasionally in the middle of the night, and talks of feeling suicidal. And yet, at the same time, Tara begins to use the foundation studio and starts to learn to play the guitar. She has been seen helping to control a tantrumming newcomer with sensitivity, and joins in a singing quartet at the Christmas Feast. One of her first paintings is displayed at the annual exhibition.

Tara's aggressive disruption of the group ceases, but she tends to fall asleep instead. She often goes to bed after community meetings and is visibly anxious when others are crying. She now actively seeks out her own member of staff for informal discussions, though almost entirely about other people's problems.

Tara is now well into her second year and is in receipt of continual complaints about her aggression. A new girl complains in the community meeting of being sexually assaulted by Tara, which she totally denies! But Tara is also simultaneously threatened by her membership of the newly established girls' group, which is trying to discuss problems of sexual identity. She is very angry when compelled to attend, and once more makes every attempt to disrupt the discussion. The community meeting, too, like the girls' group, is full of issues concerning violence between the boys and the girls. The girls declare themselves to be sexually exploited, in particular by three or four boys, who eventually actually have to be excluded from the community because of their unabated sexual exploitation and violence in reality.

Conclusions

In the previous six months, Tara's weekend visits home have all gone seriously wrong. During the first she was arrested 'for causing a public disturbance'. On the following visit she telephoned Peper Harow, incoherent and 'high' on glue. She was again picked up by the police and had to be collected by staff. On the third visit she was physically attacked by her father and so returned of her own volition halfway through the weekend. During this period, the parents asked to see the director, and they expressed their anxiety about what was happening to Tara. Father reported for the first time some of his own experiences of being in care. Stepmother reluctantly admitted to her hostile feelings towards the children, and her fear that Father would somehow 'get together again' with their mother. Apparently the issue that caused Father to attack Tara was the stepmother's complaints about 'Tara's sexy dressing'. It was unclear what this implied, but it was agreed that much more discussion needed to take place. Perhaps Tara should stay in the community, rather than go home for Christmas.

At the community Christmas concert Tara performed a simple guitar duet with her male, part-time teacher, and was amazed by the enthusiasm it received. During the holiday Tara remained very subdued, but participated in all activities, and avoided confrontations. She began a new year in a new bedroom group, with three senior girls, all of whom were engaged in university entrance examinations, for the summer. And it was soon apparent that she had become very dependent upon this group, among whom she was the youngest, as she was in relation to her actual siblings too. Tara emulated her room-mates' dress-style and speech. She went to public concerts and the theatre with them, and began daily remedial lessons.

Throughout her first and second years Tara had re-established many of the conditions for learning. She had begun to acquire a new view of herself that would eventually include successful, social, and educational attainments. Tara's educational journey had begun, with play activities in many different forms and in which her peers were also engaged. These play activities were the basis for later educational achievement, and the foundation studio was central in the transition from play to learning. None of this process arose from compulsion. Intimate relationships with senior people enabled Tara to achieve high standards of cleaning and cooking, but they simultaneously enabled the very notion of standards and values to germinate. At the same time, the eight hours a week of group discussions, often of abstract concepts, had enormously expanded Tara's linguistic ability. She had now identified with a culture that was diametric to the delinquent one with which she identified before she arrived, and she now at last felt that she belonged somewhere instead of feeling alienated everywhere. The use of the library as part of daily living, and the peer-group support of her artwork, together with her budding musicianship, was a great stimulus of her desire to become educated. Despite her endless arguments with staff in the foundation studio and in the humanities room, she did in fact take notice of her teachers. Thus Tara was rapidly developing sophisticated techniques in her artwork.

Tara's poetry contained very creative imagery, though she still had problems in basic spelling and punctuation, and was still frightened by the basic rules of arithmetic. Tara was also developing her ability to perceive and draw accurately, but her more freely expressive painting revealed that anxiety remained a major feature of her internal life.

Contact between the community and the social services department had been minimal since Tara's placement, until a new social worker became responsible for her. He began by assuring Tara's member of staff that he did not believe in residential placements! Tara began by being extremely hostile to him! A case conference had been held by those responsible for Tara's placement at Peper Harow in that local authority's offices. By an oversight, no-one had invited the community to be represented or to send reports. The area director, from whose financial budget Tara's fees were paid, felt that Tara had 'got worse'. Also he considered that the social worker should himself work with the family rather than Tara's member of staff at the community. Eventually, the Area Director was persuaded to visit Peper Harow before the next case conference, at which the community would be represented. He eventually arrived just before Christmas, but seemed sceptical and unforthcoming.

An official letter from the social services department arrived in the new year giving a month's notice of the termination of Tara's placement. An urgently convened meeting at the social services department office heard that, 'the process was taking too long'! People were concerned about 'the institutionalizing effects of residential placements'. Reference to the original letter of contract, specifying 'at least four years', was received with embarrassment by the local authority area director, but he blamed the original social worker for making 'untenable commitments'. Despite recent complaints that 'Tara had got worse', the department now felt that Tara was relating reasonably with her parents, who complained that the community was 'too luxurious' for them to keep up with. The local authority, social services department officials did not accept the director's and the community's psychiatrist's quarterly reports, though the seriousness of Tara's disturbance was reinforced verbally at the specially convened meeting.

Tara's family had visited the community immediately after Christmas and, despite their initial resistance, they once more accepted the idea that they should have regular discussions at the community with Tara and her member of staff about the family situation. Therefore, arrangements were put in hand for these discussions to take place every other month.

The psychiatrist, on behalf of the community, wrote to the director of social services spelling out the potentially catastrophic outcome of the premature termination of the placement. The area director agreed to seek a second psychiatric opinion, though the director of the community warned of the danger of these interprofessional arguments for Tara's stability. At the same time, the social worker visited and, without any prior discussion with anyone, told Tara she would be leaving in a fortnight!

Tara ran off and several days later phoned from the casualty department of a London hospital, at three in the morning, begging to be collected. The hospital, however, was concerned about her condition. She had been seriously beaten up and was badly bruised.

After discussion with the community's general medical practitioner, Tara was collected and put straight to bed. She appeared, however, to be having wild mood swings for several days. She walked around the house shrouded in a torn blanket and covered with smeared make-up and dirt, or she would appear 'dressed to the nines' and teetering on high heels. Half the time she seemed to be in tears, and the other half she was shrieking with hysterical laughter. There was no getting her near her music or her studies. Finally, Tara's peers put her under a lot of pressure at a pivotal community meeting, in which she eventually broke down and described what had happened.

She had run off in despair at her social worker's news that she was going to leave. Others asked why she had not tried to find out if she could continue to stay in the community even without the local authority's support as others were doing. Tara was equally baffled by her flight. She described how she had wandered around for two days sleeping in doorways. She eventually went home and had a blazing row with her father, so she decided to prostitute herself! She was picked up by someone and went to his flat, but she then changed her mind, so she was then severely beaten up and thrown half-dressed into the street. A police patrol car had found her semi-conscious and she was taken to hospital.

Someone at the community meeting asked where Tara's stepmother was when she had gone home. Tara said her father had told her that her stepmother had gone to visit her own mother in Leicester. Her Father had been alone in the house. Suddenly, Tara began crying bitterly and told the community that her Father had sexually abused her, before she came to the community, every time she had returned home to visit from her various children's homes. The meeting ended with enormous support being shown to Tara.

This began a new level of relationship between Tara and the group, and between Tara and her member of staff. Over the next year much discussion was devoted to clarifying Tara's view of her history, enabling the relationship between some of her behaviour and the sexual abuse she had experienced to become clear. There were many issues. Tara thought the children's homes had insisted that she went home and had refused to acknowledge her hints of abuse.

She reluctantly admitted that the foster-home placements had ended because she was so sexually provocative towards the foster fathers. As well as beginning to understand the reasons for this, Tara also began to recognize some of the reasons why she always assumed that what had happened was all her own fault. She expressed real fear of her father, who had threatened to kill her when she went home during her period of absconding.

Despite the parents' agreement to visit the community on a regular basis for family discussions, it now became impossible to contact them. Meanwhile, the area director of social services had been promoted to another local authority. The director of social services responded to the director's protests with a restatement of his authority's original commitment. A new social worker was appointed, who met a charming Tara on his visit, and who also began a regular dialogue with her member of staff. From finding it difficult to see why a comparatively sophisticated adolescent should even be in care, this social worker began to develop a supportive work strategy with the family. Agreement was reached that no legal action would be taken against father, and the social worker aimed to resurrect the family's willingness to attend the community for regular discussions.

Following her revelations, Tara was very well supported in the community, particularly in her small group and in the girls' group. The discussion in the girls' group was about identity confusion – woman and child, love and sex, father and boyfriend, mother and guilt. Tara, nevertheless, continued to have mood swings, and, as another summer arrived, two of the girls in Tara's bedroom left for university, so her depression deepened, and the staff became increasingly anxious. Nevertheless, her first O level results were better than expected. The news inaugurated a dramatic change for Tara. She restarted her guitar and piano lessons, began university entrance examination work, and aimed to take four more O level examinations at Christmas.

Tara's individual discussions with her member of staff were mostly concerned with her family. Her relationships with her brother and sisters seemed to have been permanently stunted by their early and repeated separations. Tara continually declared that the community was her 'real family'! Nevertheless, during the course of the subsequent year, Tara's proper family began their visits, accompanied by the social worker, who also saw them at home regularly. The sexual abuse was hardly mentioned. Tara found her parents' inability to discuss anything other than superficially extremely difficult to tolerate. Father occasionally talked about his own traumatic childhood, partly to try and identify with Tara, and partly to win sympathy for himself. The stepmother always responded to this implied demand, and she also seemed to find difficulty in differentiating clearly between her stepdaughter, Tara, and Tara's real mother. Despite her confusions, she was very impressed, and not a little proud, at Tara's academic development.

Eventually, Tara confronted her father directly with his sexual abuse of her, and her stepmother agreed that she had known all along what was happening. Although her parents agreed to explore this matter seriously together, they cancelled the next three meetings.

Tara finally realized that she would have to depend on her own resources, as the family was unlikely to provide any. Despite this realization, she found her lack of a 'real family' very depressing. Tara still talked of the sense of emptiness that undermined her otherwise consistent drive to achieve.

By now many new people had joined the community and Tara's role had become predominantly that of an adult, particularly in the groups and the community meetings. She took a leading part, particularly regarding male and female issues. At the same time, Tara was beginning to look beyond the community. She intended to leave at Christmas after taking her university entrance examinations. She wanted to go to university in the following autumn and was hoping to work with community service volunteers in the interim. The local authority agreed to support her with accommodation. Tara meanwhile went out to teach piano at the local children's home near the community, and had also visited Robbie, her brother, who was still living in Glasgow where he had recently married.

By Christmas, Tara had obtained acceptable university entrance results and was due to begin her course in the following September. In the meantime, it was agreed that she should return as a junior member of staff to the community holiday groups at Easter, and in the summer. All seemed well at last. Despite Tara's awareness and insight about the loss and deprivation she had suffered, the staff felt that she was still vulnerable. They were worried about her depression and anxiety, especially with regard to sexual relationships. It was hoped that she might be able to resolve these issues further at a later period of her life, perhaps within marriage. Despite her warm and relaxed relationships with staff, concern still existed about her ability to achieve an intimate relationship with a boyfriend. She expressed great anxiety about her own potential to mother a baby, though the warmth of her relationships with the younger children in the community seemed a good sign of future development.

A girl like Tara would have been regarded as a great success at Peper Harow, despite the number of questions that remain unanswerable at the time of her leaving. Perhaps the most important question would have been whether she had actually internalized sufficient sense of warmth to fuel her through the inevitable psychic stress of life events that everyone must meet. In her case, Tara's lack of family support would not help. I have not attempted to explore Tara's early adolescent behaviour fully nor the feelings that must be hidden behind it. That behaviour itself would unfortunately have confirmed some of Tara's more deeply held, negative self-perceptions. Staff would need to be clear whether or not Tara's negative self-image had finally been laid to rest. If one believes that adolescence provides access to new growth, then it is certainly possible to believe that Tara's personality could have changed fundamentally. Only time would tell.

Tara was created to demonstrate the influence both of the community and of outside factors like her family and her referring local authority. Their different significance on Tara's development and behaviour, and on what issues were set in train for her as a result, are clearly implied. And even from this minimal description, we can see that her peers were of major significance in terms of providing control over her behaviour, in providing comfort for her loss – as its realization became recognizable – and in providing models for her self-image.

Now, if each group is seen as a complete psychic entity (and yet also as part of the community as a total entity too), this would imply that Tara's relationships and functioning would also be considerably influenced by events outside herself, outside her family, and outside her history, and therefore, at times, irrespective of her own personal input. This would be the case for each person in each group, and for everyone assembled in the large group.

It should be possible to construct a similar description of a member of staff's development from the time he or she arrives at the community to when he or she leaves five or six years later. Staff tended at their point of departure to say that their experience at Peper Harow had been one of the most significant of their life. While fully appreciative of the benefits, those staff would also remember the suffering and fear they had experienced in order to achieve such benefits. Both staff and residents inevitably become caught in a collective process that makes psychic change unavoidable.

Unlike the residents though, most staff arrived with a positive self-image. Again, for most staff adolescence lay within recent memory even though they had achieved independence and academic success. Since their adolescence, they had possibly married, and become young parents. They valued their idealism that had committed them to working with the needy, and felt both privileged, but also optimistic about the life on which they were embarking. If they had trained in psychology, or in some allied subject that gave them greater knowledge about developmental psychological theories, or about dynamic social processes, they might be able to formulate a kind of explanation for the youngsters' problems. Yet, they had little understanding of what the impact would be on them personally. They, like others with less relevant training, were simply proud to join an organization that intended to address the needs of the less fortunate. It was a vocation rather than a job. Yet, coping with the diametric differences between their original self-image and the helpless one sometimes aroused by the work had never been anticipated, so their stress, albeit inevitable, was also considerable at times.

Yet, a different residential system might in fact have turned out to be far more similar than one might have suspected. Staff became equally caught up by the unconscious, organizational processes in the old approved school. What was different in an approved school, however, was that these processes were denied so that no support or staff-development schemes could be very effective, even if they were available. Staff in both kinds of institution were at the mercy of the perpetual psychological tug-of-war between the delinquent, unconscious group processes of the youngsters and their own unconscious processes and responses. However, Peper Harow's difference of approach derived from a view that one cannot impose change on people. If the way we function is dictated by our unconscious world, then change can only be brought about if that world itself changes. In the adolescent's case, if this change is to be permanent, it would be because staff and the environment had engaged with the resident's unconscious world, and had enabled change to have developed from within. Yet, if the staff group is to arrive at an enabling, enhancing mode of functioning, then it has to be released from its spellbound subjection to the unrecognized processes. These processes require institutional legitimization, not repression. A system for working with these organizational processes needs to be developed just as much as there needs to be a system to manage the youngsters' behaviour. Such a system will be essential if the member of staff is to cope with the unrealistic demands and atrocious testing out of his relationships. He will only be able to manage the stress of this if the system allowes him to explore his fears and to obtain reassurance at a profound level.

A resident needs his guru to say, 'I am here because I care about you'. However, how can he believe it when he hears it? If he does believe it, how can he know that he will not destroy the guru if he lets himself get close enough for their relationship to really matter? Atrocious behaviour will demonstrate whether or not the member of staff is capable of being hurt. If he is not merely indifferent, and even if he is angry, then perhaps this indicates both that he matters to the guru and that the guru might seem able to cope with him. The doubting adolescent might suspect that the adult will know how to cope with his hostility, and so enable him to get close and become warmed and nurtured. On the other hand, when the member of staff finds the adolescent trailing him with his inexpressible neediness – this is sometimes called attention-seeking – will the member of staff be capable of tolerating the emotional demands? When the adolescent engages in seductive charm at one moment and sneering contempt the next, threatens sexually in language plain and frightening – this is hardly the kind of relationship the new member of staff expected to have with the youngsters.

Life with our adolescents is a stormy affair. At any one moment one is at the mercy of intolerable challenges that do not appear to be based on any kind of reason. These demands feel all-consuming, so the member of staff resists them self-protectively and then feels guilty when faced with the youngster's tearful unhappiness. The reality of the youngster's suffering arouses the member of staff's tenderness, compassion, and wholehearted commitment once again.

What one feels and why one feels it, and whether it is acceptable, and whether it can be managed, and what one should be doing in this relationship, are all issues with which members of staff must grapple and eventually come to terms; and, having done so, it is to be hoped that their consequent sense of stability and strength confirms them as safe people to the disturbed adolescent. Complex though this may be, it is still too simple a description of the actual task, for it must also be undertaken as the hurly-burly of the relationship with the youngster actually proceeds. Nor has the process any definite conclusion, or even the clarity of the artificial, step-by-step development of an invented Tara McLaughlin. It requires continuous re-examination throughout the member of staff's stay.

To obtain the benefit of others' experience, and their reassurance in times of real stress, the actual exposure of one's anxieties to one's colleagues is required. As one becomes absorbed in unconscious processes, it becomes increasingly difficult to recognize that others have endured just such confusion and self-doubt, and that others have been frightened by feelings they, too, had thought long resolved. Once an organization has evolved that provides a culture in which staff can express and explore their feelings, then a truly therapeutic community can be created. But a therapeutic culture cannot evolve quickly: first, the staff will need to recognize that the normal boundaries of interpersonal social behaviour cannot be adequate enough to make them feel secure. Unlike anyone's experience in normal society, the staff in a therapeutic community are bound to be caught up by the abnormal fears and fantasies of the residents, and so are bound to experience similar, irrational, and unnerving feelings about their own relationships with each other. Only after they can acknowledge the reality of this unusual situation will they be able to comm it themselves to the serious level of supervision that will enable a nonjudgemental and perhaps kindly relationship with each other to become possible. The staff group, though, is full of rivalries, of envy, of fear, until this point of organizational maturation. If other priorities – like the need to become financially viable, and the need to contain dangerous behaviour – intrude and take up most of the staff's opportunity for reflection, then the development of the staff group's self-awareness can only be a slow process. Unfortunately, until this self-awareness is achieved, the group will be blown hither and yon by the dynamic storms of the community.

195

We know that therapeutic communities tend to oscillate, as Savalle and Wagenborg (1980) put it (see Chapter three, p. 47). Simply put, we may say that for a while a therapeutic community may cope with its residents' problems through awareness of them, and through insight into their significance. By various therapeutic resources, the community eventually promotes change and resolution of these problems. But at another point in time there appears to be little self-awareness by the community, and certainly no insight or resolution. Instead, there is a great deal of disruptive behaviour that does indicate the presence of problems, but which actually only serves to aid and abet resistance to treatment. Both positive and negative modes of functioning seem to reach extreme points and then they begin to swing back towards their opposite polarity. It may take several weeks or even months for this process to move from one extreme to the other, though there may be high and low points en route. Nor does this process proceed at a consistent rate. Only over a very long time can this alternating mode of functioning be seen to be therapeutic. Its procedure seems only to be possible by lurch and stumble. Thus, at one time a visitor will come away euphoric at the wise and loving maturity by which he has been inspired, while on another occasion he might have been met with surly apathy - a sense of purposelessness and hostility that would question the justification of the community's very existence.

Staff are often afraid that visitors will arrive in the worst troughs and not find it possible to believe in the existence of crests. The staff, themselves, have to be exceptionally experienced to accept these divergent oscillations with any kind of professional equanimity.

There may also be a developmental pattern to an organization like a therapeutic community (see also Chapter three, p. 45). It certainly seems to have been so for Peper Harow. There were always periods when everything seemed to be going well in contrast with less auspicious periods, but the community, nevertheless, continued to change and develop overall. With hindsight, Peper Harow's last eighteen years appear to have fallen into six phases. The first phase could be entitled 'ideals and revolution'. It required a total commitment to establishing a therapeutic community. We had no idea then exactly how therapy might actually be organized, or how it would actually work, but we did have a sense of the atmosphere that would be necessary and a similar intuitive sense about the kind of relationships that would need to develop.

There would be many passionate, adolescent features to these relationships, such as the ideal of self-sacrifice on behalf of others. The youngsters' very lives were seen as on the brink of disaster, except for dramatic rescue. No-one cared too much for tidiness and the good order of a well-regulated environment. Conversations could take place anywhere and at any time, and they were playful in their function, as the exploratory conversations into the middle of the night so often are in adolescence.

Anyone put off by this neo-Bohemian style would not be regarded as more adult, but as inhibitors of the young. Crises were in a sense exhilarating. Undefined success was our only goal and we eventually did reach a point where victory seemed to have been achieved. The internal organization of a therapeutically orientated programme had been established; there was a rationale for all the community's activity. The community's relationship with the outside world was on its way to being resolved. It was accepted on terms of its own definition, and youngsters were referred by psychiatrists and social workers who had a general idea about the kind of programme available at Peper Harow. The second phase, therefore, was one of 'victory'. The idealistic staff, who had come in faith that this could be achieved, could now celebrate the fact. They could take their places, as it were, at a new round table of therapeutic chivalry.

Unfortunately, the wranglings both within the staff group and between the staff and the director inaugurated the third phase. It still seems true that there had never been the opportunity to do more than follow the 'fight leader' blindly until this point. But what then emerged had always been present in the community. As soon as the adults recognized that goodwill and locker-room heartiness were not sufficient to help the residents deal with their problems, the staff began to experience the real emotional demands of the job. The staff needed the personal training and the supervision appropriate to the therapeutic task. Yet, there was not even a way to articulate what was happening, so the adult group became split. The youngsters acted out their dissatisfaction with the staff, and this dissatisfaction in turn was projected onto the director by the staff. The director responded by experiencing staff confusion and disagreement in terms of loyalty, which increased staff hostility and resentment and the director's sense of acute anxiety and hurt. There seemed to be no way to end this situation. It seemed as though new staff would arrive full of enthusiasm, only to become disillusioned.

Thus we arrived at the fourth phase in Peper Harow's development – 'the phase of maturity'. During this phase we were able to acquire consultant help to create the space in which to think.[1] The consultant enabled us to depersonalize the intergroup conflict by demonstrating its derivation from the existing organizational structure. By persuading staff to structure staff meetings with a rotating chairperson and minute taker, issues of authority, for instance, became experienced as belonging to both adult groups rather than as polarized between the all-powerful and the powerless. The staff became more authoritative in their own right, which was seen as complementary to the director's authority. It became accepted that irrational feelings were bound to be projected from individual to individual and from group to group in such a community. Instead of perceiving this process either as evidence of ill-will or simply as interesting

197

psychic phenomena, the need for responsible management of these situations was clarified to ensure that the community's therapeutic functioning could be protected. Managing an optimal psychodynamic environment was seen to be as valid a concept as managing income and expenditure accounts. This development increased the sense of personal security both of the director and of the staff. As a result, consultancy that emphasized the need to see the professional therapeutic task in terms of good management was offered to all staff. This enabled an increasing recognition by all staff of how the groups within the community, as well as its individuals, projected their anxiety and unclarified tension into other groups. If the staff group had recognized, for instance, how staff meetings mirrored the group processes in the morning's community meeting, then the staff, as a group, could begin to understand the current dynamic condition of the community as a whole. In the fourth phase it seemed as though a mature status quo had at last been reached.

The idea of not repressing behaviour or feelings but of managing them, and the idea that all the resources in the community had to be managed so as to optimize the chances of clarifying the individual and the group issues, was a very attractive one. This idea produced a very reassuring sense of order and control. Putting the idea into practice required an increased contribution from 'head as well as heart', and this was very welcome to those staff whose emotions had been in overdrive for many years.

Perhaps keeping a balance is never possible for very long. We toppled into the fifth phase – the 'Rug-from-under-the-feet' Phase – that inaugurated another conflict. This conflict was about issues of good management and bureaucracy on the one hand, and the less easily defined issues about intuition and inspiration on the other. Many people would agree that intuition and inspiration are part of the charismatic style that are necessary for a venture like Peper Harow to get off the ground in the first place. As an organization develops, however, the charismatic style becomes unsustainable in its simple initial form.

Two issues make the conflict between managerial and intuitive styles more confusing. The first is that a therapeutic community for adolescents includes a continually renewed group of incoming adolescents, not yet integrated into the community ethos and whose resistance to changing their emotional stance is enormous. The second is that, even when these adolescents have become part of a nurturing culture, this is not sufficient on its own to maintain motivation and control. We have seen in the case of Tara McLaughlin that, even when fully committed to the mature values of the community, and when truly ready to leave, she might still not possess sufficient internal security to deal with life crises without extra help. Thus, in times of personal crisis youngsters will need to fall back on their identification with all the community's values and strengths, and which are personified and so focused in the director. We have seen in Chapter four how the director above all represents the community's values and embodies its history and culture – indeed the essence of its dynamic life, as much because it is unconsciously invested in the leader by the group as because the leader chooses to represent the group's dynamic life. In such personal crises, the youngster will be able to accept the director's ultimatum about his behaviour, or will be able to jettison his determination to leave prematurely, or will find himself more easily able to conclude a period of resistance to insight. In my view it is essential that, despite the development of authority in the staff group, the director must retain and indeed nurture the community's focused investment in him. If he fails to do this, then the community's ability to contain behaviour, or even to ensure that youngsters stay in the community, will gradually evaporate. For this reason, and despite the enormous emotional cost of being in such a focal position, George Lyward even in his seventies used to enter his medieval hall at Finchden Manor from time to time, once more raising his battle cry, 'Are you for health, or for sickness?' and stirring up the personal response to a 'cause' embodied and founded in him personally. It must have been so exhausting to generate the necessary energy, when this arose more out of his cognitive recognition of need rather than from the initial spontaneity of his youth and middle age, yet that focal representation of task was absolutely needed by the residents from time to time, throughout his forty years there.

Yet, the adults in such a community also 'grow up' and no longer need to identify with adolescent functioning. They need a well-managed work situation that gives them time to come to terms with their own feelings, time to take stock of their professional interactions, and time to prepare for their multifarious tasks. It is in the conflict between the need for sensible management and the need to give the youngsters profound inspiration and hope that the dilemma occurs. Avoiding a return to inter-staff conflict requires a careful balance between such factors as staff management, delegation of authority, and the continual renewal of charisma. Perhaps there is no definitive answer.

At Peper Harow the sixth phase – 'charismatic management achieved' – has now ended, yet we are still too close to events to discern further phases.[2] The sixth period coincided with the expansion of the organization into The Peper Harow Foundation, and a second community – Thornby Hall. Events, now six years old, make undeniable our failure to manage this transition with complete success. When I left to develop the Peper Harow Foundation, there was disagreement about the extent of the authority the successor to Peper Harow's directorship should carry. Failure to resolve this disagreement left the issue about authority unmanaged and, after an apparently calm six months, the community began to fall apart. Many youngsters left and the behaviour of those remaining became unusually disruptive. This coincided with the period when referrals, for reasons of policy with regard to placements by local authorities outside their own area, fell off dramatically, so that crises occurred at every level. My successor resigned and, in the emergency, one of the assistant directors, Peter Riach and the management consultant, Penny Jones agreed to undertake a joint directorship for a limited period of time. Their task was to stabilize the community's functioning once more, and to re-establish its financial viability. This had substantially been achieved when a permanent director was eventually appointed in January 1988, who, having completed that task, and having recognized the existing limitation of the treatment programme, is now engaged long-term in the process of increasing the community's psychotherapeutic effectiveness.

There are many issues involved in the new director's task. Despite the complications of trying to balance the many existing requirements, perhaps other psychotherapeutic approaches to our youngsters' needs, such as psychodrama, might be seen to be helpful. How sophisticated in psychotherapeutic terms should the individual provision be and what could be the cost implications if more skilled individual and group psychotherapy were regarded as necessary? In association with this issue, there is obviously much more to be thought out about staff training in the many forms needed for treatment in the residential setting.

It is not surprising, either, that the changing social environment outside the community would make a difference to what psychosocial development would be seen to be essential for adolescents leaving home or Peper Harow. Undoubtedly, there is a more demanding public attitude towards the actual content and management of education, and a less flexible attitude towards obtaining work or social support, as well as less tolerant sexual attitudes. All this will surely affect responses within the community and its consequent development.

How the community might develop is difficult to predict, because the ongoing life of such a community is by its nature exploratory. The more it discovers, the more it finds out how much more there is to explore. Not fully understanding its continually new frontiers, the community will sometimes make mistakes. Yet, at its most successful, it is a process that can restore the potential to an individual for a full personal and socially successful life.

Therefore, despite the limitations of this process, our belief has been confirmed that the many aspects of the community's process indicate at least an appropriate direction for future development. Those aspects can be summed up as taking place in a total environment in which, through a variety of integrated and mutually reinforcing experiences, disturbed young people can be contained and reassured, and thus encouraged to discover how to play. By doing so, they would be able to regress psychologically and, from their new-found understanding of what has happened to them, come at last to see the world realistically. In parallel, the process must also provide the physical, emotional, and intellectual experiences of normal life so that, when they come to leave, they can have real expectations of leading normal lives.

This book set out to show how such processes are both essentially simple and yet complex. The contribution of the staff's intrinsic human qualities, and their ability to see afresh, enables a lively meaning to be drawn from the task-designed environment. The manifold, interpersonal relationships in groups of every size are vehicles for the dilemmas that the catalystic lifestyle encourages to be expressed. Unhappily, this endeavour has arisen in response only to those with the most extreme needs. Hopefully, it will enable them to live exceptionally worthwhile lives despite their exceptionally painful beginnings.

Yet, our experience indicates, too, how effective its adaptation to more familiar circumstances would be. Not only does unguessed-at talent never emerge in schools generally, but nowhere near sufficient priority is given to the organized development of a healthy, emotional adulthood, without which all society's technology will not be well used. This could be said to be the core of an educational curriculum that would truly relate to an adult life. The stress of increasing change in our society is evidenced daily in terms of violence, crime, and the breakdown of families. Technological man has never before been where he stands now. Individual parenting faces ever greater dilemmas of choice, yet traditional and largely unconscious modelling processes are still the main source of parent training for the next generation. Existing parents, in any event, can no longer feel secure that the world they have experienced will even exist when their children are parents. Even if those children have ingested a profound sense of worth in their earliest years, and the foundations of those strengths needed to take on the unknown were established, then surely their emotional maturation should be the highest priority for their adolescent education?

The one thing above all others the twenty years of experiment at Peper Harow has shown again and again is that hope can inspire apparent miracles. That hope is based upon the belief that people are capable of profound change, can come to love each other with a measure of selfless-ness, and can view with awe and wonder the limitlessness of the universe and all its living systems. To be able to reassert such optimism has seemed at times to have cost a great deal, for we can only judge with limited vision. The growth of insight is a privileged activity, providing as much for the sower as for the seed.

Notes

Chapter one: Introduction

1. The Children and Young Persons' Act 1969 intended to avoid the continuing criminalization of young offenders through court sentences. Thereafter, courts could only make Care Orders to the local authority in which the youngster lived. As approved schools orders were abolished, so were approved schools. They were to be called community homes (with education on the premises) and were to be managed by social services departments of local authorities, thus reinforcing the need for care rather than punishment. All approved schools had to change their status and become community homes, controlled either by local government or else by one of the major, national charitable organizations. Park House managers, feeling that under such authority they would not be able to become a therapeutic community, decided to apply for status as a special school. It was the only one of 130 approved schools to do so.

Chapter four: The development of community identity

1. The Duke of Edinburgh's Scheme was promoted in the 1950s to be flexible enough to catch the interest of youngsters of both sexes who would resist joining existing youth organizations. It was to promote a variety of activities and interests, such as adventure, social service, and hobbies. Skills in these areas would be evaluated, enabling participants to receive bronze, silver, and gold levels of award. It would be regarded as prestigious by employers. The scheme continues to exist.

Chapter five: The development of individual identity

1. I would not wish to underestimate the unconscious influence upon me of such writers as Bettelheim and Redl whose work is based upon their profound knowledge of psychology and psychotherapy, some of which I had already studied. I am conscious now of the great debt I owed to them and to Hadyn Davies Jones of Newcastle University for introducing them to me.

Chapter six: A therapeutic house

1. This is a common psychotherapeutic problem. Despite the most desperate unhappiness, unravelling the meaning of an individual's behaviour will face them with the roots of their difficulties. Their behaviour and attitudes at that time were unconsciously intended to defend the individual against the experiences with which he could not cope. Although they were not effective strategies, they were clung to ever more desperately and have become habitual. Dismantling these ineffective defences would leave the individual feeling as vulnerable as he felt years before. The individual is thus caught in a dilemma, whereby the path to change and happiness is itself threatening. Hence, even a well-motivated patient's 'resistance to insight'. (Rose, 1983: 22–34.)

Chapter seven: Educating anew

1. In England and Wales, at both central and local government levels, education and other social needs are provided by separate departments. If a child is sufficiently behaviourally disturbed in school, he might find his way to a special school. If social workers or the courts see him as being in need of care, he may find his way to a community home with education on the premises.

2. This reference is to a famously irreverent magazine that would have been familiar to all of those staff who had been at university in the sixties. It was called *Oz*.

Chapter eight: The treatment process of a total approach

1. I hasten to add that this approach depends on the physical potential of the institution and the particular pathology of the group. Other residential treatment environments – small units for instance – may be just as effective – indeed perhaps the only effective approach for the particular kind of individual who cannot cope at all with the particular pressures of the large group, irrespective of its unique, potential benefits.

Chapter nine: The limits of hope and inspiration

1. I would like to stress that it is not necessarily parents who inflict abuse but often other partners. The configuration of confused ideas is dictated by who the abuser is – does the child become angry with the real parent because of his failure to maintain a secure family, or to protect the child from the abuser? Nor does abuse necessarily mean either sexual or physical abuse. However, if the abuse is predominantly sexual, or physical, or emotional, it may also have a predominant effect on parallel aspects of identity. The developing adolescent may feel exceptionally uncertain about engaging in age-appropriate sexual experience, like dating for instance, or may alternatively feel there to be no boundaries between his or her initiating friendship and inevitable sexual intercourse. A self-injurious youngster

may be exploring – albeit in a totally self-defeating manner – something bad about his body image that he may suspect would confirm why he was so frequently beaten in childhood. Each case is different, and therefore requires a very careful, developing under-standing of what each child's behaviour means to him.

2. The 'part of the learning experience' referred to arises from recognition and understanding from 'within' of the dynamic interactions between the three dynamic 'groups' that make up the dynamic whole community 'group', i.e. the residents, the staff, and the director.

Chapter ten: Conclusions

1. The consultant, Penny Jones eventually became joint director with Peter Riach for an interim period between 1983 and 1987.

2. I am indebted for this phrase to Piet Jongerious of the Viersprong Clinic in Holland. He was thinking of writing a book with just such issues, and his title was to have been *From Charismatic Leadership to Charismatic Management – but Always the Charisma*!

Bibliography

(Page numbers in square brackets refer to this text)

Baron, C. (1987) *Asylum to Anarchy*, London: Free Association Books. [p. 150]

Bettelheim, B. (1967) The Empty Fortress – *Infantile Autism and the Birth of the Self*, New York: The Free Press. [p. 11 – The expression is obviously indebted to Bruno Bettelheim, even though his book is entirely about autistic children. Whilst the pathology of the youngsters at Finchden Manor and Peper Harow were not autistic, there are many similar features resulting from limited emotional growth. Bettelheim examines the concept of an 'empty centre' in some detail. The deprived youngsters of Peper Harow often erected fortress like defences to protect themselves against their hidden sense of utter emptiness.]

Bloch, D. (1979) *So the Witch Won't Eat Me (Fantasy and the Child's Fear of Infanticide)*, London: Burnett Books Ltd in association with Andre Deutsch Ltd. [pp. 117 and 149]

Burn, M. (1956) *Mr. Lyward's Answer*, London: Hamish Hamilton. [p. 30]

Curtis Report (1946) *The Report of the Care of Children Committee Council*, London: HMSO. [p. 4]

Erikson, E. H. (1940) *Studies in the Interpretation of Play, Part 1, Clinical Observations of Play Disruption in Young Children*, Genet, psychological monograph. [p. 136] p. 557–671

Erikson, E. H. (1959) *Identity and the Life Cycle*, selected papers, psychological issues (monograph), I: I, New York: International Universities Press. [pp. 80–3 and 118]

Bibliography

Foudraine, J. (1974) *Not Made of Wood*, London: Quartet Books. [p. 17]

Fox, L. (1988) '*Healing the traumatic effects of sexual abuse*', presented at 'Homes for Healing', a conference concerned with abused and denied children, organized by the Peper Harow Foundation and the Caldecott Community, London. (Dr Fox is a psychologist and a consultant in child abuse.) [p. 178]

Lennhoff, F. G. (1960) *Exceptional Children*, London: George Allen & Unwin. [p. 31]

Lucas, N. B. C. (1975) *An Experience of Teaching*, London: Weidenfeld & Nicholson. [p. 30]

Maier, H. W. (1968) *Three Theories of Child Development*, New York: Harper & Row Ltd. [p. 149]

Makarenko, A. S. (1951) *The Road to Life*, Moscow: Progress Publishers. [p. 35]

Millham, S. (1973) Open day conference at Peper Harow. [p. 100]

Morris, T. and Morris, P. (1963) *Pentonville*, London: Routledge & Keegan Paul Ltd. [p. 64]

Pines, M. (1988) '*Group psychotherapy of the borderline personality*'; unpublished paper presented at Group Analytic Society symposium, Borderline personalities – Assessment and Treatment, London. [p. 138]

Rapoport, R. N. (1960) *Community as Doctor; New Perspectives on a Therapeutic Community*, London: Tavistock. [p. 6 and 141]

Redl, F. and Wineham, D. (1951) *Children Who Hate*, New York: The Free Press. [pp. 78, 111, and 121]

Redl, F. and Winemam, D. (1952) *Controls from Within – Techniques for the Treatment of the Aggressive Child*, New York: The Free Press. [p. 147]

Rose, M. (1982) '*The potential of fantasy and the role of charismatic leadership in a therapeutic community*' *The International Journal of Therapeutic Communities* 3 (2) London: Orphans Press Ltd [p. 71]

Rose, M. (1983) *'The fear of insight – resistance to change and a residential response'*, *The International Journal of Therapeutic Communities* 4 (1) London: Orphans Press Ltd [pp. 36–7 and note 1, Chapter 6, re p. 110]

Rose, M. (1987) *'The function of food in a residential treatment process'* *Journal of Adolescence* 10: 149–62. [pp. 101–5]

Rose, M. (1987) *'The context for psychological change'*, *Residential Treatment for Children and Youth* 5 (1) Haworth [p. 10]

Rose, M. (1988) *'The need for enchantment'*, *Residential Treatment for Children and Youth* 5 (3) New York: Haworth Press Inc; also presented at the IXth Congress of the International Association of Group Psychotherapy, Zagreb. [p. 68]

Savalle, H. and Wagenborg, H. (1980) *'Oscillations in a therapeutic community'* *The International Journal of Therapeutic Communities* 1 (3) [pp. 47 and 196]

Sendak, M. (1963) *Where the Wild Things Are*, London: Bodley Head. [p. 11]

Trieschman, A. E., Whittaker, J. K., and Brendtro, L. K. (1969) *The Other Twenty-Three Hours*, New York: Aldine Publishing Co. [p. 120]

Whitelock, D. (1952) *The Beginnings of English Society*, Harmondsworth: Penguin Books Ltd. [p. xiv]

Wills, W. D. (1971) *Spare the Child*, Harmondsworth: Penguin Books Ltd. [p. 17]

Winnicott, C. (1968) *'Communicating with children'*, in R. J. N. Tod, (ed.) *Disturbed Children*, London: Longmans Green & Co. [p. 109]

Winnicott, D. W. (1964) *The Child, the Family and the Outside World*, Harmondsworth: Penguin Books Ltd. [p. 73]

Index